MW00571495

Data Analysis, Data Modeling, and Classification

Other McGraw-Hill Books in Software Engineering

ISBN	AUTHOR	TITLE
0-07-016622-6	Berk, Devlin	*Hypertest / Hypermedia Handbook*
0-07-010912-5	Charette	*Application Strategies for Risk Analysis*
0-07-010645-2	Charette	*Software Engineering Environments: Concepts and Technologies*
0-07-010661-4	Charette	*Software Engineering Risk Analysis and Management*
0-07-016803-2	Dickinson	*Developing Quality Systems*
0-07-015788-2	Dixon	*Winning with CASE*
0-07-023165-6	General Electric Co. Staff	*Software Engineering Handbook*
0-07-030550-1	Howden	*Functional Program Testing and Analysis*
0-07-032813-7	Jones	*Applied Software Measurement*
0-07-036964-X	Lecarme, Pellisier, Gart	*Software Portability*
0-07-040235-3	Marca, McGowan	*Structural Analysis and Design Structures*
0-07-042632-5	Modell	*A Professional's Guide to Systems Analysis*
0-07-042633-3	Modell	*Data-Directed Systems Design*
0-07-043198-1	Morris, Brandon	*Relational Diagramming: Enhancing the Software Development Process*
0-07-044118-9	Murphy, Balke	*Software Diagramming*
0-07-044119-7	Musa et al.	*Software Reliability*
0-07-050783-X	Pressman	*Software Engineering: A Practitioner's Approach*
0-07-055663-6	Schulmeyer	*Zero Defect Software*
0-07-059177-6	Smith	*Concepts of Object-Oriented Programming*
0-07-707241-3	Smith	*Software Prototyping*
0-07-067922-3	Wallace	*Practitioner's Guide to ADA®*
0-07-010646-0	Wallace et al.	*A Unified Methodology for Developing Systems*

Data Analysis, Data Modeling, and Classification

Martin E. Modell

McGraw-Hill, Inc.

New York St. Louis San Francisco Auckland Bogotá
Caracas Lisbon London Madrid Mexico Milan
Montreal New Delhi Paris San Juan São Paulo
Singapore Sydney Tokyo Toronto

Library of Congress Cataloging-in-Publication Data

Modell, Martin E.
Data analysis, data modeling, and classification / Martin E. Modell
p. cm.—(Software engineering series)
Includes index.
ISBN 0-07-042634-1
1. Data structures (Computer science) 2. Data base design.
I. Title. II. Series: Software engineering series (New York, N.Y.)
QA76.9.D35M64 1992
005.7'3—dc20 92-5898
CIP

1 2 3 4 5 6 7 8 9 0 DOC/DOC 9 8 7 6 5 4 3 2

ISBN 0-07-042634-1

The sponsoring editor for this book was Jeanne Glasser, the editing supervisor was Paul R. Sobel, and the production supervisor was Donald Schmidt. It was set in Century Schoolbook by Carol Woolverton, Lexington, Mass.

Printed and bound by R. R. Donnelley & Sons Company.

Contents

Preface

Many books have been written on the mechanics of producing data models. Even more books have been written on data base design. In my first two books, *A Professional's Guide to Systems Analysis,* and *Data-Directed Systems Design: A Professional's Guide,* I made numerous references to data models, and described what they are and how they are used for both systems analysis and systems design. However, like many authors I treated the problem of determining how to build one, and more specifically, what should be portrayed by the data model, rather lightly.

In the course of my career as a data base administrator, data administrator, data analyst, and data modeler, many users, managers, and prospective clients have asked me questions such as: What is the justification for developing a data model? What is the benefit of a data model? Why do we need it? What does it do for us?

These are difficult questions to answer if we concentrate strictly on the data model itself and if we answer them strictly within the context of automated systems development. These are easier questions to answer if we view the data model as the result of the process of data analysis and within the larger context of the business environment and business operations and management. However, even in those contexts the benefits are not so obvious.

Perhaps one reason is that there is no universal agreement as to what a data model is, or even why one should be constructed. There is also no agreement as to what a data model represents, what it should contain, or how to construct one. Further there is no agreement, universal or otherwise, as to the terminology which describes the constructs of data modeling, no agreement as to the concepts upon which data modeling is founded, or even any agreement on the terminology used to describe data models and their contents.

Given these conditions, and given that there are few if any formal courses in data modeling and none that I know of in data analysis, is it any wonder that the current state of confusion exists?

In this book I will attempt to provide some light on these subjects. I will discuss data analysis, and place it within the system development life cycle. Using that foundation as a basis I will provide an extensive discussion of data models, what they are, what they represent, and hopefully how to construct them.

Those who have read any of my previous books will notice a similarity in some of the text. That is because the concepts I espouse in them have not changed. This book will, however, attempt to examine those concepts from different perspectives—those of the data analyst and data modeler.

I will use some common applications as my examples and show that even when we think we know all there is to know about a subject, maybe in fact we really don't know as much as we thought.

I have been analyzing data for over twenty years, and for an equally long period I have been building data models using a variety of methods and techniques. During that time I thought I had learned almost all there was to know about these topics. I produced my data models instinctively, and they worked. However, I couldn't necessarily explain the processes I went through to produce them, or necessarily why I did what I did, and most importantly why they worked.

While working as a data analyst on a project, I was teamed with a gentleman who was billed as a lexicographer or classificationist. One day as I was trying to explain to him what I was doing, I showed him some of the material I had prepared for the client. He took it home with him and when he returned the next day he gave it back to me with the notation at the top of the page that said "we do the same thing."

As we worked together over the course of the next few months we held extensive discussions on classification as a basis for data analysis and data modeling. After our assignment ended I continued my research into classification and found that new vistas had opened up for me. I now had a vocabulary and concepts which not only helped me explain what data analysis and data modeling were all about, but I could now explain how the process worked.

All organizational activities can be divided into two categories—those that generate or create information and those that process information. Organization information that is generated requires processing and that processing, in turn, generates more information. The usual view of information is quantitative, that is, facts and figures that can be acted upon. The true scope of information is much broader and encompasses all knowledge and learning, all recording, and all transfer of knowledge.

Organizational knowledge includes numbers, facts of all types, inferences, records of actions performed, decisions made, etc.

In this book I will explain data analysis and data modeling from a classification viewpoint and show how these techniques explain what data modeling is all about.

There are probably as many different views of data modeling as there are people modeling data. Some of the fundamental questions which still remain to be answered, however, are: What is a data model? What does a data model represent? Yet, perhaps ever more important, why produce a data in the first place? This book will attempt to answer these and many other questions.

Central to the answer of many of these questions is an understanding of the differences between information and data, the relationships between business process and data, and the meaning of data itself. These themes will be the central focus of this book.

Martin E. Modell

Part

1

Introduction and Background

A picture is worth a thousand words. However, how many words does it take to describe a picture? How many ways can a picture be described? How many words does it take to describe the description of a picture?

Chapter

1

What Is Data Analysis?

Introduction

Business processes and data are tightly interlocked. Processes, or more specifically the sequences of tasks that business personnel engage in, collect, use, and generate data. Data is both the raw material which feed business processes and the product of those processes. Most business activities either collect, maintain (update), file, or disseminate data directly, or indirectly. That is, the data is a direct result of, or describes the actions of, the person performing the process, or it is indirect in that it is about some action someone else has performed. It may be data about some object that the person is working with directly, or an object someone else is working with.

Data, however, is not tangible. It is not something that can be picked up and handled. Data only becomes tangible when it is recorded on some media, which itself can be picked up and handled. Data thus is most often synonymous with the media used to record it. In most cases, the form data takes is highly dependent on the media on which it is recorded. In addition, and perhaps more importantly, the form data takes is highly dependent upon the perceptions of the person recording it, and its use is highly dependent upon the perceptions of the persons using it.

But what is data? *Data* is the name given to those words and numbers we use to describe the things we work with, the types of actions we take, and the results of those actions.

Strictly speaking, data are facts. Within the context of business activities and data processing (in its broadest sense) data are the words, phrases, and numbers we use to create those descriptions and record those results. To the extent that those words and numbers are meaningful, and accurate, they constitute information. There are some writers that make a distinction between data and information, and to some extent that distinction is valid.

Data and Information

Most dictionaries define data in terms of information, but they do not necessarily define information in terms of data. Information is defined in terms of the communication of knowledge.

Information is the representation or recording of knowledge derived from study, experience, or instruction. Data is information organized for analysis, reference, or used as the basis for a decision. Data are facts suitable for processing. Information is data that has been organized and recorded in such a manner as to become meaningful. Information is organized, recorded knowledge of a specific thing, event, or situation. Information is that which communicates knowledge. Knowledge is defined as specific information about something. From these definitions we can derive the relationships between data, information, and knowledge as follows: Information is data (or facts) about a specific subject or event, organized to convey or communicate knowledge. That is, information is data that is organized to tell us something.

Data that does not tell us something is not information. Data is not always organized, or more importantly, may not be defined. The number 23666 is data, which means nothing, per se, until we attach to it the explanation (or definition) that it is the zip code for Hampton, Virginia. Data only becomes meaningful when some definition or explanation is assigned to it. We might also go so far as to say that words and/or numbers without definition are not even data.

Note that the word *data* itself is plural (datum is the singular form although this is hardly ever used). This use of the plural form also tells us that a single fact (a single word or number) is usually not enough to convey information, we need multiple facts, multiple words, multiple numbers or combinations of words, numbers, and definitions to convey information.

For instance, a single word or number (as in the zip code above), or even a list of words or numbers in and of itself is usually meaningless without some explanation as to what those words or numbers represent. In the case of the above five-digit number we must also give it a precise name, in this case it is a five-digit zip code, to distinguish it from the nine-digit (five plus four) zip code.

In the case of lists, we require some explanation as to why the specific entries in the list were assembled, and what significance if any can be attached to the order of the entries in the list. At minimum, a single word or number requires some definition or explanation before it becomes meaningful.

From the above discussion we can arrive at the following definitions:

Definition. *Data* are words and or numbers which have specific meaning. Data derive their meaning from a precise name and agreed upon definitions.

Definition. *Information* is data that have been organized and arranged to convey knowledge.

A Brief History of Data

From the earliest times, people have attempted to describe the things around them and to create records of their actions. These records were intended to preserve for later use, information about what happened, what was happening, and what was expected to happen in the future. These records cover every aspect of human interaction, both private and public, personal and interpersonal.

Some of the earliest forms of records appear as notches on sticks and bones, and to some extent as various forms of art—cave paintings and statues.

The word *history* itself means a narrative of events, or a chronological record of events. To record is to set down for preservation, in writing or in other permanent form. A record is thus an account of information or facts, set down in writing or pictorially as a means of preserving knowledge. If data are clearly defined words and or numbers, if information is organized data, if information is knowledge, and if records are a way of preserving knowledge, then we can see that there is a direct link between data and the recording of knowledge.

Records were, and still are, created for many different reasons. Aside from recording observations and the results of human activity, people have also attempted to record their ideas for posterity; ideas about life, beauty, nature; ideas about how and why things work the way they do. These records are the stuff and essence of the physical sciences, art, philosophy, the social sciences, etc.

The Difficulties in Describing Things

Some of the things people have sought to record were relatively easy to set down, others much more difficult. It is easy to record the steps one goes through to perform some physical activity. It is somewhat more difficult to describe something physical, such as a house, a tree, an animal. These things can be seen and felt, and although most people see these things the same way, there are slight differences in perspective, orientation, and experience, which make those perceptions different, and these differences make the descriptions different.

There are also differences in people's ability to make those recordings. These differences show up in vocabulary, use of words, sentence and phrase construction, style, technique, and a myriad of other things which differentiate the ordinary from the brilliant. In addition, some people are more observant than others, and some are more meticulous in their description. Some, as noted above, just have a wider vocabulary or make better choices of words and can thus describe things in a more picturesque manner—more meaningfully, more clearly, or in more detail.

If problems and differences of perception, and thus of description, arise when people describe the physical, is it any wonder that even more problems arise when they venture into the realm of ideas, the things which cannot be seen or felt.

It is in the realms of art, writing (fiction and nonfiction), theoretical science, and philosophy that the portrayal of ideas is attempted most frequently. Artists must first select their subjects, and then the perspectives they wish to portray. The artist must then choose the media—oils, pastels, charcoal, etc.—and then the colors to be used. The artist must determine what to highlight and what to make subdued, where to place emphasis and where to draw focus.

The writer, scientist, and philosopher must develop an understanding of their ideas, solidify those ideas into words, and present those ideas logically. The choice of words, perspectives, and emphasis is as important here as in the realm of art, perhaps even more so. Writers, unlike artists, must rely on mental imagery to convey their ideas.

When we look at a painting or a sculpture we see what the artist saw, or more specifically what the artist wanted us to see. When we read words, we do not necessarily understand what the writer wanted to convey. We do not know how closely, nor how completely, our understanding of the ideas matches that of the writer. Because ideas are intangible and usually not based upon something real (tangible) they are difficult to describe, even when pictures and diagrams are employed.

Describing a System

Business systems are concepts or ideas. One cannot pick up a business system, in most cases one cannot see a business system, although one can see many of its components—activities and recorded data.

Systems analysts and systems designers, although they use both words and pictures (diagrams or models) to describe the results of their analysis, and the requirements and specifications of the business systems they create, are in many ways more like writers than artists. They use words and diagrams to describe ideas, intangibles, things which exist and things which do not exist. Unlike the artist, and, in some cases, the writer who describe things that are fixed, or static, systems analysts and systems designers attempt to describe things which are dynamic. That is, they try to describe things which are constantly changing or constantly moving. They describe actions being performed, and actions as they should be performed. They describe work flows, document flows, and the documents and reports that carry business data. However, they must also describe the environment that they are creating these business systems for and in which these business systems exist. They describe the environment that these business systems create. All of these descriptions are conceptual; they are ideas and perceptions of a reality. More importantly they must describe the data that fuel the business, the data that are carried on the documents and reports. This description of data is not of the words and numbers, but of the meaning of the words and numbers. In many cases they must also determine, or select, the words and numbers to be used to create these descriptions and then determine the definitions to be used to apply meaning to them.

The analyst must look at data and the meanings assigned to data from several perspectives. The first perspective is that of the business community being supported by the system and who therefore use the data. For these people the analyst must determine the requirements for data, for information, and most importantly for knowledge. The second perspective is that of the programmers and the computers they work with. For these people, the analyst must determine coding structures, automated record contents, and other automation-related requirements.

It is the analysis of data requirements and the description of those data requirements that is the concern of this book, for as we have seen, data are just facts—words and numbers with definitions attached.

The analyst must address several problems—first, the selection of the appropriate facts to use; second, the determination of how to organize those facts to make them most useful; and third, how to present or record those facts, and what recording media to use.

Thus we arrive at another definition.

Definition. *Data analysis* is that set of activities that determines a business's requirements for information, determines the data and data definitions required to represent that information, and determines the most effective and useful method for organizing and recording the data.

Background of Data Requirements Analysis

In order to understand both data analysis as it is practiced today—as a part of the systems analysis—and systems design processes, and to understand the problems inherent in data analysis, one must have some understanding of its history.

Modern data analysis practices are the result of many parallel and interrelated trends. The effects of these influences are not uniform in all organizations, but they are present to some degree in just about every organization today. They are

The movement from permanent data recording technology (WORM—write once, read many times) to update-in-place technology

The movement from single record design to fragmented or segmented record design and the growth in the number of record types contained in application files

The movement from an application or process orientation of file design to a central file or entity orientation of file design—from single user function/single user organization application files to multi-user function/multi-user organization application files

The movement from standard file access methods to data base management system (DBMS) management of data and still further, from single DBMS organizations to multiple DBMS organizations

The movement from batch processing to on-line processing of data and the growth in the number of users of those on-line systems

The movement from cyclic to real-time currency of data

The movement from generalized responsibility for data-related activities to specialized responsibility for data-related activities in the systems life cycle—from systems analysis and systems designers to data base administrators to data administrators to data/information resource management organizations

The movement from predominantly manual generation of systems analysis and design documentation to CASE (computer-assisted software engineering)-assisted system life cycle documentation

The movement from operationally oriented data files to data files which must support all levels of the organization, and the growth in the demand for data within today's corporations

The growth in the number of files used in each application and the size of these files

Each of these trends (Figure 1.1) are having substantial and recognizable effects on the techniques for developing systems and on that set of system development activities known today as data analysis.

In the early days of data processing most applications of automation were scientific, and thus statistical or highly mathematical. That is, the computers were programmed to solve complex formulas or computations. These computations relied on relatively (by today's standards)

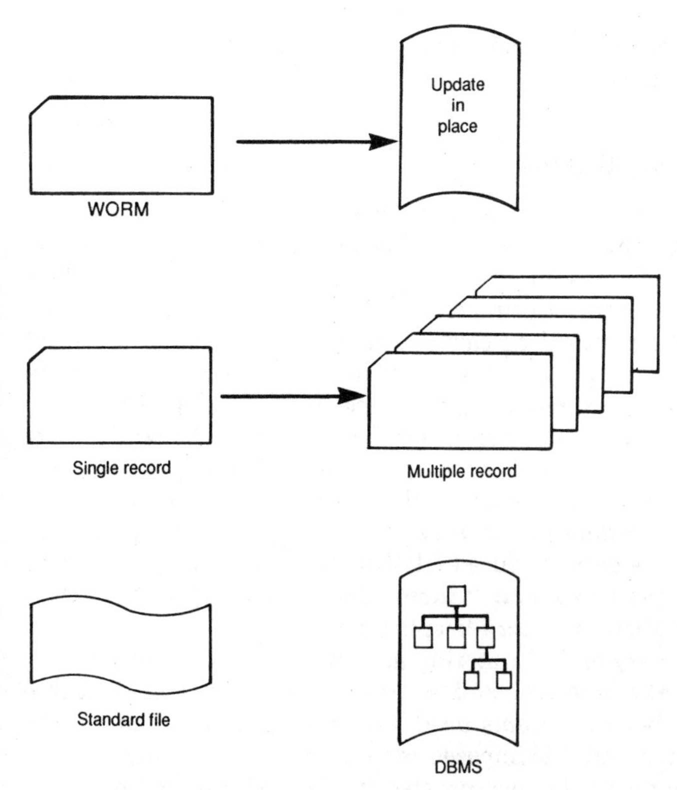

Figure 1.1 Trends in file design.

small amounts of data (numbers). Data were entered into the machine for computation in one of two forms, punched cards or punched paper tape. Most punched cards held either 40 or 80 columns of data (Figure 1.2). Paper tape held more data but was less commonly used because it

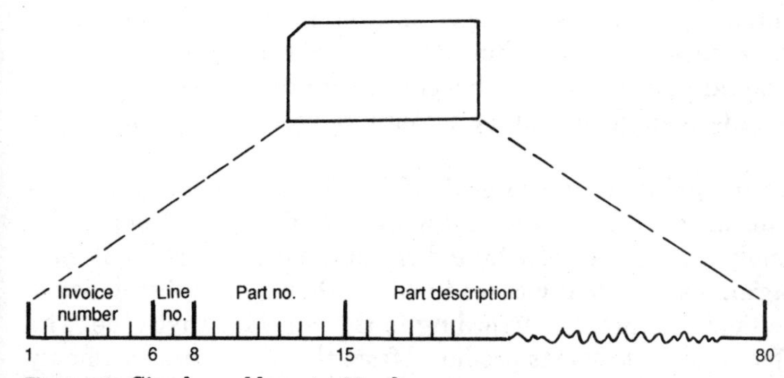

Figure 1.2 Simple card layout—80 columns.

was delicate (more so than cards) and was difficult to change (again, more so than cards).

Punched Card Data Storage

Although the data was vital to the proper functioning of the applications, the volume of data read in was low in comparison to the volume of data produced. Several hundred punched cards of data could produce several thousand pages of printed data. Data tended to be single use, that is, data was punched on cards for a single calculation pass and then discarded. In some cases, the programs produced new data for the next calculation pass by punching numbers into cards or paper tape.

The advent of electronic accounting machines brought with it new kinds of applications—commercial applications (hence the name accounting machines). These applications were still predominately mathematical, but the computations were not as complex, and the ratio of data read in to the data produced fell drastically. Computers retained their primary function as computational devices but they also began to take on new functions as record-keeping machines.

Since the primary form for storing data was still the punched card, data space was at a premium, and wherever possible data was coded to reduce the number of columns used. Central processor memory was also at a premium and this imposed restrictions on the amount of processing logic that could be incorporated into a program. Coding structures and schemes were used to compress data where possible, and this compressed, coded data was passed on to the output reports. Codes were used most frequently when the potential values for data item contents could be represented by, and thus selected from, a relatively short list of entries. Codes were usually developed such that a single (or in the case of a long list—two)-digit number (or character) corresponded to each entry in a list.

Because each update cycle of the application (each execution of the program) produced changes to these records, requiring a new set of cards to be produced, many systems designers devoted extensive effort to developing card formats in which a single card corresponded to a single item record—a single inventory account, payroll account, or budget account.

This data compression had several effects. First, it reduced the processing time, since card readers, and more specifically card punching, was extremely slow (especially by today's standards). Second, it simplified program logic in many cases to "If . . . then . . . else" style logic: Test a code field and process according to the rules for that code. The adverse effect was that reports produced from this data were extremely cryptic, unless one had extensive reference sheets to decipher the code meanings.

This problem of highly coded information was ameliorated to some degree by merging the coded data with more descriptive data cards for reporting purposes and by producing reports with headings which assisted the reader in the deciphering chore.

Data was thus segregated into two kinds—static data (data used for reference purposes such as names and addresses) and used to provide descriptive information on reports and forms and dynamic data (used for totals, quantities, payroll deductions, payments and receipts, etc.), data that was highly coded or otherwise compressed.

This segregation allowed data used for reference and descriptive purposes (on reports) to be maintained apart from the dynamic data. Dynamic data was normally maintained by machine, where each cycle or run of the programs generated a new version of the data records, while the static, or reference data was maintained predominantly in manual form, with cards being pulled from the master decks, changed, and replaced, as necessary.

As card processing technology progressed, and as processing units increased in memory and speed, application programs became more complex and could thus process more data in a single pass. User demand for more informative reports also increased the need for more data, and more complex data. The need for more data was accommodated in two ways: First, more highly encoded data was used, and second, more cards were used to accommodate the additional data items.

As both static and dynamic data expanded across multiple cards, each card had to have a data item to identify the account, employee, inventory item, invoice, etc., that its contents represented, and additional data items to reflect the card type and card sequence number.

Where multiple cards were used to store both dynamic and static data each card had a specific format, field layout, or kind of content. As applications and thus data became more complex, sets of cards were used to store a single record's worth of data and more and more codes had to be added to identify the kind of data on each card; that is, the programs had to be able to identify what kind of card they were reading so that they could determine the kind of data that was expected on that card.

Each different format was identified by a code such that the programs could interrogate the code and determine what data items were expected on that kind of card. In some cases, sets of cards were used with the same layout. Where the application required these cards to be processed in a specific sequence an additional data element was added to ensure that that sequence was maintained. This type of card-set design was used most frequently on order and invoice processing systems, where multiple lines of address and multiple item lines were needed for a single document, and each address line or each item line was represented by a single card.

Magnetic Media Data Storage

With the introduction of magnetic storage media—disk, tape, and drum—systems designers were able to effect several major changes in data file design. Although drum storage was around for a substantial period of time, it was slow, had relatively limited capacity, and was moderately expensive. Drum technology never really gained the popularity that tape or disk (DASD) enjoyed and today except for isolated instances drum applications are almost nonexistent.

Magnetic media, more so DASD than tape, allowed systems designers to make many significant changes to their designs. First they were able to build longer records, having been released from the 40- or 80-character limitation of cards. Second, they were able to build larger files and were able to process them faster due to the speed of the recording devices. Third, they were able to develop update-in-place applications, at least with drum and disk. They were also released from several other limitations; one being the number of concurrent files which could be input into an application program, and the second the requirement to process all files sequentially rather than randomly.

These media allowed for the introduction of randomly accessed reference files, easy resequencing of data files, more frequent updating of data files, and enabled the movement to on-line style applications.

Limiting Factors on Magnetic Media

As systems designers designed applications using this new technology they incorporated the same data file design techniques as they used in the card environment. Data that were migrated from card to tape and disk retained its format and eighty position flavor. Many early file designs retained the same concepts and tape records appeared in multiples of 80 characters.

Although tape and disk technology were introduced at much the same time, much of the processing was tape oriented. This was due to the relative speed and capacity of the tapes versus the disks, and more importantly the cost of the media. Tapes could be removed and stored easily, and tapes were much less expensive and had a higher capacity than disks. Tape was also a sequential processing media and most systems designers had extensive experience in the techniques involved in sequential file processing.

Many of these applications were oriented around the "old master–new master" processing, with one or more transaction files and master files being input to the applications and a new, updated, master being the primary output. This method of systems design also carried forward the cyclic processing nature of earlier card systems—that is, the currency of the data in the files reflected the timing of the processing cycles.

These early magnetic media files also carried forward the multiple-record format of the card processing systems. The difference being that the records on magnetic media were not restricted to 80 characters. This mode was known as master-detail processing in that the data for a given subject (invoice, purchase order, employee record, etc.) was contained on multiple coded records each of which was identified by the subject identifier and as with the card formats some code which identified the type of record being processed. Usually the first record contained static information and the detail records contained variable, dynamic, or multiply occurring groups of data.

The processing logic for these kinds of files was difficult and cumbersome, and prone to errors of file processing logic, due to the variable number of record occurrences—and thus the variable amount of data. In order to obtain the complete set of data for a given subject the application had to process all of the records associated with that record identifier.

Magnetic processing also introduced variable-length record processing and while this resolved some of the problems with processing multiple-record-type files, they introduced other processing problems resulting from the effort to decode field identifiers and the determination of which fields were and were not present.

Variable-record-length processing was effective where variable record lengths were combined with fixed record formats. That is, files were designed in such a manner that each record was fixed in length but each record type contained a different-length record.

As disk storage processing technology advanced other access methods were introduced which combined the advantages of sequential processing with random processing strategies—that of associating indexes with either sequential or random access files so that the data could be accessed in either mode. Indexes, however, were initially limited to single-record-format files and to fixed-length records.

Data Base Technology

As they gained experience with disk processing techniques supplied by the hardware and operating system vendors, many large companies, including some hardware and software vendors, experimented with new disk access techniques and methods for providing even more flexible file processing. These combined indexing mechanisms with both fixed- and variable-length record formats and with the earlier master-detail, or multiformat, record file processing concepts. These new access mechanisms or access methods added file processing logic which allowed for chaining records together via pointers (physical record location addresses) contained in one record which pointed to the next record in sequence. This allowed for more flexible formats (Figure 1.3) since the individual record types comprising the complete subject record no longer had to be physically contiguous but could be scattered throughout the physical file. This processing worked provided that the pointer chains remained in tact.

As these early experiments evolved, the complex file/record management, access, retrieval, and update logic was extracted from the processing programs and replaced with common code which could be in-

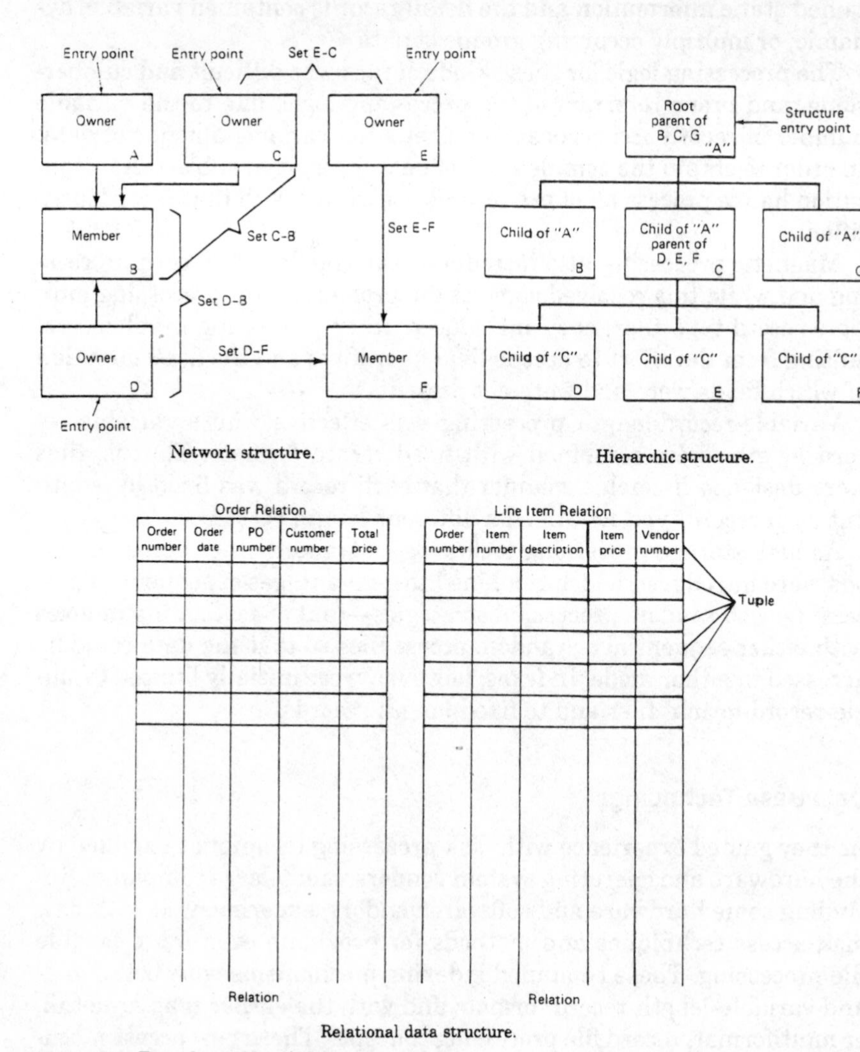

Figure 1.3 Data base file models.

voked from the application programs and could be directed to perform specific tasks through strings of parameters passed during the invocation processing.

These new complex file processing techniques were commercialized in the late sixties and early seventies under the general name *data base management system* (DBMS).

The Effects on Data File Design

As each of these advances in technology was introduced and absorbed, they added new and more complex considerations to the problems of file design. As file design options increased, specialists emerged for each type, first tape and disk file processing and design specialists, then later data base design specialists. Although initially these people were technicians who specialized in physical design considerations, physical file implementation, data base management system parameter selection and coding, and file access performance, other advances and concepts were introduced which caused these technicians to assume other analysis and design responsibilities within the systems life cycle.

Chapter

2

Data Analysis and the System Development Life Cycle

The framework and sequence of activities used for the development of systems is called the system development life cycle. The processes and activities within this framework are usually performed according to well-defined and comprehensive sets of procedures called methodologies. These methodologies include specific activities for the analysis and design of both the data and process portions of the system.

While some of these activities can be uniquely designated as data or process most overlap and combine aspects of both. As these methodologies developed, the activities defined by them became more and more separated into those specific to data and those specific to process. This differentiation of activities into either data or process has led to the rise of the term data analysis, as opposed to systems analysis, as a way of both categorizing the activities and of assigning responsibility for them.

We have used the term *system development life cycle,* and the implication of the name is that it is used specifically for system development, rather than for system maintenance or system enhancement. Although maintenance and enhancement are different from development in many respects, they are in reality subsets of the full development cycle of activities.

Maintenance is the term applied to those activities which correct flaws or errors in both systems design and implementation with respect to system requirements and system specifications. That is, maintenance makes the system conform to original requirements.

System enhancement falls between system maintenance and system development in that it also corrects flaws in requirements and specifications. System enhancement adds to system capability by incorporating new or augmented requirements.

The major differences between the three kinds of life cycle lie in the scope of their activities, in the extent of the changes each produces, and in the considerations each must address with respect to the existing system implementation. Maintenance changes the existing system, enhancement adds to the existing system, and development replaces the existing system.

Because the data-related activities for development are the most comprehensive we will concentrate on the development life cycle and point out the differences in those activities as they apply to both maintenance and enhancement.

Before we begin our discussion of data analysis and the system development life cycle we should set some perspective.

1. Since most business activities involve the gathering, manipulation, presentation, or dissemination of data or information, any system development life cycle must concentrate on those activities.

These data-specific activities should be clearly defined and have clearly assigned responsibilities.

2. Since many business procedures are or soon will be automated, or semiautomated, any system development life cycle must acknowledge, account for, and provide for automation considerations.

This is especially true for data, in specific, for the design of the automated files, the physical storage of those files, and for the identification and specification of all file access and maintenance procedures and issues.

3. The development of business systems is a business function and as such should be subject to the same management and controls as any other procedure. Its processes and activities should be performed within a framework and according to a well-defined set of procedures.

The management of data and the controls applied to it should be at least as stringent as those developed for either the business processes or any other business assets.

4. The development of business systems, as a business function, is subject to the same types of changes which affect other business functions, and the systems and procedures which govern how it operates are subject to the same change agents as any other business systems or procedures.

Although business data, and specifically business data files, change less rapidly and less frequently than do business procedures, those changes which do occur have a more severe impact, and thus data file changes must be closely monitored and controlled.

What Is a System Development Life Cycle?

In order to accomplish any given set of tasks effectively one must have a work plan or procedure. Without such a procedure or work plan, activities are performed in a haphazard manner and with little if any coordination. The results are that the various intermediate products rarely fit together into a cohesive whole, and worse yet, the finished product rarely meets the initial specifications. In some cases because of a lack of a work plan there are no initial specifications.

The overall work plans for systems development are called system development life cycles, and the detail plans are called methodologies. In some cases, the system development life cycle is also called a methodology, but for our purposes we will make a distinction between the two.

Definition. A *method* is a means or manner of procedure, a regular and systematic way of accomplishing something—an orderly and systematic arrangement. A method is a set of procedures that follow a detailed, logically ordered plan.

Definition. A *methodology* is a system of principles, practices, and procedures applied to a specific branch of knowledge.

The Purpose of a Methodology

Methodologies, specifically system development life cycle methodologies, provide the framework and the sets of procedures within which the myriad of development tasks can be performed. Most methodologies cover the entire span of development activities from project initiation through postimplementation review.

Depending upon the methodology, they may or may not include specific activities for data. In many cases, identification of data element requirements and specification of data file design are incorporated into the procedural design and specification activities. This data-related design and specification is not documented separately but often appears as an appendix in the procedural documentation.

Methodology

Generally speaking, the analysis portions of a methodology must include and provide for

Business organizational analysis

Business function analysis

Business process and activity analysis

Business data analysis

This analysis portion forms the first and perhaps the most critical phases of the development project. It is the analysis phase that identifies and documents the business requirements for change. In other words it is the analysis phase which defines the problem to be solved and the scope of the problem environment. In many cases these phases are the project itself since the information developed may show that no further work is either necessary, feasible, or desirable. In all cases, the results of the analysis phases determine

1. If there is a problem to be addressed
2. If there is a feasible solution to the problem
3. If developing a solution to the problem is cost beneficial to the user and to the firm as a whole

Analysis projects are initiated to change the business procedures of a business, but more often they are initiated because the firm requires both procedural change and data change. This data change can come in many forms, from reorganizing the data to make access more efficient, to making wholesale additions to the kinds of data available for use by the business.

System Development Life Cycle Phases

Assuming that the project proceeds in a normal and orderly fashion, it can be expected to follow the following general phases:

A. Project initiation
B. Analysis
   1. General business analysis
   2. Detail business analysis
C. Examination and study
   1. Evaluation of existing system components
   2. Problem identification
   3. Feasibility analysis of alternative approaches
D. Design
   1. Development of general business system design
   2. Development of detailed business system design
   3. Development of procedural solution specifications
E. Implementation of the procedural solutions

F. Testing of the procedural solutions
G. Implementation of the procedural solutions into the normal business processing schedule (production)
H. Postimplementation review of results.

Although the preceding list contains many project phases, it can be simplified to

1. Analysis
2. Design
3. Implementation

These three (Figure 2.1) are bracketed by project initiation, and project conclusion and review. Additionally, all five activities include the administrative tasks of planning, scheduling, and control.

Each phase has its associated data activities (Figure 2.2), each of which is designed to identify a specific aspect of business data, or to assist the analysis and design teams in defining that data, organizing that data, or determining the various implementation-specific aspects of the physical data file storage. In some cases these activities are completely separate, and in other cases they are tightly interwoven into the procedural activities.

Definition. *Analysis* is the separation of an intellectual or substantial whole into its constituent parts for individual study; the stated findings of such a separation or determination.

Definition. *Systems analysis* is, by extension, the study of a group of interacting, interrelated, or interdependent business functions, processes, activities, or elements forming a complex whole. It is also the separation of these functions into their constituent parts (the procedures which govern them) for individual study.

Definition. *Data analysis* is that set of processes and activities whereby the user requirements are identified and the data elements necessary to satisfy those requirements are identified, defined, specified, and organized.

A business system is intended to be an orderly, harmonious group of interacting, interrelated, and interdependent procedural components. Each of these components and each of these procedures in turn generate, use, or disseminate data. All business procedures process data. All business procedures are data processing procedures, that is, they all process data in some manner.

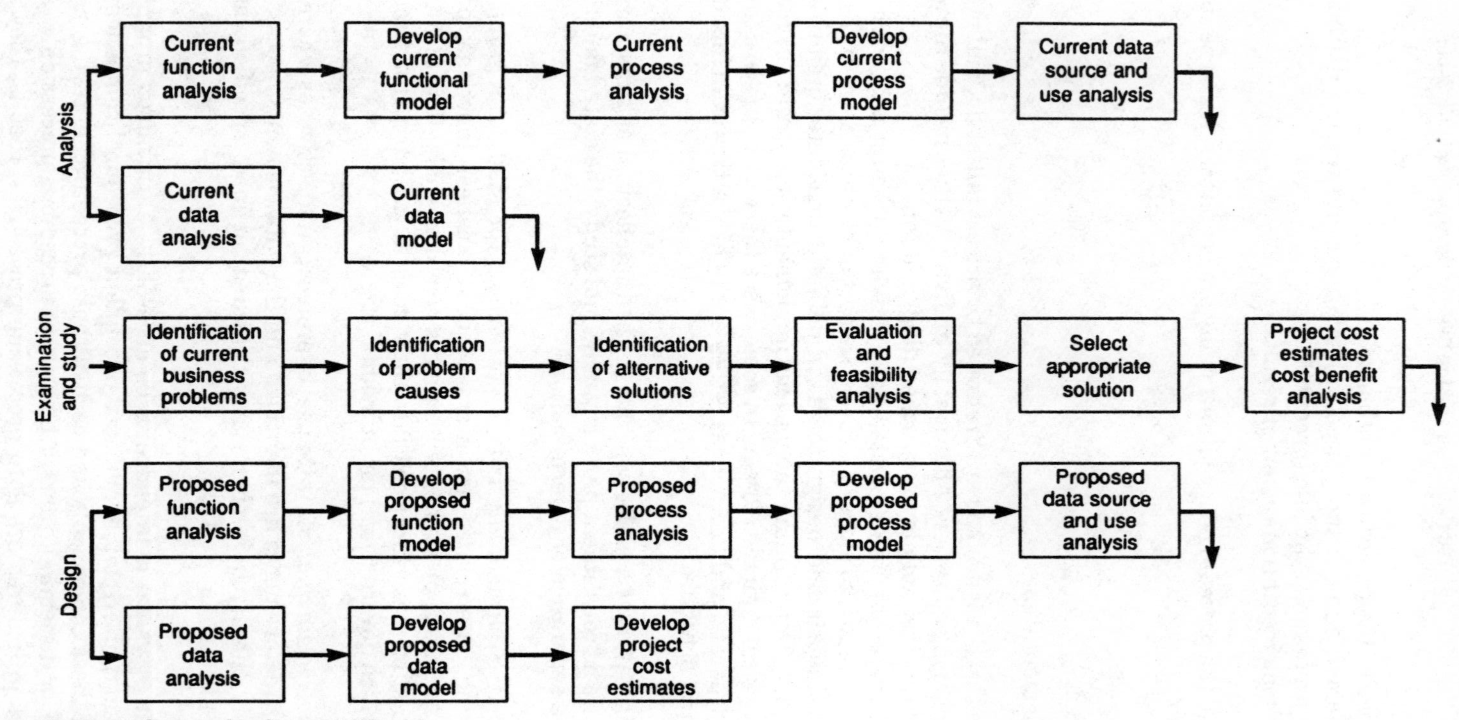

Figure 2.1 System development life cycle.

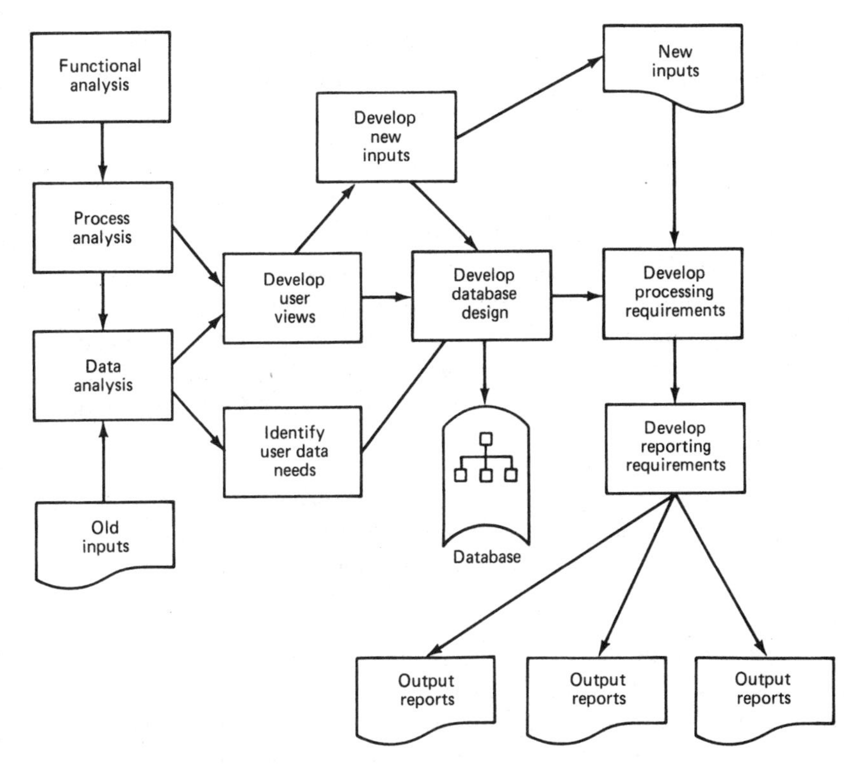

Figure 2.2 Data analysis view of the system development life cycle.

Over time, internal and external business changes cause gradual, individual procedural changes such that the component parts of the system either no longer interact harmoniously or those individual components can no longer be changed except with great difficulty. These changes also cause new or different requirements for data to arise. These new data requirements may be for additional data not previously available, for existing data to be made available in new ways, or to different parts of the organization, or it may be for changes or modifications to existing data.

When that point is reached the system itself, and all its component parts, must be taken apart, modified such that all the parts work harmoniously, and put back together. During the process of modification, the disorderly, disharmonious, independently acting procedures are changed. At this time new procedures for new processes, activities, and tasks are developed and can be added into the revised system.

A major result of this process are the additions, modifications, and reorganizations made to the business data files which support those procedures. Sometimes these changes to the business data files are minor, sometimes radical, and in some cases extensive new files are added to the business data inventory.

Systems Analysis versus Systems Design

If systems analysis is the process of separating a system into its component parts (individual procedures) for study, examination, and repair or replacement, then system design is the process of taking those component parts *after examining, studying, and making changes to them,* and putting them back together into a harmoniously interacting complex whole.

Definition. *Systems design* is that set of processes and activities whereby the specifications as to how that data is to be gathered, maintained, processed into information, and made available to the user are articulated.

One can see from the above that there are in fact substantial differences between systems analysis and system design. In fact it could be argued that we are not talking about two processes, but in fact three processes—analysis, examination and study, and design.

Systems analysis works with tangible things and activities and how they act and interact today. Systems analysis also works with data and procedures and their interaction. In many cases the analysis uncovers many areas of miscommunication of information. This miscommunication is due to differing definitions, differing interpretations, and differing use of organizational data. The analysis also frequently uncovers many inconsistencies in data, personal files which do not correspond to public corporate files, data which has been extracted from one context and used in another, and the use of different or at least highly modified procedures in different parts of the firm to perform the same activities.

These business activities can be observed, examined, and described, and that description can be compared to the original for verification and validation. The description either conforms to reality or it does not. The analysis is correct to the extent that it is complete and to the extent that it compares accurately to the original. Systems analysis works in the present, and to an extent in the past. It works with and attempts to understand and describe what is.

Examination and study works with the results of analysis, looking for ways to improve. It attempts to identify the problems and the opportunities for change. It also attempts to document the needs and requirements for what should be changed or added. The examination and study phase attempts to identify the sources of both procedural and data problems, and to the extent possible to identify which data to use, and which procedures to follow, when conflicts are identified.

Systems design, on the other hand, works in the future. It is a plan for what activities should be performed in the future, how they should be performed (the procedures), and what resources are needed for the performance of those activities. Most importantly, it is the development of a framework within which those activities must be performed. That framework is what provides order and harmony to the whole. The design may be taken to any level of detail necessary, or possible, to fully describe what changes must be made and how, when, and where they must be made.

Systems design must also address business data, its storage, and its use. The design documentation must resolve the problems of conflicting definitions, conflicting use, inconsistent processing, questions of data ownership, data currency, and perhaps most importantly the questions of data responsibility; who must collect the data, who must maintain the data, who may access that data, and who determines when it is no longer of value to the firm. In some firms these issues are addressed when new data is identified and the systems are designed for its processing. In other firms these issues have been deferred for many years and are only addressed when the organization embarks on a system redesign project.

Obviously, the lines between systems analysis and systems design are blurry at best. Most authors have treated the two topics as one, and to the extent that design is a continuation of the analysis process, it is correct to do so. However it must be stressed that there are in fact, three processes.

These processes are not separable. Analysis, and examination and study are performed so that we can make modifications and come up with a new design. The reason for a new design is because we need to make modifications, and the scope and extent of those modifications are based upon analysis, examination, and study. We cannot do any one without the other two, and in fact have little if any reason to do any one without the other two.

Most of these authors have presented systems analysis and system design in the form of a methodology—a fixed set of processes, activities, and tasks which when accomplished will produce a design. To the extent that analysis and design are two ends of the same process they were also correct in developing a common methodology.

Design and analysis differ in distinct ways. The goal of design is to construct from component parts. The goal of analysis is to break down into component parts for examination.

System Components

Given the above, the components of a business system consist of

1. A *framework* which specifies the processes, activities, and tasks which need to be performed, and how those processes, activities, and tasks are related and interdependent. It also specifies the interprocess, interactivity, and intertask rules to which all processes, activities, and tasks must conform in order to operate in an orderly and harmonious manner.
2. The *individual procedures* which specify in detail how each process, activity, and task is to be performed and how each is to interact with all other related and interdependent processes, activities, and tasks.
3. The physical, personnel, and monetary *resources* which are used by each procedure. It also specifies the limitations or constraints in terms of time, personnel, budgets, data, and standards upon each procedure.
4. The data which are the raw materials of business processes, the schemes under which that data is organized, and the files in which that data is stored. Business data also include the methods of presenting that data, either on screens, reports, forms, or other media. Business data, in keeping with our previous definition of data, also includes the definitions, explanations, and agreements which provide common meaning and value to that data.

Although we have defined data as an integral part of a business system, and obviously it is, we must also recognize that business data transcend most business systems. A processing procedure is little more than a formalized series of instructions describing how to accomplish some task, and a system itself is little more than a framework for organizing those procedures so they work in an orderly manner. Within the framework of a given user application, there may be different kinds of systems and different kinds of design environments. Each type of system and each type of systems environment has a different set of considerations and thus no one design approach will suffice for all.

Business data, however, represents both information and knowledge. Businesses can operate with inconsistent procedures, most do so every day. Businesses can operate with chaotic procedures, again most business have areas where their procedures are less than perfect. Businesses cannot operate without information, nor can they operate without correct information. That means that businesses cannot operate if the data from which they derive their information is defective. They cannot operate for long without consistently defined information, for to do so is to construct a corporate version of the tower of babel.

Business data is also the means for corporate communications. If the data is correct, business communications—both horizontally and vertically—will be clear and precise.

Systems versus Applications

There are two additional terms which are used somewhat interchangeably within the data processing community: system and application.

Definition. An *application* is the way in which a specific technology, such as data processing, has been used to solve a specific user business problem.

Some examples of applications are order entry processing, inventory record processing, payroll processing, personnel record keeping, customer statement generation, and accounts receivable or accounts payable processing.

In these examples, data processing technology has been used to support and accomplish a set of use area processing activities. These activities have not been wholly automated, only some of the highly structured, repetitive, well-proceduralized, well-defined, specific tasks of the data collection, filing, record keeping, calculation, printing, and reporting have been taken over by the computer. Many of the other tasks within the same processes remain manual.

Definition. A *system* is the complete framework within which mutually supportive processes, activities, and tasks operate.

A good system is one in which these processes, activities, and tasks operate in a cooperative, harmonious, efficient, orderly, timely, and controlled manner. The processes, activities, and tasks encompassed by a system may or may not be automated, and if automated may not be completely automated.

From the process perspective, new system development is undertaken for one or more of the following reasons. To enable

1. New activities to be performed
2. Existing activities to be performed in a more efficient, cost-effective, rapid, or timely manner
3. More iterations of a given activity sequence to occur in a specified period of time
4. Greater management control
5. More efficient use of company resources

6. Greater cooperation between the various activities which have to be performed
7. A greater level of integration between system components
8. The use of new technology or the replacement of obsolete technology
9. A faster response to future changes

From the data perspective, new system development is undertaken for one or more of the following reasons. To enable

1. New data to be acquired
2. Existing data to be enhanced or modified by the addition of new or modified coding structures
3. Data to be more accessible, or more flexible accessibility to data
4. Greater management control over data
5. New data to be added to existing files
6. Data from several files to be cleaned up, scrubbed, or otherwise consolidated into one central file
7. A greater level of integration between system data files
8. The use of new technology or the replacement of obsolete technology as the means for storing company-automated data

Chapter

3

Data Analysis and Systems Analysis

Analysis

Systems analysis, and thus those data activities associated with it, is essentially a fact-gathering phase. It looks at what is happening in the business area under study and it develops documentation of the current environment which, in turn, acts as a foundation or starting point for any further analysis or redesign activities. Since systems design is essentially a redesign of the current environment, making changes to improve current effectiveness, efficiency, and capability, as well as correcting flaws which may exist and adding capability which is lacking, the analysis team must have an accurate starting point.

There are multiple levels of business activity. These levels of business activity can be roughly categorized into a strategic (or planning) level, a managerial (or monitoring and control) level, and an operational level. Each of these levels represents a different level of perspective on the firm; each of these requires a different level of data aggregation and a different kind of data. Stated in a different manner, each has different data needs and different ways of viewing that data. Each level also uses data in different ways.

Just as there are multiple levels (Figure 3.1) of business activity, so are there differences in the way data is both viewed and used between businesses. These differences are obvious when one looks at a manufacturing concern versus a service provider, and less obvious when one compares two firms in the same line of business. Differences also exist when one looks at two firms with the same product lines and who share the same customer base. Differences exist even when one looks at different divisions or even different departments of the same company.

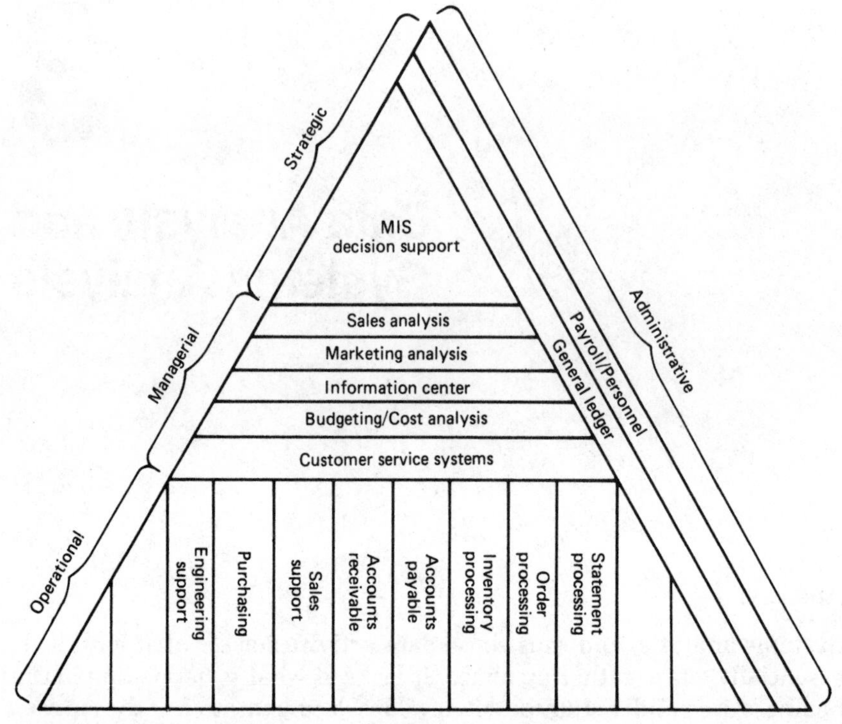

Figure 3.1 Multiple levels of business systems.

Most methodologies recognize some of these differences and allow for analysis on multiple levels. Most methodologies do not allow for differences in data perspective or data use. Almost all allow for multiple-level analysis. Although there can be many levels, or successively more detailed iterations of analysis, for practical purposes most discussions are limited to three.

The first is usually labeled the general or business environmental analysis level (Figure 3.2) and it concentrates on the firmwide functions, processes, and data models. This has been called, by some, enterprise analysis. The analysis at this level has the widest scope in terms of numbers of functions covered, and looks at the highest levels of the corporation. This level corresponds to the strategic level of the firm. It does not treat data as such, but rather looks at higher levels of data abstraction—usually those persons, places, things, and ideas which are labeled business entities.

The second is usually labeled detail business or client environmental analysis, and concentrates on the functions, processes, and data of the individual client or user functional areas. This analytic level is narrower in scope than an enterprise level analysis, and may be limited to

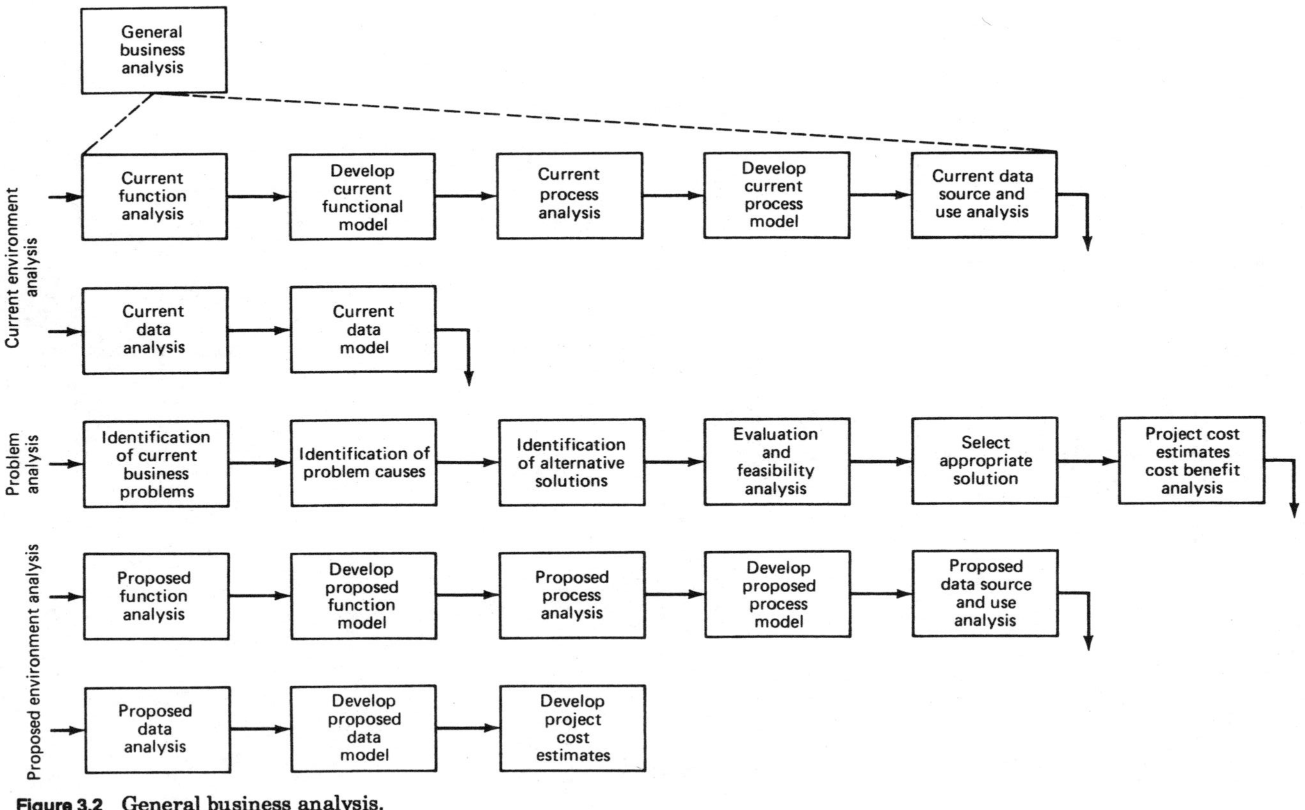

Figure 3.2 General business analysis.

a single high-level function, such as human resources, finance, operations, marketing, etc. This type of project corresponds to the managerial or administrative level of the firm. Data references at this level are a mixture of abstract high-level business entities and more concrete, specific groups of entities and entity roles, and in some cases data files (also for some reason treated as entities) used by the user areas.

The third is the most detailed, and can be considered as the application level (Figure 3.3) which addresses the analysis of specific user-processing systems. This level of analysis has the narrowest scope and usually concentrates on a single-user functional area. It is within this analytic level that individual tasks, individual file records, and data items are addressed. This analytic level corresponds to the operational level of the firm. Data at this level is highly specific, reflecting its usage in user processing.

Regardless of the level being addressed or the particular methodology employed, analysis must examine the current environment from all three perspectives—functional, process, and data. The intent and goals of the analysis phase are to document the existing user functions, processes, activities, and data. The activities of this phase could be loosely equated to those of taking inventory of what is present and then trying to rationalize or make sense of what is found. This is especially true of the data activities.

It is the need for more, better, or more complete data that drives most system redesign projects. Most existing business systems use data

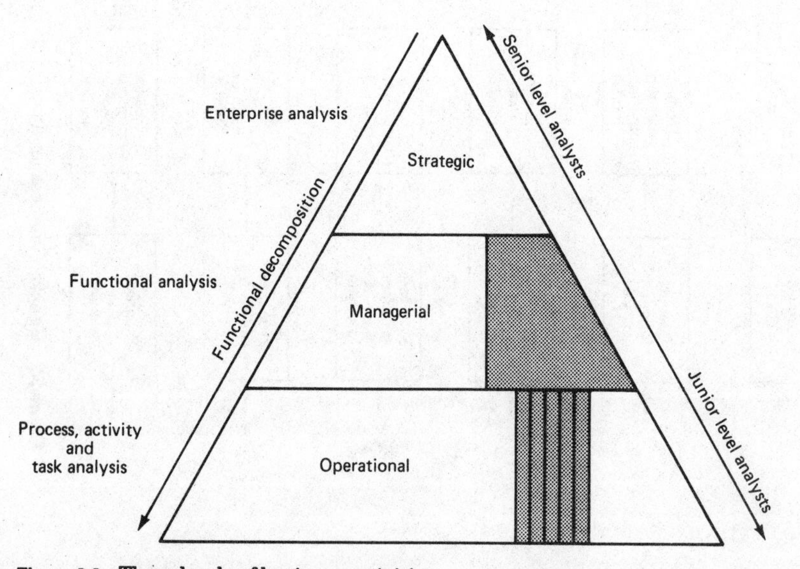

Figure 3.3 Three levels of business activities.

which reflect old requirements, old business systems, or old business philosophies. What almost all analysts uncover as they progress through the analysis activities is that many of the concepts which form the foundation of the firm are not clearly understood, or worse have multiple definitions. Much of the data, because it is used primarily under local control, developed local definitions, which over time caused miscommunication between the various areas of the firm. This local definition caused even more miscommunication between the various levels of the firm, and in time hindered or completely prevented management's efforts at reorganizing, or changing, the business activities and data availability to meet changing business needs.

The data analysis activities of the system analysis phase attempt to identify these data differences in preparation for resolving them and designing a consistent communication structure for the firm. Business data with consistent meaning, and appropriate organization, form the heart of the business communications process.

The initial analysis or inventory identifies all current data and all current sources of that data, in all of its idiosyncratic forms, and more often than not, it identifies gaps in the company's data. These gaps take the form of user requirements for "new" data. New data can actually be new data, or as is more often the case, it is existing data in a different form, a different organization, different levels of detail, different time frames, or in different combinations than currently are available.

This inventory of "what is" added to the user's new requirements and need for revisions to existing files and data sources is the primary product of the analysis phase and the raw material of the examination and study, and design phases. The phrase "what is" with respect to the analysis phase is contrasted to the phrase "what will be" which typifies the design phase. Thus the analysis phase concentrates on the current environment while the design phase concentrates on the future environment. This statement is true to the extent that analysis looks at current systems. It is untrue to the extent that analysis also gathers requirements (unfulfilled needs) which are part of, or may become part of, the future system.

The major activities (Figure 3.4) for the analysis phase are

1. Current function analysis
2. Development of the current function model
3. Current process and activity analysis
4. Development of the current process model
5. Current data source and usage analysis
6. Current data analysis
7. Development of the current data model

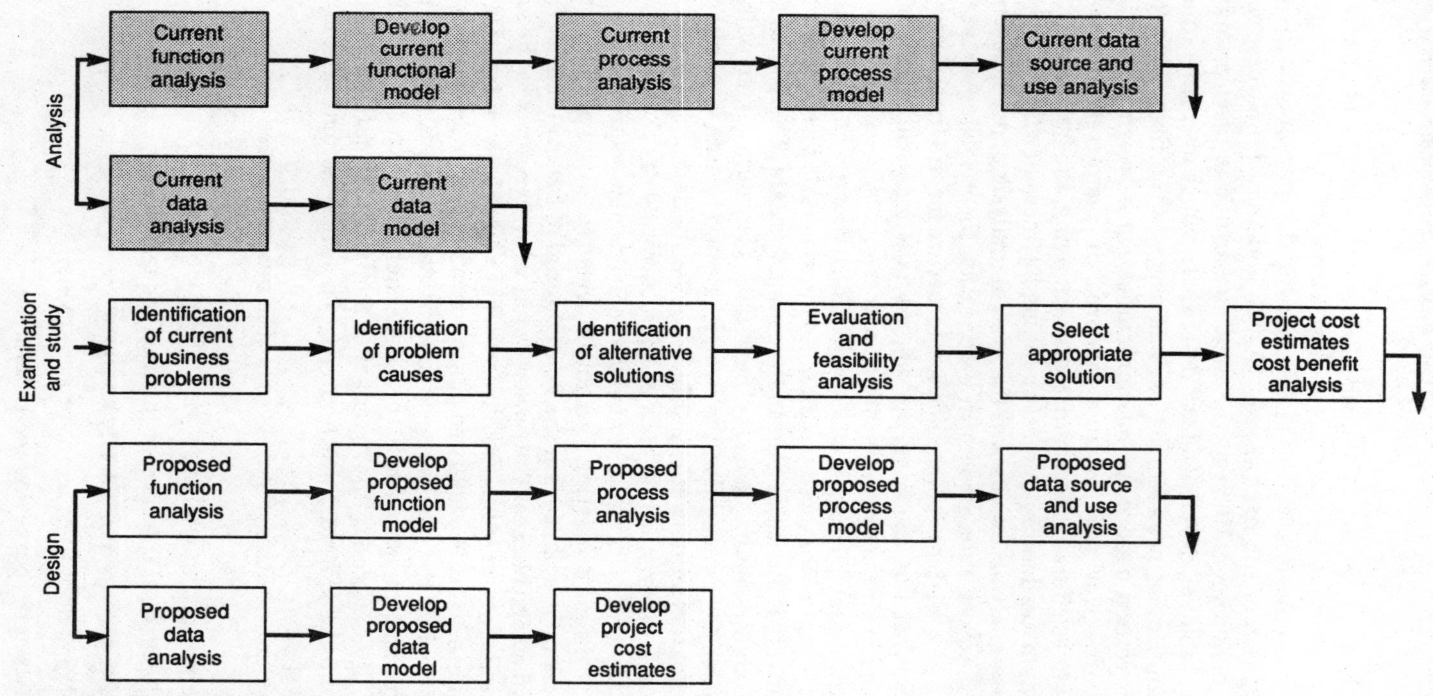

Figure 3.4 Major activities of the analysis phase.

Each of the above major activities involves either process or data or both. Obviously the last three are data-related analysis activities. Depending upon which methodology was chosen, the third and fourth activities could also be considered data analysis activities. This is especially true if the data flow diagram method has been chosen over the process decomposition method. Each of these activities focuses on some aspect of the current environment or some aspect of user requirements, and each develops some product [either a narrative or a graphic model (Figure 3.5)].

The design of any new system must be predicated upon an understanding of the old system. The only exception to this is where there is no old system. It is the migration from account to customer orientations (a new philosophy or way of looking at the business) that drove many major banks, insurance companies, and brokerage houses to major development projects to redesign and reorient their systems. This type of major change caused these firms to require the performance of completely new sets of activities—activities with which the firm has no prior experience.

Many of these firms however, had a very difficult time in developing

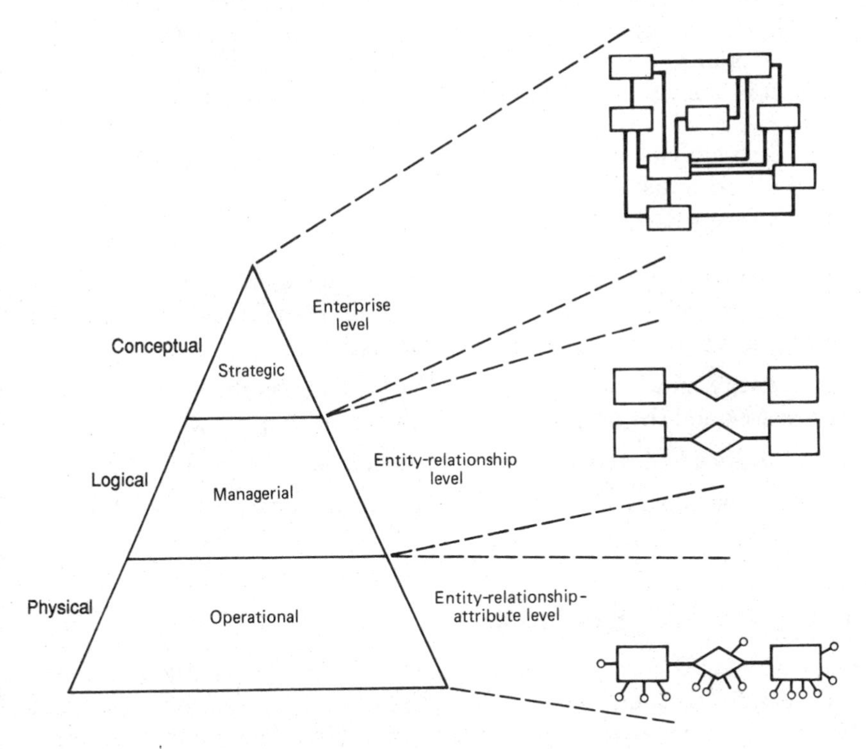

Figure 3.5 Various data models produced during the analysis phase.

these systems, especially in the analysis and design stages. This difficulty arose because many of them could not or did not understand who or what their customers were. That is, they could not create a definition of a customer such that they could identify and describe one. Many of the firms had many different types of customers with ill-defined differences between them. For instance, many brokerage houses could not distinguish, practically, between retail customers and institutional customers. Many insurance houses could not differentiate between customers and policy holders.

The bulk of the analytic activities in these firms were focused on determining how and where customer data were currently acquired, and not on what a customer was, that is, not on what kinds of people or organizations made up the customer base but on what kinds of information the firm needed to acquire and maintain about those customers. Without an understanding of what the customer was, many of the systems designs that resulted were inadequate for the firm's needs.

Process-Related Activities

During the analysis phase, each function is described in detail in terms of its charter, mission, responsibilities, authorities, and goals.

Each major grouping of business processes, or system, within each function is identified and described in terms of the processes which are within it.

For each activity there is a description of the tasks involved, and the resources being used.

For all processes it seeks

- To trace the processing flows and their component tasks, both individually, in relation to each other, and in context of the user function and the overall functions of the organization
- To identify and describe all current data inputs which trigger those processes and the outputs which result from those processes
- To identify and describe all current results of the individual processes
- To place each process within the larger context of the functions of the firm

Data-Related Analysis Activities

The easiest and most common data activity during the analysis phase is to look for data elements and list them, that is, describe their data processing incarnation (size, shape format, etc.). Many analysis teams come up with long lists of these data elements, gleaned from file and reports. This activity, while it has some value, is meaningless unless the analysis team also takes the time (lots of time) to define each element (or as is more often the case to identify each of the multiple, and sometimes conflicting, definitions of each element) and to determine which elements are in fact the same, regardless of the label attached to them. Most older systems, both manual and automated, have their own data files. These files may be electronic or paper, or some combination of both.

These files contain data, designed for that business system, and named according to the whim, logic, or even standards of the team responsible for their design. Individually, the data in these files are consistent and usually minimally redundant; however, in combination with files from other systems, the results are chaos. In almost all cases, there are no clear definitions of these data elements, and without clear definitions, there is no way to determine when elements are the same or different. In many cases without clear definitions there is no way to determine what the data element content represents, or even what it should represent.

Within the analysis phase, all sources of data and information must be identified and all uses to which that data and information are put must also be identified. All data forms, reports, and files must be identified and their contents inventoried.

All data flows between functions, processes, activities, and tasks must be identified, researched, and described.

The analysis process (Figure 3.6) seeks to decompose a complex whole into its component parts. It seeks to

- Trace the data flows into, from, and through the organization
- Identify and describe all current data inputs
- Identify and describe all current data outputs
- Identify all current data stores (on-going files)

Input/Output Analysis

This type of data analysis begins with all entry points of data into the system and traces all flows to the final outputs. It includes transaction analysis, data flow analysis, data source and use analysis, and data event analysis. For these methods each data input to the system is flowed to its final destination. That is, the path of each input, and sometimes each data element is traced through the firm, and documented. Where there are multiple paths that specific data can take, each path is documented, and the conditions under which that path is or should be taken is documented. This type of analysis and documentation is dif-

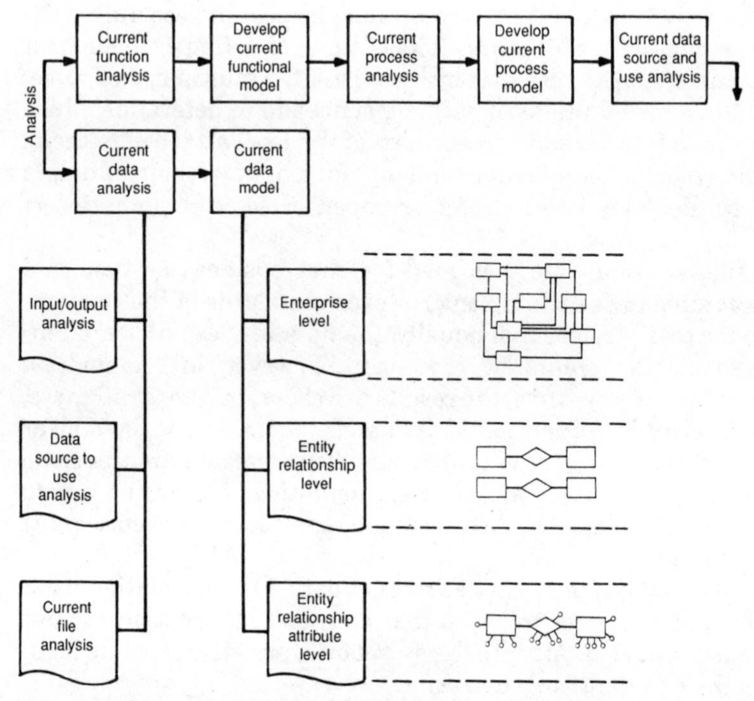

Figure 3.6 Data analysis products of the systems analysis phase.

ferent from the traditional structured analysis techniques, also called data flow diagrams, which are in reality data flow decomposition diagrams. Data transformations and manipulations are examined (using data flow diagrams) and outputs are documented. This type of analysis is usually left to right, in that the inputs are usually portrayed as coming in on the left and going out from the right. Data flow analysis techniques are used to depict the flow through successive levels of process decomposition, arriving ultimately at the unit task level.

Analysts performing these tasks must take care to include in their documentation all copies made of input forms and reports, and all points within the firm that data contained on forms and reports are reentered into other reports and personal computers. This type of activity is especially prevalent in staff offices where analysis of company performance is accomplished for the firm's management. The path of each copy of each multipart form must be traced and documented, along with the reason for each copy, and careful notes should be taken as to when these forms, reports, and copies are annotated with additional data, or when corrections are made.

Validation of these methods requires that the analyst and user work backward from the outputs to the inputs. To accomplish this, each output or storage item (data items which are stored in on-going files—also an output), is traced back through the documented transformations and processes to their ultimate source. Output-to-input validation does not require that all data inputs be used, however all output or stored data items used must have an ultimate input source and should have a single input. Input-to-output validation works in the reverse manner. Here, each input item is traced through its processes and transformations to the final output.

Validation of output to input, or input to output, looks for multiply sourced data items, and data items acquired but not used.

Data Source–to-Use Analysis

This method of data analysis is approached at the data element level and disregards the particular documents which carry the data. The rationale for this type of data analysis is that data, although initially aggregated to documents, tends to scatter, or fragment, within the data flows of the firm. Conversely, once within the data flows of the firm, data tends to aggregate in different ways. That is, data is brought together into different collections, and from many different sources for various processing purposes.

Some data is used for reference purposes, and some are generated as a result of various processing steps and various transformations. The result is a web of data which can be mapped irrespective of the processing flows. The data flow models, and the data models from the data analysis phases, are particularly useful here. The analyst must be sure to cross-reference and cross-validate the data model from the existing system.

Validation of the Analysis

Although not a definable phase within the system development life cycle, the validation of this stage of the data analysis is important enough that it deserves separate treatment.

The completed analytic documentation must be validated to ensure that

1. All parties agree that the conditions as presented in the documentation accurately represent the environment.
2. The documents generated contain statements that are complete, accurate, and unambiguous.

The validation of the products of the analysis phase must address the same two aspects of the environment: data and the processing of data.

A system is a complex whole. Old systems are not only complex, but in many cases, they are a patchwork of processes, procedures, and tasks which were assembled over time and which may no longer fit together into a coherent whole. Many times needs arose which necessitated the generation of makeshift procedures to solve a particular problem. Over time these makeshift procedures become institutionalized. Individually they may make sense, and may even work; however, in the larger context of the organization, they are inaccurate, incomplete, and confusing.

Most organizations are faced with many of these systems, which are so old, and so patched, incomplete, complex, and undocumented that no one fully understands all of the intricacies and problems inherent in them, much less has an overview picture of the complete whole. The representation of the environment as portrayed by the analyst may be the first time that any user sees the entirety of the functional operations. If the environment is particularly large or complex, it could take both user and analyst almost as long to validate the analysis as it did to generate it, although this is probably extreme.

Validation seeks to ensure that the goals of analysis have been met, and that the documents which describe the component parts of the system are complete and accurate. It also attempts to ensure that for each major component the identified subcomponent parts re-create or are consistent with the whole.

To use an analogy, the processes of system analysis and system design are similar to taking a broken appliance apart, repairing the defective part, and putting it back together again. It is easy to take the appliance apart, somewhat more difficult to isolate the defective part and repair it, and most difficult to put all the pieces back together again so that it works. The latter is especially true when the schematic for the appliance is missing, incomplete, or, worse, inaccurate.

If during the repair process new, improved, or substitute parts or components are expected to replace some of the existing parts, or if some of the existing parts are being removed because they are no longer needed, the lack of proper documentation becomes a problem almost impossible to overcome.

The documentation created as a result of the analysis is similar to the creation of a schematic as you disassemble the appliance. The validation process is similar to making sure that all the pieces are accounted for on the schematic you created. However, because your intent is to repair and improve, the documentation you create must not only describe where each component fits, but why it is there, what its function is, and what if any problems exist with the way it was originally engineered and constructed.

Validation must not only ensure that existing procedure is correctly documented, but also that, to the extent possible, the reasons or rationale behind the procedures has also been documented. The validation of the products of analysis seeks to ensure that the verifier sees what *is* there and not what *should* be there.

Systems analysis by its very nature works to identify, define, and describe the various component pieces of the system. Each activity and investigation seeks to identify and describe a specific piece. The piece may be macro or micro, but it is nonetheless a piece. Although it is usually necessary to create overview models, these overview levels, at the enterprise and functional levels, seek only to create a framework or guidelines for the meat of the analysis, that which is focused on the operational tasks. It is the detail at the operational levels which can be validated. The validation process of both data and process work at this level. Each activity, each output, and each transaction, identified at the lowest levels, must be traced from its endpoint to its highest level of aggregation or to its point of origination. In the analysis, the analyst is fact gathering and seeking to put together a picture of the current environment.

During validation the analyst begins with an understanding of the environment and the pictures or models he has constructed. The aim here however is to determine

- Whether the analyst's understanding of the environment is complete and correct
- Whether the depiction of the current environment matches what is actually there and matches the user's understanding of his environment

It must be understood that the analysis documents represent a combination of both fact and opinion. They are also heavily subjective. They are based upon interview, observation, and perception. Validation seeks to assure that perception and subjectivity have not distorted the facts.

The generation of diagrammatic models, at the functional, process and data levels, greatly facilitates the process of validation. Where these models have been drawn from the analytical information, and where they are supplemented by detailed narratives, the validation process may be reduced to two stages.

Stage one. Cross-referencing the diagrams to the narratives, to ensure that

1. Each says the same thing.
2. Each figure on the diagram has a corresponding narrative, and vice versa.
3. The diagrams contain no unterminated flows, there are no disconnected figures, no ambiguous connections, all figures and all con-

nections are clearly and completely labeled and are cross-referenced to the accompanying narratives.

4. The diagrams are consistent within themselves, that is, that data diagrams contain only data, process diagrams contain only processes, and that function models contain only functions.
5. Each diagram is clearly labeled and a legend has been provided which identifies the meaning of each symbol used.
6. When the complexity of the user environment is such that the models must be segmented into multiple parts, each of the parts has consistent labels, titles and legends, the connectors between the parts are consistent in their forward and backward references, and names of figures which appear in multiple parts are consistent.

Stage two. Cross-referencing across the models. This includes ensuring that

1. Processes are referenced back to their owner functions, and functions reference their component processes.
2. Any relationships identified between data entities has a corresponding process which captures and maintains it.
3. All data identified as being part of the firm's data model has a corresponding process that captures it, validates it, maintains it, deletes it, and uses it.
4. All processing views of the data are accounted for within the data models.
5. References to either data or processes within the individual models are consistent across the models.
6. All data expected by the various processes are accounted for in the data models.

Walk-Throughs

Walk-throughs are one of the most effective methods for validation. In effect they are presentations of the analytical results to a group of people who were not party to the initial analysis. This group of people should be composed of representatives of all levels of the affected user areas as well as the analysts involved. The function of this group is to determine whether any points have been missed. In effect this is a review committee.

Since the analysis documentation should be self-explanatory and nonambiguous, it should be readily understandable by any member of the group. The walk-through should be preceded by the group's members reading the documentation and noting any questions or areas which need clarification. The walk-through itself should take the form of a presentation by the analysts to the group, and should be followed up by question and answer periods. Any modifications or corrections required to the documents should be noted. If any areas have been missed, the analyst may have to perform the needed interviews and a second presentation may be needed. The validation process should address the documentation and models developed from the top two levels—the strategic and the managerial—using the detail from the operational.

Each data item contained in each of these detail transactions should be traced through these models, end to end, that is, from its origination as a source document, through all of its transformations into output reports and stored files. Each data element, or group of data elements contained in each of these stored files and output reports, should be traced back to a single source document.

Each process, which handles an original document or transaction, should be traced to its endpoint, that is, the process-to-process flows should be traced.

Chapter

4

Data Analysis and the Examination and Study Phase

Evaluation and Study

The examination and study activities are not normally separated into a separate phase, instead most methodologies combine them with either the systems analysis phase outlined in the last chapter, or with the systems design phase outlined in the next. They serve as bridge activities in which the analysis and design team looks at "what is" and makes its preliminary decisions as to what the "should be" will look like. Problems uncovered by the analysis are examined, design approaches identified, and implementation alternatives evaluated.

During this phase (Figure 4.1) of the system development life cycle the results of the analysis are examined, and using both the narratives and models, the analysis team identifies the procedural and data problems which exist. These problems may be as a result of misplaced functions, split processes or functions, convoluted or broken data flows, missing data, redundant or incomplete processing, and nonaddressed automation opportunities. They also identify those data items and data problems that cause miscommunication within the firm.

The activities for this phase are

1. Identification of current data problems
2. Identification of the causes of data problems
3. Identification of alternative solutions
4. Evaluation and feasibility analysis of each solution
5. Selection and recommendation of most practical and appropriate solution

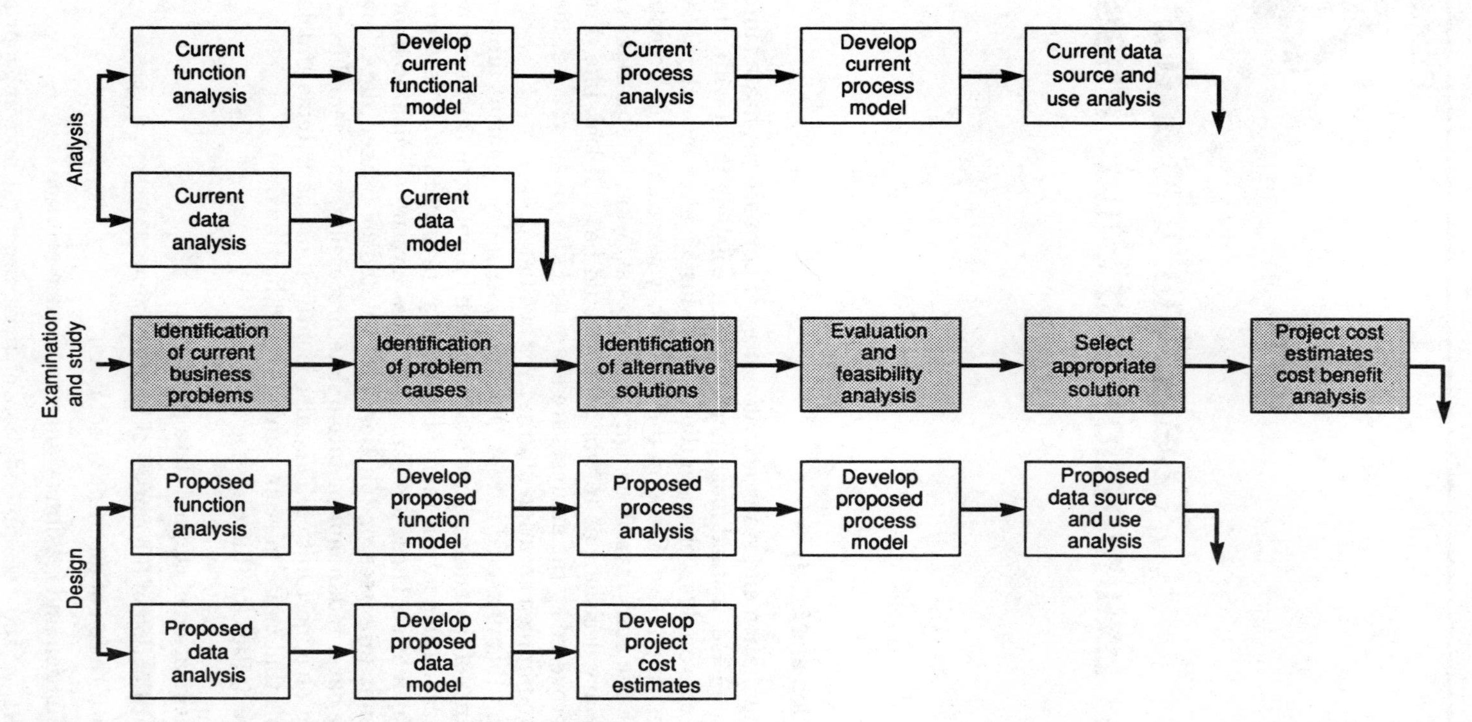

Figure 4.1 Data analysis and the examination and study phase.

6. Project cost estimation and cost benefit analysis

Each activity examines both data and process, since for the most part they are interwoven. Problems with data and problems with process are inseparable and in most cases one cannot change one without changing the other.

Data components are evaluated to determine whether the data gathered by the firm is

1. Needed
2. Verified or validated in the appropriate manner
3. Useful in the form acquired
4. Acquired at the appropriate point, by the appropriate functional unit
5. Complete, accurate, and reliable
6. Made available to all functional areas which need it
7. Saved for an appropriate length of time
8. Modified by the appropriate unit in a correct and timely manner
9. Discarded when it is no longer of use to the firm
10. Correctly and appropriately identified when it is used by the firm
11. Appropriately documented as to the type and mode of transformation when it does not appear in its original form
12. Appropriately categorized as to its sensitivity and criticality to the firm

Most importantly, data items are evaluated to determine whether they are defined properly and consistently, if at all.

The evaluation of the data components seeks to achieve an end-to-end test of the analysis products, looking for inconsistent references, missing data or processes, missing documents or transactions, overlooked activities, functions, inputs or outputs, etc.

In many respects this evaluation should be conducted in conjunction with the other evaluation processes. The analyst and the user alike should be looking for "holes" in the analysis documentation, both to determine "correctness" and completeness.

Identification of Current Data Problems

Just about every business system has problems with respect to data. The differences between newer systems and older systems are reflected in the types of problems and the number of problems.

Older systems have problems with inaccurately defined data, missing data, and data which has become too inflexible to support current needs. This is typified by forms containing fields which are used by different areas for different reasons, multiple-copy forms where data on the various copies changes independently of each other, and forms which have been supplemented by addendum, and continuation forms used to contain information not provided for on the original version.

In some cases, older coding structures have become vague, or worse, have codes which have changed their meaning over time without corresponding changes in procedural documentation.

Newer, usually automated systems employ codes whose meaning is embedded in program code and procedures which have become so complex that only the programmers are fully versed in them, and thus the operational and managerial personnel are forced to rely on the data processing staff to resolve problems whose solution rightly belongs elsewhere.

The newer systems in many cases have had "intelligence" built into identifiers which have become inadequate for current business needs. Account-based firms (banks, etc.) have long constructed account identifiers from a combination of office number and some qualifier (usually a sequential number or a series of codes) which identify not only the unique account, but also the type of account, account responsibility, etc. Over time these codes have lost their meaning due to account movement, expansion of code ranges beyond the limits of the valid values (e.g., single-digit numeric codes with more than ten possible values), or changes in code meaning which affect some accounts and not others.

Perhaps the most prevalent type of data problem is that of missing or inadequate data. This happens in just about every firm. Original assumptions as to the kinds of data which must be collected and maintained have been invalidated due to changes in business conditions or business requirements. This is most readily evident with respect to customer demographic information, which is used for marketing analysis, and customer service needs.

Perhaps the second most prevalent problem is data which has been collected and filed by the firm, but never maintained (kept up-to-date). This out-of-date data is usually kept in paper files for reference although in many instances it may be found in automated files as well. Aside from being largely inaccurate, this data is also expensive to store, and dangerous if it is used for current processing or analysis. Much of this data is maintained on original employment applications, account-opening forms, and other one-time use forms which are filled out and filed away. Other file problems arise from different kinds of data being stored in the same files and in some instances the same records making data maintenance inconsistent at best and impossible at worst. Examples of this are found in payroll systems which also carry employee data, account files which also contain customer data, policy files which contain customer data, and order files which also contain product data. Still other types of problems come from files where different data in the same records has different currency, that is, different parts of the records reflect different instances in time, and files containing the same data reflect different instances in time, making data reconciliation and amalgamation difficult if it can be done at all.

Some current data problems are related to growth in both the size of the files themselves and in the number of operational personnel who need access to the same data. Increases in transaction volumes, changes in the complexity of those transactions, and the slow evolution of business systems due to continual minor (and sometimes major) modification all cause the performance of older systems (their ability to support current needs) to degrade. Operational personnel who were originally satisfied with same-day response to queries now demand multisecond response. Managerial personnel who were originally satisfied with printed reports now require personal access to the data files for analysis.

The evolution of personal computing and the concurrent migration away from centralized data center support have caused heightened user awareness of both data and processing, and has increased the demand for data in ever-increasing quantities and levels of detail. Firms which used to file data on microfiche or tape after relatively short periods of time beyond its use in current business processing are now being asked to keep increasing amounts of this data available for longer periods of time for immediate access by business personnel.

Technology has also played a part in causing real or perceived data problems in many firms. Newer, more flexible, more friendly data base management systems and the increased use of nonprocedural languages and more friendly data manipulation techniques (fourth-generation languages) coupled with the increased computer literacy fostered and supported by desktop microcomputers of all types have caused new interest in data and its availability by business personnel. This proliferation of small, powerful processors with disproportionately large capacities for data storage and the evolution of newer methods of automated communication between processors of all sizes, regardless of location, and the ease of data transfer between these processors has weakened corporate control over its data and in many cases reduced the reliability of data which reaches management's attention.

Microcomputer-based data base management systems which allow the user to collect new data, retrieve data from other processors, and mix this data together for analysis, along with new tools for data analysis and manipulation, all heighten corporate conflict over data. Microcomputer systems, departmental systems, and centralized mainframe systems, along with manual (paper-based) systems, barely coexist and have created a quagmire of data problems, many of which were unforeseeable when the only data processing was performed on mainframes.

Causes of Data Problems

Although each analysis team must identify the specific set of problems and the specific set of causes (Figure 4.2) for their environment, generally data problems are caused by one or more of the following:

1. Lack of current procedures
2. Lack of corporate data policies
3. A slow erosion or breakdown of communication between business areas
4. The introduction of new concepts into the organization without careful analysis, documentation, and explanation to all personnel
5. Frequent and rapid changes to the business environment without allowing time for business personnel to digest and assimilate those changes

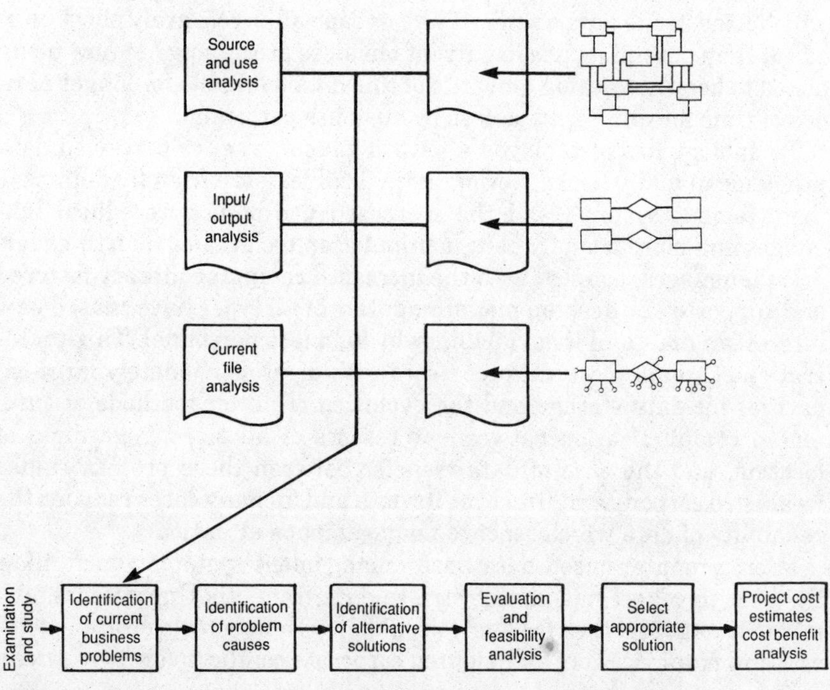

Figure 4.2 Data analysis inputs into the examination and study phase.

6. Erosion of management awareness of basic business processes and the concurrent divergence of perception and reality

Carrier to Data Evaluation

Carrier to data evaluation focuses in on the data transactions to determine whether the data on the documents (data carriers) which enter the firm are passed consistently and accurately to all areas where they are needed.

It seeks to determine whether or not the firm is receiving the correct data, whether it understands the data that it is receiving (i.e., what the transmitter of that data intended), and whether it is using that data in a manner which is consistent with its origin.

Since, with few exceptions, the firm collects data on its own forms, and with even fewer exceptions, the firm can specify what data it needs and in what form it needs that data, this level of evaluation should compare the firm's use of the incoming data with the data received to ensure that the forms, instructions, and procedures for collection, acquisition, and dissemination are consistent with the data's subsequent usage.

Zero-Based Evaluation

This evaluation approach is similar in many respects to zero-based budgeting, in that it assumes nothing is known about the existing data. It is a "start-from-scratch" approach. All user forms, data, and files are reexamined and rejustified. The reasons for each are documented and all data flows are retraced.

Zero-based evaluation should always be undertaken where the analysis indicates that the systems, processes, activities, and procedures are undergoing resystemization or reautomation. It should also be undertaken where the analysis indicates that the existing systems and automation may have been erroneous, or the business requirements may have changed sufficiently to warrant this start-from-scratch approach.

In any case, the analyst should never assume that the original reasons for data being collected or being processed are still valid. Each data transaction and each process must be examined as if it were being proposed for the first time, or for a new system. The analyst must ask

1. Are the business areas addressing the appropriate data and is it correct data?
2. Are all the steps performed to process each transaction correct? And, are they all necessary?
3. Are the appropriate business areas collecting the firm's data?

4. Does the value of the data being collected or processed justify the resources being devoted to it?
5. For each report:

   Is this report necessary?

   If it is necessary, is it necessary in its current form?

   To its current level of detail?

   Should it be produced as frequently as it is?

Problem Identification

Although many of the problems, especially data problems, with the existing system may have been known or suspected at the time of project initiation, the scope and extent of those problems, and in many cases the reasons for those problems, may not have been accurately known.

The analytical results not only represent the analysts' understanding of current environment, and the analysis team's diagnosis of the problems inherent in that environment, but also their understanding of the users' unfulfilled current requirements and projections of user needs for the foreseeable future. The combination of these four aspects of the analysis will be used to devise a design for future implementation. Thus it is imperative that it be as correct and as complete as possible.

It is at this point that the analyst and user should have the detailed analytical documentation before them, as well as the results of the evaluation of that analysis.

During the interviews conducted during the data analysis activities of the systems analysis phase, each user should have been asked questions which sought to identify one or more of the following data problems:

Missing data

Difficulties in data access

Data at an incorrect level of detail

Data which means different things to different user areas

Data which is owned by multiple user areas

Data which is not current

Data which is not timely

Data which is changed by multiple user areas

Data which is transformed and altered without management knowledge

Data which is being reentered into computers from incorrect media

Users were asked to identify areas where responsibilities for activities were either not specified, or where responsibility for certain activities were accompanied by the appropriate authorities. Activities where responsibilities were split—where responsibility was shared across multiple functions—were identified.

Identical or highly similar activities which were performed in multiple areas were identified. Activities which appeared to be aimed at accomplishing the same purpose but which were performed in highly dissimilar manners were identified, and the causes for those dissimilarities were identified.

During the interviews, the users were also asked to enumerate processes and activities which were not currently being performed, and which could not be performed or could only be performed with great difficulty in the current environment, but which the users felt should be performed, especially if that difficulty had to do with missing, incorrect, or unaccessible data.

As the analysis progressed, the analysts should have been able to identify areas of opportunity. Areas of opportunity result from the synergy between data and process, data and data, process and data—synergy which has created the ability to achieve a corporate mission or goal, or to provide a new service, or create a new product, or provide new information about the firm's products, competitors, customers or markets—but where that opportunity has not as yet been identified or taken advantage of.

System Design Requirements Document

The product of the examination and study phase is a document which is usually referred to as a system design requirements document, or a client requirements document. This document classifies, catalogs, and enumerates all existing and identified problems and opportunities, by function, processes, activity, task, and procedure. For each of these it lists the change requirements or specifications—the specifications and requirements for correcting the problems or the possible methods of taking advantage of the identified opportunities. Simply stated, this is the verified documented list of all the places and ways where system and procedural changes have fallen behind the business activities which they were intended to support. It also documents all the ways where the users anticipate changes to occur, or where changes which have occurred have created opportunities to take advantage of recognized synergies within and between business activities and among the resources of the business.

Prioritizing of Changes

Each item pair—problem and requirement or specification, or opportunity and proposed method or approach—is evaluated against all other pairs and prioritized. The prioritization may be performed by any one of a number of available methods such as

1. A simple high, medium, or low priority—reflecting perceived importance to the firm and the user.
2. A simple scalar prioritization—where each item is assigned a number which places it in rank order such that the first item pair in the list is the most important, the second is next in importance, etc.
3. A complex scalar prioritization—where each item pair is assigned a degree of difficulty to implement, or a degree of importance, or both, and within the first a scalar prioritization. The result is a ranking of the most important items within another ranking method, i.e., most important high-priority item (assuming there are multiples).

The above methods (and variations thereof) are the most prevalent ones and while they accomplish part of the goal of analysis, and are necessary, there are two other rankings which should be performed by both the user and the analysis and design team. These are dependency ranking and synergy or impact/benefit ranking.

Dependency Ranking

Dependency ranking seeks to determine item dependencies, items which form the foundation for other items, or which items must be accomplished before certain others. This assumes that there are three types of changes which must be made during any new system design.

Foundation changes. Changes upon which all others are based. These include changes in charter, responsibility assignment, or technology; development of a new product or service, new technology; selection of a new market; finalization of corporate reorganization, movement to new location, or modernization of existing location, etc.

Architectural and procedural changes. Changes which once the foundation items are determined can be designed and developed. These are basic structural changes, and form the bulk of the difficult and usually time-consuming system design tasks. These include changes in data gathering, validation, verification, storage, and evaluation procedures. They also include all the activities which aggregate and regroup those procedures to activities, the activities to processes, and the processes to systems.

Presentation, display, or cosmetic changes. Many changes which have been identified result from changes in user perception and perspective, or from increased user awareness of his environment and needs. These result in requests for changes in report form and content, faster access to existing data, or improved methods of accomplishing existing tasks. These changes usually do not require structural or architectural changes. Each of these changes while small in itself, when added to the vast number of other similar changes may require the largest part of the design team energy.

Synergy or Impact/Benefit Ranking

Synergy or impact/benefit ranking is the most difficult task to perform in this phase but it is also the one where major benefits to the firm exist. Although it is termed a ranking, in reality it is the examination of each item or combination of items (the items in this case being proposed changes or modifications) to assess

A. The number of specific, recognizable, direct, or indirect benefits which are expected to be achieved from this change.
B. The extent of the positive impact, that is,
   1. The number of other changes which could be accomplished if this change is made.
   2. The number of other changes which would not be necessary if this change is made.
   3. The number of other changes which would be made easier if this change were made.
C. The number of additional (and unanticipated) things which could be accomplished or goals which could be achieved if this change or combination of changes were made.
D. This change in combination with one or more other changes, if all made at the same time, would increase any of the above (synergy).

Cost-Benefit Ranking

The examination and study phase usually includes a cost-benefit analysis of each proposed change and an evaluation of the costs and benefits of each change with respect to its various rankings and prioritizations. The item-by-item cost-benefit analysis provides another (and sometimes the most definitive) method of evaluating the proposed change in specifications and requirements.

Cost-Benefit Analysis

The examination and study phase is completed when a cost-benefit analysis is developed for the system design phase for the selected approach.

From the data perspective each item of data that is collected, and each procedure put in place to collect, maintain, or present data has a cost. Since each data item must have all three types of procedures to be useful, the cost of data, at a minimum, is the cost of the procedures and the effort necessary to perform those procedures. There is additional cost associated with storage and media. These costs must be assessed during the cost-benefit analysis.

There are additional costs which must also be ascertained, most of which accrue from the costs of new technology, which are usually associated with significant upgrades in data capability. These costs include

1. The cost of the new file management software, usually a data base management system (DBMS) or a relational data base management system (RDBMS)
2. The cost of retraining, or cross-training existing staff in the use of this new software (developers and users alike)
3. The costs of upgrading all existing applications software to take advantage of the new products
4. The costs of new specialists to support the new software
5. Any costs associated with new hardware to house and support the new products

The benefits are achieved from reductions of those costs through more efficient processing and higher data availability.

In some cases the benefits may be achieved through actual increases in revenue, or faster collections, or more rapid turnover, or increased productivity. Some examples of benefits to be looked for, and estimated, in this area are

1. More rapid processing of customer invoices decreases the time between shipment and billing thus decreasing the receivables period and increasing the cash flow.
2. More rapid identification and payment of vendor invoices offering discounts allowing the firm to reduce its purchasing costs.
3. Faster access to information allowing employees to process more transactions in the same period of time.
4. Reductions in work due to reducing the number of processing steps or resulting from simplified procedures.
5. Improved editing or validation procedures which reduce errors.

Indirect benefits are those which cannot be quantified, or assigned a monetary value, but which nonetheless result in desirable outcomes from the project. These might include

1. Access to previously inaccessible or missing information
2. Faster access to information
3. More flexible processing, or additional processing capability or ease
4. Additional functionality
5. Standardization of information
6. Improved communications or reporting procedures
7. Improved, clearer, or more accurate reports or screens
8. Reports providing more detail, or reports removing unneeded detail
9. Improved understanding of the basic functional or processing interactions within the firm
10. Improved documentation of the basic functions and processing within the firm

A cost-benefit analysis may be as short as a single page or may cover many pages. In format it is similar in style to a standard budget, with costs being equated to the expense side, and benefits being equated to the income side. All cost items should be subtotaled by category and an overall total cost figure computed. All benefits should be subtotaled by category and a total benefit figure computed. In more complete cost-benefit analyses, both the costs and the benefits would be "spread" across the project or phase time frame, with the costs and projected benefits.

The data requirements of the operational level units, while extensive, rarely change since they are contingent upon fixed sources of input. However, when the data requirements do change, the result can sometimes be chaotic for it usually means some basic aspect of the business has also changed.

Chapter

5

Data Analysis and the Systems Design Phase

The design phase of the system development life cycle is sometimes called the proposed environment analysis phase. Systems analysis is the decomposition of the current environment into its component pieces for examination and study. The design process is the development of a plan for the building up of a larger harmonious unit from component parts. Design is also the business systems repair phase. That is, during design, all of the problems, or as many of them as can be addressed given available resources, time and technology, are corrected. Although this book makes a distinction between analysis and design it should be obvious that some analysis occurs during the design phase as well.

The systems analysis phase looks at the current environment and dissects it to identify existing problems. During the design phase, additional problems arise which also require analysis. Requirements are uncovered which were not identified during the preceding phases and these requirements must be examined for impact and to determine whether they should be addressed and, if so, how.

In some cases as the design proceeds, assumptions made during earlier phases must be reexamined and corrected. In other cases the design team finds that it must extend its scope further than originally assumed because of previously unidentified relationships between various processes, data, or both.

Most design techniques use a top-down approach, performing successive decompositions of the desired and expected final product to determine the component composition and structure of that final product.

From this decomposition the designer can determine where and how the existing components must fit, which components must be changed and how those components must be changed to fit the new design, what new components must be built, and what old components must be discarded. The final plan shows why and how all the component parts must fit together.

However, decomposition, or the breaking down of a whole into its parts, is also the way analysis works. Thus design can be considered a special form of analysis—analysis of the future or proposed environment. Many of the tools and techniques of the analyst are used by the designer as well.

The difference between analysis and design is that the analyst uses these tools to describe what is, whereas the designer describes what will be. The analyst works with components as they are today, the designer works with many of the same components, most of which however have little tags on them indicating how they must be changed.

Because of its goals, system design works best in a top-down manner. Once completed, however, that design is implemented from the bottom up. All the components are changed on an individual basis, and these changed components are assembled with new components into successively larger and more complex subassemblies until the final product is completed.

During the development of a new system, systems designers, along with analysts and user liaisons, work with business data flow, function and process models, and narratives to develop the concepts and ideas, the context, structure, framework, and detail plans for the new procedural system. They are the architects, the planners, and controlling force of the design process. They specify design, structure, usage, and materials. They translate business context, functional requirements, process, activity, and user task requirements, along with business data and information requirements into meaningful design.

Their relationship to the application development groups is one of architect/consultant to contractor, and their relationship to user management is one of architect to employer. They can design, suggest, modify, and implement, but the end product, in the final analysis, must meet the needs of its occupants, not vice versa. When the design is successful, all parts work in harmony, each piece performing its required function.

The data analysts, an integral part of the design team, work with the systems analyst's documentation of existing data and data files, along with the documentation of as yet unfulfilled user requirements for new data, to determine

1. The most appropriate data organization.
2. The level of data granularity.
3. How data should be defined.

4. How data must be used.
5. How data conflict can best be resolved.
6. How data must be edited, validated, and verified.
7. How data should be stored.
8. What technology should be used to store data and how it should be used.
9. How current data should be modified or changed to meet new or changed business requirements.
10. What procedures must be followed to convert data from its current form to its proposed form.
11. What are the most appropriate procedures and business areas to gather the data required by the new design.

Some of these items are technical issues and it is those which illustrate the principal difference between systems analysis and data analysis. Although the systems designer may (some say must) develop a procedural system to satisfy the requirements of the business first and should make technical (automation) decisions only after all business procedural issues have been resolved, data analysts must always consider the automation implications of data storage and access when they develop their design recommendations. This is true whether a process-directed or a data-directed design approach is taken.

Many of the recent developments and much of the research with respect to data arose from the laboratories of vendors of automated data processing equipment, data base management systems, data management systems software, and from those researchers who concentrated in the information sciences. Still other advances and understanding of data came from research in semantics and data modeling.

Multilevel Design

Almost all system development life cycles (Figure 5.1) recognize and allow for design as a multilevel undertaking in the same manner that they must allow for the analysis of the existing environment to occur in a multileveled manner. As with the analysis phase, although there can be many iterations of design, for practical purposes we usually restrict ourselves to three (Figure 5.2).

The first is usually identified as the general or business environmental design level and it focuses on the firmwide functions, processes, and data models. This has been called by some, enterprise design. This level of design has the widest scope in terms of numbers of functions covered,

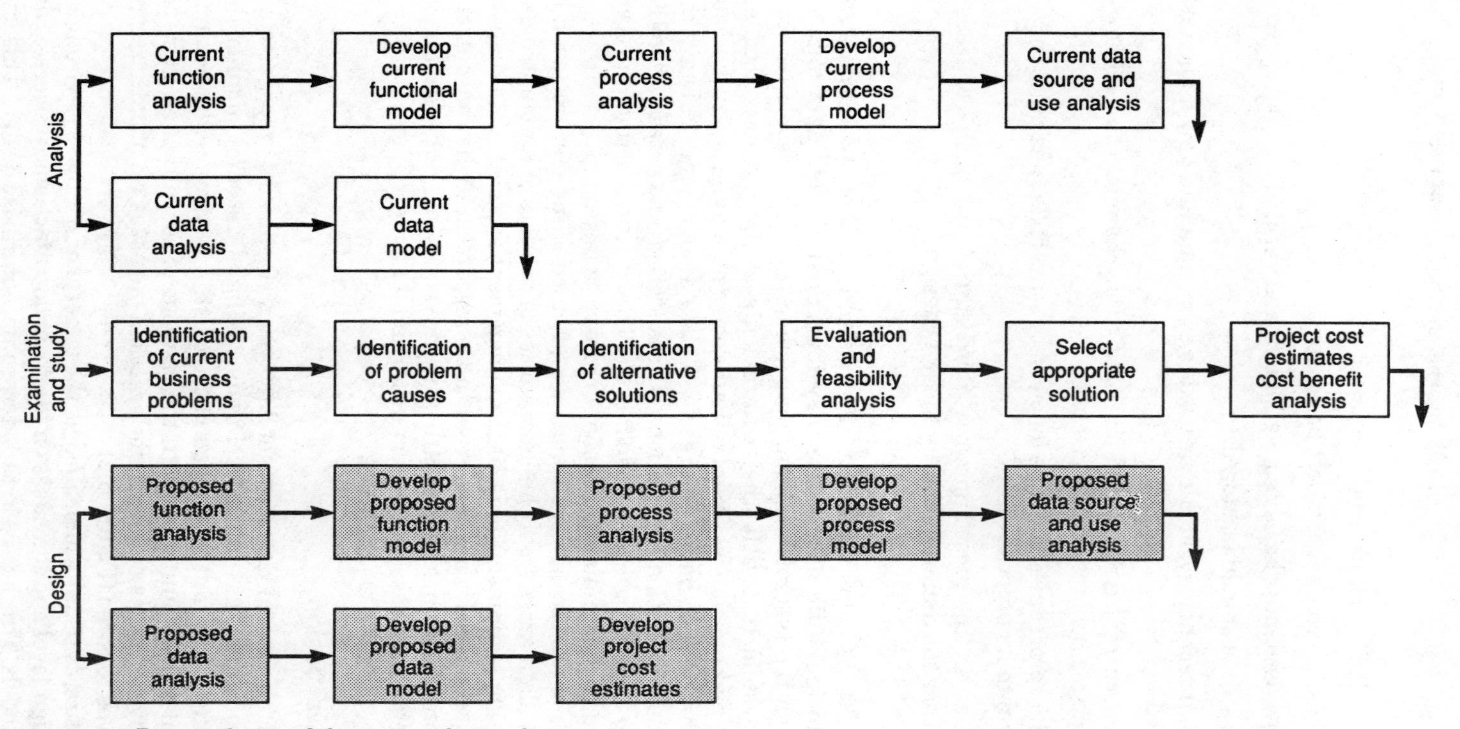

Figure 5.1 Data analysis and the systems design phase.

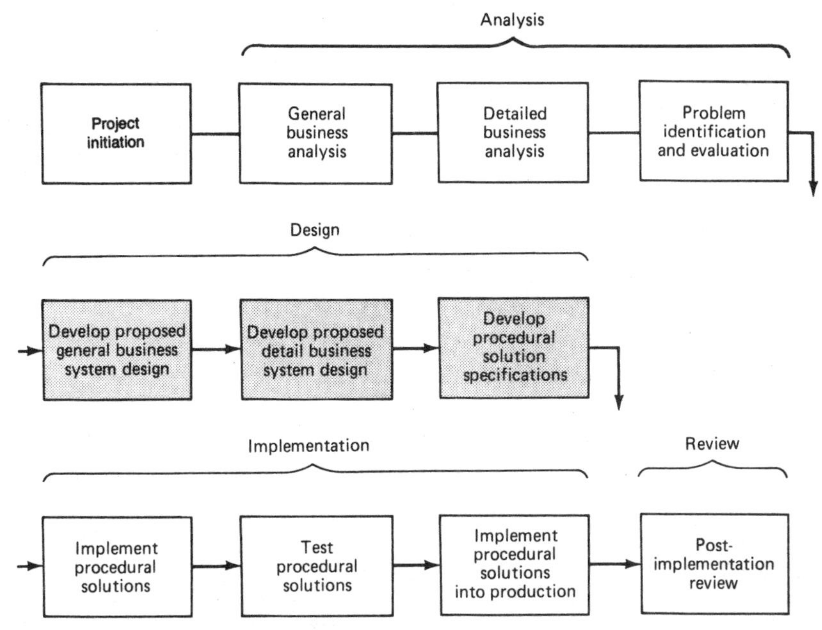

Figure 5.2 The three levels of design within the system life cycle.

and looks at the highest levels of the corporation. This level of design corresponds to the strategic level of the management pyramid (Figure 5.3). It establishes the general context within which the individual functional and system frameworks can be developed.

This design level also establishes the standards which will be followed in the design process, the methodology which will be employed, the technology which may (or must be) used, and the financial and other resource constraints which will effect the design team.

Within this level of design, corporatewide data models are developed. These models incorporate data perspectives from all sectors of the firm, all levels of the firm, and most include both internal and external data. The principal focus at this level is identification of data subjects and definition of those data subjects. A data subject is some set of things, persons, places, or concepts deemed of critical relevance to the strategic and senior level managers of the firm. In some cases this identification is restricted to highly limited sets of numbers, ratios, or other indicators which management feels determine the relative health, stability, and prosperity of the firm. These indicators are sometimes called critical success factors.

This level deals mostly in concepts, relationships, assignment of responsibility, and setting of priorities. It is at this level that management determines overall strategy and direction. The models and products at

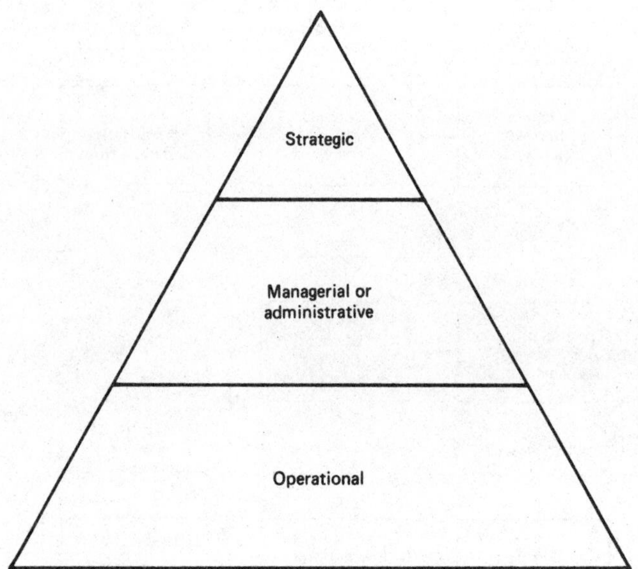

Figure 5.3 The three-level organizational pyramid.

this level document policy, goals, objectives, and allocation of resources. This level also determines schedules and mileposts for all additional work.

The second design level is identified as detail business or client environmental design, and focuses on the functions, subfunctions, processes, and data of the individual client or user functional areas. This design level is narrower in scope than an enterprise level design, and may be limited to a single high-level function, such as human resources, finance, operations, marketing, etc. This level of design corresponds to the managerial or administrative level of the managerial pyramid. It defines the specific functional and system framework for the design which is being developed.

Within this level the conceptual data models and the corporate definitions of the high-level data concepts and data subjects are decomposed (analyzed), refined, and more detail is added. Additional information is added and multiple perspectives are examined.

The single corporate model is usually decomposed into multiple function-specific models (in many cases these models may cross or span functional lines). Here again there are differences between the system designer and the data analyst. The system designers must retain focus on the satisfaction of the requirements of the functional user. Theirs is a procedural focus, and procedures (whether derived from the data or process perspectives) are specific to a user. The data analyst must retain the corporate focus and continually examine specific user data requirements within the context of the corporation as a whole. The corporate data model and the corporate data framework dictate for the data analyst how to define, organize, and store data. The data analyst must continually look for impact on other users and for additional perspectives when making data design decisions.

Data is one of the primary mechanisms for integration of procedural systems. Data is a corporate asset, and all data ultimately belongs to all corporate areas. The data analyst is the advocate for those areas which might be impacted by specific functional area system designs, but which are not direct participants in the systems design process. Data models and documentation at this level are more detailed than those at the higher level, but not as specific as those required by the designers of the specific user processing systems.

The third design level is the most detailed, and can be considered as the application level which addresses the design of specific user processing systems. This level has the narrowest scope and usually focuses within a single user functional area. At this level of design individual tasks are addressed. This design level corresponds to the operational level of the managerial pyramid. It defines and describes the specific procedures which will be developed and the resources, in terms of data, information, personnel, and materials, which are needed by each procedure.

This level focuses on the data items required for processing and the data items which require processing. That is, this level focuses on those procedures which import new data into the firm and the existing data which must be retrieved from the firm's files to correctly edit, validate, and process this new data. This area also focuses on those procedural systems which maintain or update existing data files with internally generated data (data which results from internal activities and must be added to imported data or external data). All systems, whether they bring new data into the firm or process internally generated data, must also retrieve and present data for information, monitoring and control, or analysis purposes.

This level must also resolve the issues of data conversion and where, how, and who should gather the data required by the new system. This level must also resolve the issues related to the procedures for changing data which already exists. These issues include

1. How to develop new coding structures for data
2. How to revise existing coding structures
3. How to decompose aggregated data into more elemental units
4. How to aggregate data which is at too fine a resolution

5. How to group, or regroup, data to eliminate or reduce data ambiguity
6. How to group, or regroup, data to ensure needed levels of data integrity and security
7. How to resolve issues arising from differences in data perspective, data definition, data usage, data timeliness, and data currency

The data models and documentation at this level contain details of file and record organization, data item definition and interpretation, data responsibility, and data use.

The application or detail design phase uses the results from phases one and two to devise and design a proposed environment for the user. This proposed design presents the user with a revised function model, a revised process model, and a revised data model. It is this phase which produces the final products of the analysis and design process.

Design Components

Regardless of the level being addressed—the general business level, the detailed business level, or the application level—or the methodology employed, each design level should include the following activities:

1. Proposed function design
2. Development of the proposed function model
3. Proposed process and activity design
4. Development of the proposed process model
5. Proposed data source and usage design
6. Proposed data analysis
7. Development of the proposed data model
8. Development of project implementation cost projections

In addition, to the above which are predominantly process-related items, the following data analysis activities (Figure 5.4) must also be included:

1. Data conversion plans
2. Development of a dictionary of definitions containing concepts, terms, entities, roles, data groups, and data elements
3. Data file method design
4. Data file organization model
5. Data acquisition plans

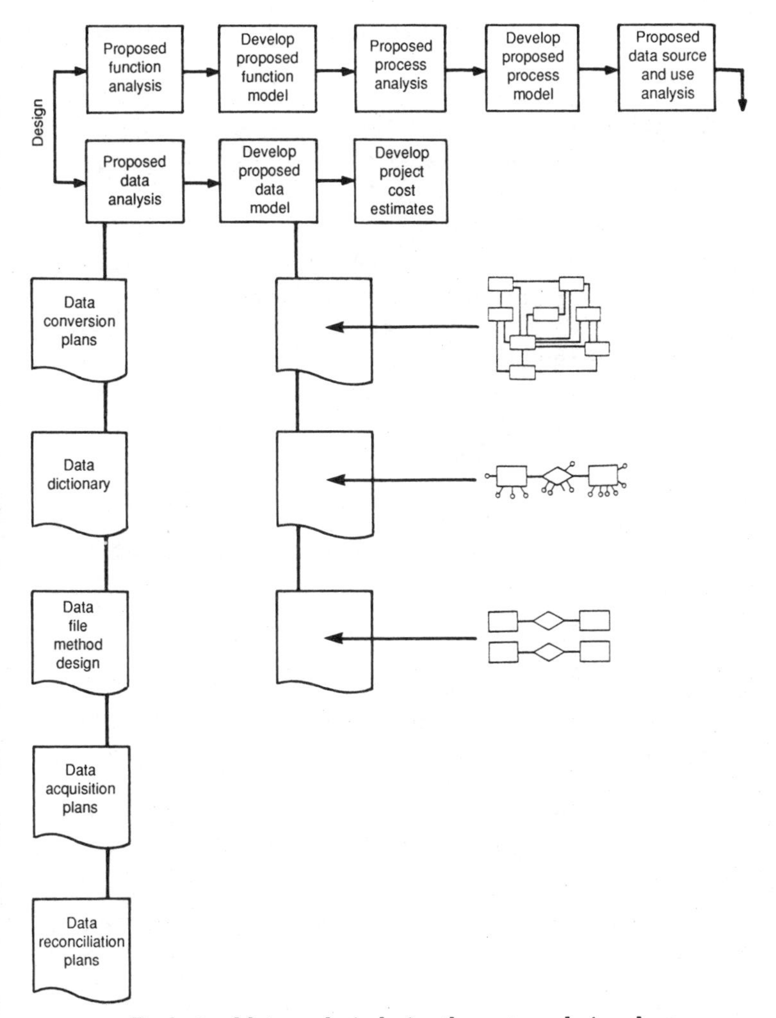

Figure 5.4 Products of data analysis during the systems design phase.

6. Data reconciliation plans
7. Data roles and responsibilities models
8. Data validation and verification plans
9. Data administration plans
10. Data forms and reports documentation

Integration

One of the terms which is used extensively in systems development projects is "integration." Just what is integration, and what do we mean when we say a system is integrated? How do we design an integrated system?

Definition. To *integrate* is to make into a whole by bringing all parts together, to unify, to join with something else, the organization of all parts into a harmonious whole.

It would seem then that by definition all systems are integrated since a system is a harmonious whole as well. It would seem further that the process of system design is also the process of integration. But we have said that integration is the bringing together of all parts. In a system what parts are we talking about? What do we bring them together for? How do we bring them together? And finally why must we bring them together at all? Why do we need to design systems? Another question and equally important in our discussions is—when is a system fully integrated? At what point is a system complete?

The answer to these questions requires the introduction of a few more concepts.

Goals of System Design

There are various goals which are common across most system design projects. These are

1. To increase the level of integration among the functions, systems, processes, activities, tasks, and procedures of the firm.
2. To increase the level of visibility management has into the activities of the firm, and to increase the level of control that management has over those activities.
3. To increase the responsiveness of the firm's systems and to increase their flexibility such that systems and procedural changes can be accomplished when business changes warrant.
4. To concurrently decrease the conditions which cause changes to the firm's systems and procedures when business changes occur. In other words, to make the firm's systems and procedures more independent of change.
5. To increase the level of standardization and conformity between systems and procedures.
6. To increase the level of systems and procedural documentation.
7. To increase the quality, accuracy, consistency, and timeliness of the information needed by the business.

What Is an Integrated System?

All systems by definition are integrated. But to paraphrase one of the animals in George Orwell's *Animal Farm*—all systems are integrated but some systems are more integrated than others.

Systemization began with early efforts to apply a concept known as methods and procedures analysis to business activities. These methods and procedures analysts examined the tasks performed in offices and factories and developed improved, that is, more efficient and more effective, ways of accomplishing them. As new and improved procedures were developed for more and more of these tasks, they were collected into larger procedure sets to reduce the redundant activities, and to make each activity more unified with the whole. Activities were separated and rearranged to accomplish the tasks in a faster, more efficient, and more controlled manner.

As more and more procedures were collected under one control mechanism, and as more and more procedures were developed in a mutually supportive, interrelated, and interdependent manner the systems became larger and larger and more and more integrated.

The larger the system became, the more integrated the system became. The more integrated a system became the wider its span of control, and the wider the base of company functions it supported. The drive to integration has led some to design systems which attempt to incorporate all procedures which appeared to be even remotely connected under a single control umbrella.

To accomplish this integration, to design these super large systems, various mechanisms have been developed to assist the system designers in their tasks. These mechanisms have not concentrated on the procedural level, nor on the activity or even the process level, instead they have attempted, with varying degrees of success, to focus on the framework level.

The most completely integrated systems are those which attempt to look at the corporate environment from the highest or broadest perspectives, from a top-down, cross-functional, or cross-business-unit perspective.

To illustrate, a completely integrated system would be one which looks at human resources rather than payroll and personnel as separate processes, or at general ledger rather than at balance sheet, accounts payable and receivables, etc. Completely integrated systems are modeled along functional, business, and strategic lines rather than along process and operational lines.

Completely integrated systems recognize the interdependency of user areas and try to address as many of these interrelated, interdependent areas as is feasible. These integrated systems are usually oriented along common functional lines, common data requirements, or along some other business thread which can serve to tie all the separate processes together in a unified manner.

Integrated systems are usually developed using a top-down design since it is easier to determine overall requirements, and because integrated systems development makes it necessary to understand, at a very high corporate level, the interdependencies and interrelated nature of the various applications which must be hooked together.

The most completely integrated systems are very difficult to design and generally require more time to implement than if the separate parts were developed in a less integrated manner.

Since integrated systems cross functional and, thus, user boundaries, many user areas must be involved in the design and implementation phases. A multiuser environment is much more difficult to work with, since although the system will be integrated, the users are normally not. Each user brings his or her own perspective to the environment, problems and requirements, and these differing perspectives may often conflict with each other. The designer must resolve these conflicts during the design process, or during the later review and approval cycles. In addition to the conflicting perspectives, there are normally conflicting system design goals, and more importantly conflicting time frames as well.

There are no hard and fast guidelines which distinguish candidate systems for integration. Systems which appear to be totally standalone, that is, systems which may appear to be totally complete in and of themselves, can be integrated with other systems if the correct integration mechanism is found. There are no size or complexity distinguishing characteristics.

Integration Issues

The level of integration which a firm can introduce into its systems is dependent upon the following issues:

1. The location of the firm on the growth cycle. Firms in the early stages of the cycle should not attempt to develop highly integrated systems, whereas firms in the late stages should always strive for them.
2. The ability to assemble all interested and relevant users, and the ability to get them to agree to participate, compromise where necessary, and to jointly fund the project.
3. The commitment from user management to devote the time and resources to a complete top-down analysis and to participate in the design of the new system.

4. The ability to get all users to share the stored data and to share the tasks of data acquisition and maintenance.
5. User understanding of the processes and functions which the system would ultimately be designed to service.

As businesses change and as the need for systems changes occur on a more and more frequent basis, firms are taking the opportunity to expand the scope, control capabilities, and level of integration of those systems. This desire to move these systems further up into the corporation and further out on the growth and maturity curves, and to incorporate more and more information capability into them, makes it more and more necessary, and in fact imperative, to redesign the framework of these systems, the manner in which the individual procedural components operate separately and interdependently, and the manner and type of resources which are used in the performance of those procedural operations.

Thus we see that we cannot repair nor even in many cases renovate these systems, but we must completely redesign them from all perspectives. Because we are effecting change, we must work with the existing environment, we must include those items of change which have been identified during the analysis as needing to be included, and we must include all the items which we can anticipate will be needed in the future.

Development versus Maintenance and Enhancement

All data processing projects can be assigned to one of three major categories—development, enhancement, and maintenance. Although the phases involved in each type of project are approximately the same, they vary in degree of difficulty and scope. Even among projects within the same category, there may be large differences in scope and difficulty. Generally, however, each of these types of projects requires some degree of analysis, design, coding, testing, and implementation.

Applications maintenance and enhancement projects differ from development projects in one substantial way—that being that the analysis and design personnel assigned to these projects must also assess the impact of the proposed change on an existing system. These maintenance or enhancement projects usually leave large parts of the base system intact. The remaining parts are either modified, or "hooks" are added to the additional code. The requests for maintenance or enhancement changes normally originate with the user, although they may originate with the development team itself. There are numerous reasons for these system modification requests, among them are changes to the business environment, user-requested additional capability, correction of erroneous processing, and user-requested refinements, or cosmetic changes, to the existing system.

Those changes which originate from alterations to the business environment are the most difficult to implement, followed closely by those which add new capability. The implementation difficulties arise because these types of changes not only require new analysis of the user area but also reanalysis of the original system design to determine where, and how, the changes can, and should, be made. Maintenance or enhancement which is necessitated by correction of erroneous processing, user-desired refinements, or other cosmetic changes usually require little in the way of new analysis.

The analysis and redesign efforts required by business environment changes and additions of new functionality can be almost as extensive as that which was required in the original systems development. The most difficult aspects of any change to an application system are those which are directed either toward changes in underlying system design and the resulting processing logic, or toward changing the structure and contents of the data base.

When the maintenance or enhancement project is directed at a system in a data base environment, and the data base must be changed, that analysis must not only cover the application in question, but also any other applications which use the same data base and in particular the same data records or data elements. In some cases, the immediate enhancement or maintenance project will require data which should logically be captured by a different, unrelated, application. The "chain reaction" or "cascading" of changes can increase the scope and impact of the initial request by orders of magnitude. The greater the integration or interdependence, the greater the potential impact of any change.

We can see from the above discussions that it is not enough to have analyzed and to understand the individual procedural changes but we must also understand the impact of the changes on the system, the direction in which system design must be taken, and the reasons why those directions are valid. We must understand the various ways in which frameworks for these new systems can be developed and what the mechanisms for increasing the level of systems integration are.

Intangible Nature of Design Components

There is one final point which needs restating here. Of the three components of system design, only two are observable and based upon physical reality. Of the two only one is consistently real—the individual procedures. While some of the resources are physical—the people, and money, the data is conceptual—hard to visualize, hard to identify and describe.

Because we are building a plan in advance of implementation—a set of specifications which we want to be able to verify and validate—we must rely heavily on narratives and even more heavily on diagrams and pictures which describe that which we wish to put in place. These diagrams and narratives form models of the proposed environment, an environment which does not and will not exist until we are sure of what we wish to develop.

These models provide us with something to look at in lieu of reality. They provide us with a mechanism for understanding, testing, and validating. There are many different types of models, many different types of diagrammatic notation. We should remember as we use them however that there are limitations to notation and limitations to any model. No model can fully represent reality or even one aspect of reality. The more conceptual the component to be modeled, the more difficult it will be to model it.

We must therefore remember that while we must stress clarity of notation, we must also remember to separate modeling notation from model content. If we need to change the notation of the modeling technique we are using to improve content and clarity of meaning then we should be free to do so. If by mixing and matching different notational styles we improve clarity of content we are free to do so. Most notational styles exist to assist the designers, not to restrict them.

We must also remember that models are usually built to allow us to isolate certain components within the design for examination and study, and that they also allow us to separate structure from detail. Certain types of models only allow certain levels of detail, and certain types of models will only portray certain aspects of the design. Models show us how the pieces fit together, and what the final structure will look like when all the pieces are in place. They allow us to make changes easily and quickly without impacting the real world.

Logical Design

One last system design concept before we move on to other topics. One term which is used very frequently and very inconsistently is the term "logical." We have logical data models, logical systems, logical designs, logical this and logical that. Logical has become one of those overused terms which have lost their meaning through inconsistent usage.

The term "logical" is used extensively to qualify certain aspects and components of the design process. In order to ensure that clarity is maintained and in keeping with the theme of this book which is that the definition of concepts is crucial to all analysis, and especially to data analysis, the following definition will be used for logical, along with the the general context within which the term will be used.

Definition. *Logic* is a mode of reasoning which is based upon the relationship of element to element and to the whole in a set of objects, individuals, principles, and events.

A thing which is *logical* is that which shows consistency of reasoning, and is reasonable based upon earlier statements or events.

A *logical system* or *logical design* is one which is built upon consistency, and is based upon a consistent line of reasoning. A system which is based upon a framework where all the elements have a reasoned relationship between them and all fit together based upon a common set of reasoning can be considered to be a logical system.

Logic is built upon rules which determine underlying fact and cause and which provide the basis for drawing reasoned conclusions. All logical models must be explainable and consistent. They must be based upon facts and reality, easily discernible, and easily provable. All cause should have effect, all effect should have cause. All components of the model must have a reason for existence.

Thus we can see that logical systems, integrated systems, even the concept of a system itself are all based upon the need and desire to develop a framework within which business activity can be performed in a harmonious, interrelated, interdependent manner, where all components are brought together according to a unified line of reasoning, according to a common set of rules, or because of some unified thread.

Chapter

6

Effects of Prior Automation

Introduction

Although referred to as the system design process, a more appropriate name is system *redesign*. Normal business change causes procedures and resource usage to change over time. All procedures and resources operate within an existing system which while appearing to be stable and unchanging is in reality undergoing constant gradual change. Moreover, although business systems may appear to be inflexible, they are in fact very informal, flexible, tenuous, and limited in nature.

When the number of changes to an individual procedure reaches critical mass (that is, new changes can no longer be applied, or the user can no longer function effectively) the individual procedure must be changed. When the number of individual procedures which must be changed reaches a critical mass all the procedures and the framework within which they operate must be changed. When the change encompasses all the procedures, the resources used by them, and the framework within which they operate, we are changing the system.

One of the reasons which make procedural changes difficult or impossible is that the system within which they operate is not flexible enough or cannot provide the resources which are needed for their operation. In most cases unless the procedural changes are mostly cosmetic, they must be accompanied by some system modification, that is, the system must be redesigned to a certain extent.

Although the effects of gradual procedural change and the need for more extensive procedural change can be tolerated by the firm for relatively long periods of time before critical mass is reached, there is much less tolerance for gradual data change. When data requirements change, those changes by and large must be implemented as soon as possible. However, whereas procedural change can be developed and implemented rather quickly and with low impact on the firm, the data change takes time and has a substantial impact on the firm. This is true whether the changes required are for new data or for changes to existing data.

Data change is similar to changes in language, and in fact as we shall describe in later chapters, there is a strong parallel between language and data. Changes in meaning of words can make existing texts obsolete, or meaningless. The lack of the appropriate words to describe something or some event renders communication ineffective. Use of the wrong word can have extremely negative effects in any communication situation.

In very similar ways and for very similar reasons changes in the meaning or use of data can render information or business communication ineffective. As with words, the meaning of data changes over time, often subtly, gradually, and unintentionally. While this happens with all data in whatever form it is stored, its effects are most strongly felt when it is computer-stored data that changes.

Different Redesign Environments

There are substantial similarities between all redesign efforts, but there are also substantial differences. These differences are apart from the obvious applications or functional area differences which make payroll different from order entry, and inventory different from accounts receivable. These differences are those which are due to the effects of prior automation (or the lack of it), and the level and extent to which automation will be used in the redesigned system.

These differences occur most strikingly where data is concerned. Conversion from manual to automated data record keeping, from card media to tape and disk media, and from files stored using basic operating system file storage and access methods to files stored and managed by data management software. These software products are known as data base management systems, or simply as data management systems. There are even differences which occur when data is transferred from one data base management system to another, or when data is allocated between several different data base management systems.

Additional considerations occur when data and processing are moved from the centralized or mainframe environment to the decentralized or distributed environments, and still others are introduced when data and processing are migrated still further to microcomputers (also called personal computers or workstations). Each of these entails different design decisions and requires a different set of criteria to be analyzed when determining where and how data should be collected, maintained, and stored. However, these differences not only occur when data storage and processing mechanisms are changed, but also when data philosophy changes (usually based on some new business or competitive need).

Reasons for Initiating a System Design Project

Aside from the need to apply the accumulated backlog of business changes, design projects may be initiated for a variety of other reasons. These reasons may be attributed to (1) a change in the basic aspects of the user's functional role, (2) a change in company strategic objectives, (3) a need for increased performance from the automated systems, (4) a need for more direct and immediate access to the firm's automated files, (5) a desire to upgrade the system to take advantage of more current technology, or (6) a need to clean up the system.

These reasons reflect the procedural needs. In addition, and in many cases more importantly, there are strong data reasons for initiating such projects. Almost all of any given firm's business procedures have been developed to acquire, maintain, or disseminate data, or its derivative—information. The techniques used to analyze and design procedures have been developed and refined over time. These techniques may be data directed or process directed, but all focus on the end product of procedural development. Many of these techniques, however, treat data as a by-product, or an afterthought. This is true even of the newer "engineering"-based techniques and CASE-based techniques.

These approaches to design generate data models because data models are called for and they link, or associate, the components of the data model with the process components. In many cases, however, the data model itself is ignored after that, and there is no methodological or support techniques for developing the data model itself or analyzing it for validity, accuracy, or completeness. In fact, many of these approaches begin with a top-down–generated data model, and then proceed to complete it from the bottom up by populating it with known data items, or data items suggested or requested by the user participants in the design process.

Regardless of whether the scope and magnitude of the functional, process, activity, and procedural changes are fairly narrow or wide reaching, in almost all cases the data changes are substantial, or have the potential for being substantial. In some cases, aside from streamlining and updating the procedures of the system, there may be only minor changes to either the data architecture or in additional business processing capability aimed at providing more meaningful or usable data to the firm. Very few of these projects look at data opportunities, or evaluate existing data to determine whether it was correct in the first place. In other words, data in existing files very rarely get discarded or dropped from the files of the firm.

Aside from the variety of reasons for a project being undertaken, we must also recognize that the technical base differs from project to project. This technical base reflects the differences in current user-processing environment technology, the current level of user automation, and current residence on the maturity curve. Because of these differences in current user-processing technology and user automation, and because the goals of any system design project normally include (1) movement along the maturity curves, (2) an increase in the level of system integration, and (3) an increase in the level of information which can be obtained about business operations, systems design project activity must reflect or at least be cognizant of the level of technology and automation of the current environment.

These automation levels can be categorized into three types which reflect both their existing level of technology and the technology of the redesigned system. These categories are

1. Basic systems—wholly manual
2. Intermediate systems—partially manual and partially automated
3. Mature systems—fully automated

From a design perspective, each of these three automation levels involve different, and yet similar, work. The work is similar in that the development activities, which are involved in each, follow the same general phases and approach. They are different in that each of the starting or current environments that the system designer must use as a base have substantially different characteristics.

The following is an overview of the design activities in each category of system.

1. The basic system environment—wholly manual procedures

In a very few cases today, the current system is manual and the design team has determined that the redesigned system should remain manual. This is the simplest environment, from the designer's viewpoint, in that all the procedural components of the environment are overt as is the framework. That is, they are clearly visible for observation and validation.

Data records are usually paper and stored in massive cabinets using a variety of filing systems, and these systems are characterized by extensive redundancy of data. That is, data records are generated on multipart forms and each copy is disseminated to different areas of the firm, often changing independently of each other. These purely manual systems tend to be small, containing relatively few procedures. The procedures themselves, however, may be exceedingly complex. These procedures tend to fall into identifiable categories

a. Procedures which involve the handling of physical items, such as materials or original documents
b. Procedures which involve the operation of machinery
c. Procedures which involve high degrees of human interaction, or human judgment
d. Procedures which are highly complex and apply to very few cases, which have to be modified for each case

In manual systems, all work will be performed by user personnel, who work directly with physical files, forms, documents, and materials. The proposed processing of these forms and documents, the work flows, and the individual steps can be simulated and modeled relatively easily. The creation of work flows, data flows, and physical material flows form the heart of the system design.

In the manual environment, there is a direct, in most cases one-to-one, correspondence between user task and procedure. Aside from the obvious use of machinery, this is one of the the primary differences between manual and automated systems.

From a system design perspective, all systems are concerned with what are, or once were, essentially manual operations. In fact, it is helpful during the design process to view all the activities of the user as if they were still being performed by hand. This allows the designer to review, in detail, each task being performed, each data operation, each data movement, and each data carrier. (A data carrier is a piece of paper, a form, a report, a worksheet, a transaction, etc.)

The designer's task in the manual environment is to rewrite the procedures which govern task performance and the work flows to streamline the processes, reduce redundant processing, and rearrange the tasks so as to ensure more orderly processing. The designer must also ensure that the forms, documents, and reports which both enter and leave the user area contain all necessary data.

The procedures for each task, and each task step, must be placed in perspective within the user area and the user's surroundings to determine its appropriate definition, position, and level and mode of performance.

The designer must ensure that each new procedure conforms to existing standards and that the procedures are collected and appropriately indexed, cross-referenced, and documented.

Any new or revised standards and procedures which are included in manual systems must clearly define the processing sequence for the task to be performed, the rules which govern their performance, and the responsibilities and authorities of the person or persons to whom they will be assigned. The designer must also revise any user-enabling documents such as job descriptions, unit charters, and mission statements. In addition the designer must develop new input forms, control procedures, monitoring procedures, and reports. The designer must also develop new or revised work and data flows diagrams.

Procedure content and form. Each procedure must include standards of performance. Standards of performance describe the quality (and sometimes the quantity) of the work to be performed, the time frame within which the work should be performed, the amount of time which should be devoted to each unit of work, and the number of exceptions which can be tolerated.

Each procedure should include responsibility and authority information. This information describes who is responsible for performing the work described in the procedure, and what authorities are vested with the person or persons performing the work. Each procedure should include descriptions of the security and control aspects of the work. All steps to ensure the security of the materials and resources used in the work should be described, and each resource should be classified as to its security level, storage, use, and disposal criteria. All controls which are included in the procedure should be clearly described and should show how the control is enforced. Controls can be simple financial controls, such as the addition of various balancing steps, to more complex batch preparation and verification steps. Controls can be applied to materials, documents, reports, and and other physical materials, which must be counted and accounted for.

Each procedure should include information which shows how it relates to other procedures. All materials, data, and information sources which are external to the procedure should have their source documented, including the source of each form, report, document, or other information source. All materials which have their source in the procedure or which are processed by the procedure and which must be passed to another procedure should have their destination clearly indicated.

It should be noted that while some user information processing systems are and will remain wholly manual, even in these cases they may interact with, and either receive data from, or pass data to, systems which are partially or completely automated. In these cases, while these other systems might remain unaffected by the new manual system, the designer must examine the impact on them, and may have to tailor the new manual procedures where these interfaces exist to conform to what is being delivered to or received from the automated systems.

2. Intermediate systems—partially manual and partially automated

For many currently manual systems the determination is made by both the user and technical members of the design team that some of the current activities, in whole or in part, can be cost effectively augmented by automation. In other cases, the current system is already partially automated, and the new design will maintain or probably increase the level of automated support.

One major difficulty in this mode arises when a normally integrated, or straight-line, procedure must be partitioned into manual and automated segments. The system designer must always consider the impact on the timing and execution of the manual segments when making the determination as to how to apply automation to those segments to be automated. The designer must always look to the larger, and more global user process within which the automated segment fits when making these implementation determinations. These framework or global user process considerations affect implementation choices, such as hardware and software choices, batch versus on-line execution, and other similar technical selections.

The analysis phase and the subsequent examination and study phase will have identified those current manual procedures where it is feasible to substitute automated processing for manual processing and where such automation is suitable. For each suggested area of automation, the designer must break each process, each activity, and each task down into its component steps, and determine if the rules for performing the step are sufficiently well defined and if there is a sufficiently low level of exceptions to allow the procedures to lend themselves to machine automation.

The designer's product for this type of project closely resembles that produced for a strictly manual system design. However, here the designer must also develop new input forms suitable to an automated environment, file content requirements, for on-going master, transaction and reference files, report layouts and a processing flow which intermixes the original, and unmodified manual processes, new manual processes, and new automated processes.

When preparing the design for procedures where some segments will be automated and others not, or where new automation is being applied, the designer must prepare supporting plans for "conversion" procedures. Conversion procedures are those which must be developed for single, or, in some cases, on-going use, and which are normally used to prepare data in manually maintained files for ultimate storage in machine readable form.

In mixed-mode environments (partially manual and partially automated) a decision must be made as to whether data is to be kept in wholly automated form or in both automated and manual form. In the first case, wholly automated files, the designer must make provisions for procedures which produce and distribute file content reports, edit, validation, maintenance activity, and reference reports which would be needed to support the manual segments. In the second case, the designer must make provisions for all of the above procedures, and for additional procedures which must be performed to ensure that the contents of the manual and automated versions of the user's files are coordinated.

The designer must also make a determination as to the costs involved in the automation process, project schedules, and hardware and software recommendations.

3. Mature systems—fully automated

Although we like to consider that some user systems are completely automated, in reality no system is completely automated. Mature systems are in reality those where all procedures which are capable of being automated cost effectively have been automated. These systems still have many manual procedures, but whereas in the prior environments automated procedures supported the essentially manual character of the system, here the manual procedures support the essentially automated character of the system.

In today's business environment, most firms of any size have many user areas with heavy levels of automation. Many in fact have progressed from concentrating system design efforts on initial automation to design efforts which concentrate on re-automation.

In these user areas, most of the existing processes and procedures are either totally or partially automated. Automated procedures and the manual procedures which support them are the most complex, most highly integrated, and the least visible (or overt) of any business procedures, and thus are the most difficult and time consuming to change. They are also the least amenable to change. Consequently they usually lag furthest behind the on-going business changes.

The nature of information processing technology is such that, in many of these systems, changes which would be trivial in a manual environment become monumental in the automated environment. Interestingly enough in many cases it is changes in data requirements definition or format which have the greatest impact on automated systems, and it is these which appear to be the primary impetus behind many re-automation design efforts.

Effects of Prior Automation

The effects of this prior automation on the re-automation design efforts must be fully understood by the design team. This prior automation impacts all forms and documents currently used by the business area users, all automated and supporting manual procedures, and the structure and contents of all data files used by the automated system. The technology used to construct these automated systems may now be outdated or inefficient or, worse, obsolete. Business changes which occurred since these systems were originally developed may have completely changed the user requirements or business environment which the system was originally designed and developed to support.

The difficulty of changing automated systems is such that it is usually easier to twist and contort the user processing to fit the system than it is to change the system to fit user business processing needs. As the business changes mount, the contortion or twisting in the user area is such that when the tension is released by the initiation of a new design effort, the emergent processing requirements bear little if any resemblance to the system being replaced. Procedural forms, documents, reports, and file contents which were the result of some prior designer's efforts may no longer reflect the current information or data needs of the firm.

The natural user procedural processing flows themselves may have become unnatural, to the extent that they were modified to reflect the intrusion of less-than-effective automated processing sequences, minor attempts to repair systems which no longer function properly, and the normal contortion of business procedures which occurs when individual task procedures are consolidated to accommodate efficient and integrated automated processing. These automated processing flows may have been structured to accommodate the needs of the then prevalent technology, rather than the needs of the business and as a result the user processing was changed to accommodate the needs of automation.

Each of the individual task procedures both automated and manual, the process flows which have been established to govern and control the procedures, and the documents, transactions and data files all must be reexamined in the light of the current business environment, the current business processing needs, and the currently available and usable technology. Because of the combined effects of the changes necessitated by business changes, those changes necessitated by technology changes, those changes which result from the natural pressures to move forward along the maturity curve, the increase in the levels of integration among the firms processing systems, and the needs of management to have increased access to and availability of business management information (control information, monitoring information, etc.) the most common decision by the design team is to scrap the existing system entirely in favor of a new and more streamlined processing flow, new procedures, new data files, new documents, forms and reports, etc.

These re-automation projects are very difficult, complex, and time consuming, because the replacement systems are almost always larger, more complex, more global (more integrated), more technologically sophisticated, and have more capability than the system or in most cases systems which they replace.

Forms of Re-Automation

Re-automation project activities may take the following forms:

1. Basic changes—simple procedural rewrite

The procedural rewrite is one of the simplest aspects of re-automation. Procedural rewrite does not use major framework or architectural changes in the design of the current business system and thus entails very little structural change to the user business processing capability. Procedural rewrite normally results in the exchange of the old version of procedural component with a new version—a component for component substitution.

Procedural rewrite does not involve change to the interprocedural processing flows nor does it add to system complexity. It is simply a clean up of the procedural processing within the existing flows usually in a more up-to-date language or with more streamlined logic within the automated procedures themselves. Because the opportunity exists, many of these efforts incorporate those business changes which can be accomplished within the context of the original system structure and with existing system resources.

In the process of the procedural rewrite, minor changes may be made to existing file structure, data content consistency may be cleaned up, report layouts, screens, and transactions may change to a minor extent, but generally speaking the changes are predominantly cosmetic in nature and as such file and report content, the availability and accessibility of data to management, and system business support capability usually do not increase. There is usually little of any impact on the user area. A procedural rewrite may eliminate processing anomalies ("bugs"), remove unused, obsolete, or outdated code, and may add *minor* new data presentation capability to the system. The emphasis here is on minor.

Procedural rewrites are usually done for the benefit of, and at the initiation of, the information processing area, specifically for either the system maintenance personnel who need a "cleaner" system to maintain, or the data processing operations personnel who have requested operational changes to streamline the processing, or to make it perform more efficiently.

2. More complex changes—procedural enhancement

Procedural enhancement has many characteristics in common with procedural rewrite. One of the main ones being that it usually requires minimal framework or architectural changes to the system. Procedural enhancement may result in increased user-processing capability, increased user access to existing data files, or the introduction of new procedures into the system framework.

These types of changes require all the activities which need to be performed at the procedural rewrite level, and additional activities to assess the impact of the proposed changes on an existing system and to make those architectural, framework or other procedural changes (automated and manual support) which are needed to enable the additional or enhanced procedures.

These procedural enhancement projects usually leave the majority of the system framework intact. They also leave intact, and usually unchanged, the bulk of the system resources. The framework may be modified slightly to reflect the new or expanded capability of the existing procedural components as well as to accommodate newly added procedural components. Other procedural components may have to be slightly modified to support the added capability and to provide the needed interface capability with the new and revised procedures.

The requests for procedural enhancement normally originate with the user, although they may originate with the development team itself. There are numerous reasons for this level of system modification requests, among them are changes to the business environment, user-requested additional capability, correction of erroneous processing, and user-requested refinements, or cosmetic changes, to the existing system. In most cases these changes are relatively easy to make (that is, easy in relation to a full-blown system redesign project) and incorporate a sufficient level of business changes and new capability. These types of changes are normally sufficient in stable user areas (areas which are not subject to a high degree of change), and can normally be accomplished within a short period of time.

Of these, the procedural enhancements which originate from alterations to the business environment are the most difficult to incorporate into an existing system design, followed closely by those which add new processing capability. These implementation difficulties arise because these types of changes not only require new procedural design but also selective modification of the original system design to enable the procedural changes to be made. Procedural enhancement which is necessitated by the need to correct erroneous processing, by the need to add user-requested refinements or other cosmetic changes, usually require little in the way of system design modification.

The redesign efforts required by business environment changes and additions of new processing capability can be almost as extensive as those which were required in the original systems development even though many system components and large parts of the system framework remain untouched or are only changed in minor ways.

The most difficult types of procedural enhancements are those which also require changes in underlying structure, format, or contents of the system data and reference files or the system data base.

Procedural changes which require additions or modifications to portions of the system files or data base may not only affect the system being changed, but any other system or application which uses the same files or data base, and in particular those which use the same data records or data elements.

In some cases, the desired or needed procedural enhancement will require data which can only be procedurally captured by a different, unrelated, application. The "chain reaction" or "cascading" of changes can increase the scope and impact of the initial request by orders of magnitude. When data base technology has been used as a means to achieve system integration, this integration by its nature causes a greater interdependence between what might otherwise be separate systems. The greater the level of integration or interdependence between systems, the greater the potential impact of any change to the integration mechanism.

These data-driven changes, when the files or data base must be modified, can have a major impact. The more extensive the use of the data base, the more thorough and painstaking the system modification efforts that are required. Minor changes in format or content definition may require changes in all procedures which use the modified data items. These include data acquisition, data editing and validation, reporting, retrieval or other data access or presentation facilities which may be impacted by these data structures, content, or processing logic changes. Although the individual procedural changes may be minor in each case, the cumulative effort to make these changes may severely impact the time needed to effect the changes.

3. Most complex—complete system redesign and redevelopment

The complete system redesign and redevelopment project is the most comprehensive and difficult type of re-automation and thus is the most difficult and comprehensive of any of the variants of system design projects. It involves

a. The procedural modifications and redesign of a "new" development project

b. The additional activities of data file and data base conversion

c. Reintegration of the newly designed system into the global family of systems under which the firm operates

System redesign and redevelopment requires a start-from-scratch design, which must at the same time acknowledge

a. The presence, capabilities, and limitations of the existing system

b. The needs and desires of user areas who have lived with an increasingly restrictive system, and who have an increasing backlog of business, cosmetic, and ease-of-use changes to be included in the next version of the system

c. The pressures and lure of newer and more attractive hardware and software technology

d. Pressures from management to provide more useful and timely information, more service, more flexibility and more accessibility to information, to provide more integrated information, more monitoring and control capabilities

A project of this magnitude is usually undertaken when

a. The backlog of pending changes reaches critical mass.

b. A single radical change has occurred, such as a corporate takeover, or the introduction of a new product or product line by either the firm or its competitors.

c. The firm undergoes a radical reorganization, or restructuring, or a radical change in senior management. This internal restructuring may have been as a result of a shift from a centralized to a decentralized environment, or as a result of the addition of major new lines of business, or of a change in orientation of the firm, such as from an account to a customer orientation, or from a sales force–based organization to a direct mail marketing organization.

d. The capability of the existing system "runs out of steam"—that is, it can no longer process the growing volume of information.

e. The organization's information processing technical staff and management make a determination to replace the existing hardware and/or software technology base with a newer, more sophisticated, and usually radically different technology base, which is expected to offer increased processing flexibility and capability and which is expected to be easier to change.

Any single reason may be the trigger for such a redesign effort, but more often than not, once started, the project takes on a life of its own. The growing integration of systems brings many users under the same systems "umbrella" and thus there are many interested areas of the firm seeking to incorporate as much of their backlog of business changes into the new system as possible. Given the complexity of the issues which affect such a project, it is not surprising that the size of these types of projects mushroom to tremendous proportions.

Chapter

7

The Various Types of Data Models

To begin our discussion of data models we should first begin with a common understanding of what exactly we mean when we use the term. A *data model* is a picture or description which depicts how data is to be arranged to serve a specific purpose. The data model depicts what data items are required and how that data must look. However it would be misleading to discuss data models as if there were only one kind of data model, and equally misleading to discuss them as if they were used for only one purpose. It would also be misleading to assume that data models were only used in the construction of data files.

Some data models are schematics which depict the manner in which data records are connected or related within a file structure. These are called record or structural data models. Some data models are used to identify the subjects of corporate data processing—these are called entity-relationship data models. Still another type of data model is used for analytic purposes to help the analyst solidify the semantics associated with critical corporate or business concepts.

The Record Data Model

The record version of the data model is used to assist the implementation team by providing a series of schematics of the file that will contain the data which must be built to support the business processing procedures. When the design team has chosen a file management system, or when corporate policy dictates a specific data management system, these models may be the only models produced within the context of a design project. If no such choice has been made, they may be produced after first developing a more general, non-DBMS specific entity-relationship data model.

These record data model schematics may be extended to include the physical parameters of file implementation, although this is not a prerequisite activity. These data models have much the same relationship to the building of the physical files as program specifications have to the program code produced by the programmers. In these cases, the data analysis activities are all focused on developing the requirements for and specifications of those files. These models are developed for the express purpose of describing the "structure of data."

This use of the term presupposes that data has structure. If we assume for the moment that data has structure, or that data can be structured, what would it look like. For that matter what does data look like? The statement also presupposes that there is one way, or at least a preferred way to model data.

Practically speaking however these models depict the "structure" or logical schematic of the data records as the programmer must think of them, when designing the record access sequences or navigational paths through the files managed by the data management systems.

With the above as an introduction, we can begin a discussion of data and data models. We will use the above as a common starting point and a common perspective.

Early Data Models

Although the term data modeling has become popular only in recent years, in fact modeling of data has been going on for quite a long time. It is difficult for any of us to pinpoint exactly when the first data model was constructed because each of us has a different idea of what a data model is. If we go back to the definition we set forth earlier, then we can say that perhaps the earliest form of data modeling was practiced by the first persons who created paper forms for collecting large amounts of similar data. We can see current versions of these forms everywhere we look. Every time we fill out an application, buy something, make a request on using anything other than a blank piece of paper or stationery, we are using a form of data model.

These forms were designed to collect specific kinds of information, in specific format. The very definition of the word form confirms this.

Definition. A *form* is the shape and structure of something as distinguished from its substance. A form is a document with blanks for the insertion of details or information.

Almost all businesses and in fact almost all organizations use forms of every sort to gather and store information.

Why are forms used? A form is used to ensure that the data gathered by the firm is uniform (always the same, consistent, without variation) and can thus be organized and used for a variety of different purposes. The form can be viewed as a schematic which tells the person who is to fill it out what data is needed and where that data is to be entered. Imagine, if you will, what would happen if the firm's customer orders arrived in a haphazard manner, that is, in any way the customer thought to ask. Most of the orders would take a long time to interpret and analyze, much of the information that the firm needed to process the order would probably be missing, or at best be marginally usable by the firm.

In many firms, especially those who receive a large number of unsolicited orders, a large amount of time is spent in trying to figure out what the customer wants, and whether in fact the customer is ordering one of the firm's products at all.

This is in contrast to those firms where orders come in on preprinted order forms of the company's design. While this doesn't ensure that the customer will fill out the form correctly, at least there is the hope that the firm has communicated what it wants and needs.

Forms and Automation

As firms began to use automation to process their data, it became more and more important to gather standardized data. Early computing machinery had little if any ability to handle data that was not uniform. Data was taken from the paper record forms and punched into card records which were then fed into machines—machines that had minimal (by today's standards) logic capability. These machines performed the mechanical functions of totaling, sorting, collating, and printing data but had little ability to edit that data. In fact these machines were highly sensitive to data which was not exactly in the expected form.

The card records to which the data was transferred for machine processing were initially designed to follow the sequence of data as it appeared on the form. New forms were designed on which the analyst could lay out or structure the data fields (the components of the automated records) on the cards. Additional forms were designed to assist the analyst in designing the reports to be produced from that data. This process of designing card record and report layouts was probably the earliest examples of data modeling.

Although the media dictated the length constraints of the data entry and storage records (mainly 80-column cards), the analysts had some latitude within those constraints. The amount of data to be entered from a given form dictated the number of card records needed. The number of cards and the complexity of the data placed further constraints on the card layouts, the number of columns available, and the positioning of the fields on each card. Further constraints were imposed by the mechanical processing that had to be performed (sorting, merging, collating of cards), requiring control fields, sequence fields, and fields for identifying specific card formats. Multiple card formats were used to accommodate different kinds of data cards—name and address cards, account balance cards, order item cards, etc.

The Influence of Magnetic Tape Media

The introduction of magnetic tape media removed many of the constraints of size from data record layouts, but left many of the field sequence and record identification requirements. Although new record layout techniques were being developed, many of the early magnetic record layouts looked remarkably similar to their predecessor cards. Magnetic tape media also reduced the number of record format indicators needed to identify the various types and layouts of records. As experience with magnetic tape media increased many analysts experimented with larger and larger records, and introduced more descriptive data to accompany the process support data in the original files. This descriptive data allowed systems designers to provide more meaningful data to the business users.

Tape also allowed data to be more easily sorted, and data from multiple files to be merged and collated. Because of its ease of use and high capacity, many critical processing systems were, and still are, based on tape-based files.

Tape however still retained several limitations:

1. Tape could not be modified in place. Maintenance of data stored on tape required the old data to be read in, modified in machine memory, and new records written out on a new tape. This type of "old master–new master" processing is still in use today.
2. Tape records could not be retrieved randomly or selectively. The sequential storage of records on tape required that the tape be read from beginning to end every time data was needed, even when the data needed constituted only a small part of the file.
3. Modification of tape-based data records was achieved by adding fields on to the end of the record layout.
4. Although tape storage introduced the concept of variable-length records, and in some cases variable-length data fields, processing of those files was cumbersome and resource intensive, and placed additional restrictions on the mechanical aspects of processing such as sorting, etc. Because of this most tape processing was restricted to fixed-length, fixed-field record layouts. This restricted the manner in which repetitive, but variable-occurrence data could be handled.

   For instance, retention of monthly data required either one tape per month to be generated, thus requiring multiple tapes to be read to accumulate multimonth reports or month-to-month comparisons, or provisions had to be made within the tape record for monthly fields (commonly called "buckets") in which case depending upon the month, one or more "buckets" would be empty or filled. The designer however had to make these layout choices during the design phase and then develop the processing procedures to accommodate that design choice.

Direct Access File Storage

Almost concurrently with the introduction of tape record storage, the vendors introduced another magnetic storage media—commonly called disk or direct access storage devices (DASD). This form of media used rotating or spinning drums (a form that never really became popular because of its limited capacity and large size) or platters coated with magnetic material to store data, and used movable arms equipped with heads for reading and writing data to the media.

The early versions of these devices were faster than tape, and allowed for direct access to data (facilitated by the moveable arms) but had fixed capacity which was much smaller than that of the tape units of the same period.

Although these devices allowed for greater processing flexibility, early record design techniques for them were almost identical to those used for tape records.

These devices however allowed vendors to develop and introduce additional methods of storing and accessing data based on the direct and random processing capabilities. These devices allowed data to be located based on physical media address and thus indexes could be constructed which allowed for both sequential and random processing. These addresses also permitted various records to be tied together using the physical address as "pointers" from record to record. The standard vendor-supplied file access mechanisms however still required that all records in a given file have the same layout. Because the record access was relatively fixed, and because the record layouts were also relatively fixed, there was no real need for a data model as such since all that was really necessary was to know what fields were contained in each record and to understand in what order the fields appeared.

Data Management Systems

Until the introduction of data management systems (and data base management systems) data modeling and data layout were synonymous. With one notable exception data files were collections of identically formatted records. That exception was a concept introduced in card records—the multiformat-card set, or master detail set. This form of card record layout within a file allowed for repeating sets of data within a specific larger record concept—the so-called logical record (to distinguish it from the physical record). This form was used most frequently when designing files to contain records of orders, where each order could have certain data which was common to the whole order (the master) and individual, repetitive records for each order line item (the details). This method of file design employed record fragmentation rather than record consolidation.

To facilitate processing of these multiformat record files, designers used record codes to identify records with different layouts and redundant data to permit these records to be collected (or tied) together in sequence for processing. Because these files were difficult to process, the layout of these records and the identification and placement of the control and redundant identifier data fields had to be carefully planned. The planning and coordination associated with these kinds of files constituted the first instances of data modeling.

The concepts associated with these kinds of files were transferred to magnetic media and expanded by vendors who experimented with the substitution of physical record addresses for the redundant data. This use of physical record addresses coupled with various techniques for combining records of varying lengths and formats gave rise to products which allowed for the construction of complex files containing multiple format records tied together in complex patterns to support business processing requirements.

These patterns were relatively difficult to visualize and schematics were devised to portray them. These schematics were also called data models because they modeled how the data was to be viewed. Because the schematics were based on the manner in which the records were physically tied together, and thus logically accessed, rather than how they were physically arranged on the direct access device, they were in reality data file structure models, or data record structure models. Over time the qualifications to these names became lost and they became simply known as data models.

Whereas previously data was collected into large somewhat haphazardly constructed records for processing, these new data management systems allowed data to be separated into smaller, more focused records which could be tied together to form a larger record by the data management system software. This capability forced designers to look at data in different ways.

Data Management Models

The data management systems (also called data base management systems) introduced several new ways of organizing data. That is, they introduced several new ways of linking record fragments (or segments) together to form larger records for processing. Although many different methods were tried, only three major methods became popular: the hierarchic method, the network method, and the newest, the relational method.

Each of these methods reflected the manner in which the vendor constructed and physically managed data within the file. The systems designer and the programmer had to understand these methods so that they could retrieve and process the data in the files. These models depicted the way the record fragments were tied to each other and thus the manner in which the chain of pointers had to be followed to retrieve the fragments in the correct order.

Each vendor introduced a structural model to depict how its product is organized and tied data records together. These models also depicted what options were chosen to be implemented by the development team, data record dependencies, data record occurrence frequencies, and the sequence in which data records had to be accessed—also called the navigation sequence.

The hierarchic model

The hierarchic model (Figure 7.1) is used to describe those record structures in which the various physical records which make up the logical record are tied together in a sequence which looks like an inverted tree. At the top of the structure is a single record. Beneath that are one or more records each of which can occur one or more times. Each of these can in turn have multiple records beneath them. In diagrammatic form the top to bottom set of records looks like an inverted tree or a pyramid of records. To access the set of records associated with the identifier, one starts at the top record and follows the pointers from record to record.

The various records in the lower part of the structure are accessed by first accessing the records above them and then following the chain of pointers to the records at the next lower level. The records at any given level are referred to as the parent records and the records at the next lower level that are connected to it, or dependent on it, are referred to as its children or the child records. There can be any number of records at any level, and each record can have any number of children. Each occurrence of the structure normally represents the collection of data about a single subject. This parent-child repetition can be repeated through several levels.

The data model for this type of structural representation usually depicts each segment or record fragment only once and uses lines to show the connection between a parent record and its children. This depiction of record types and lines connecting them looks like an inverted tree or an organizational hierarchy chart.

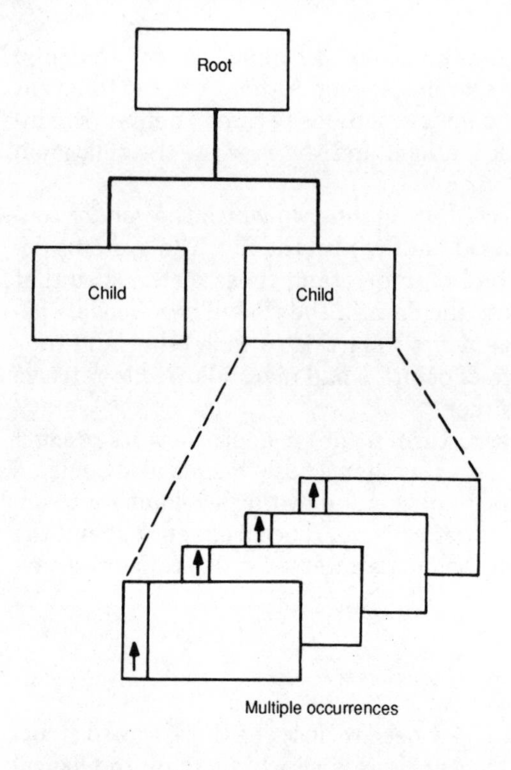

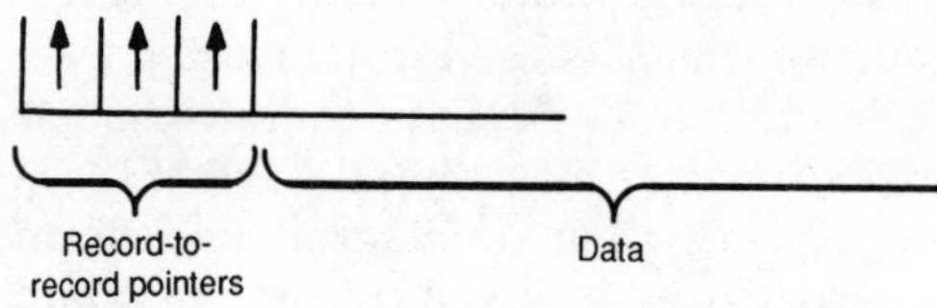

Figure 7.1 Logical and physical views of the hierarchic model.

Each file is said to consist of a number of repetitions of this tree structure. Although the data model depicts all possible record types within a structure, in any given occurrence, record types may or may not be present. Each occurrence of the structure represents a specific subject occurrence and is identified by a unique identifier in the single, topmost record type (the root record).

Designers employing this type of data management system would have to develop a unique record hierarchy for each data storage subject. A given application may have several different hierarchies, each representing data about a different subject, associated with it and a company may have several dozen different hierarchies of record types as components of its data model. A characteristic of this type of model is that each hierarchy is normally treated as separate and distinct from the other hierarchies, and various hierarchies can be mixed and matched to suit the data needs of the particular application.

The network model

The network data model (Figure 7.2) has no implicit hierarchic relationship between the various records, and in many cases no implicit structure at all, with the records seemingly placed at random. The network model does not make a clear distinction between subjects, mingling all record types in an overall schematic. The network model may

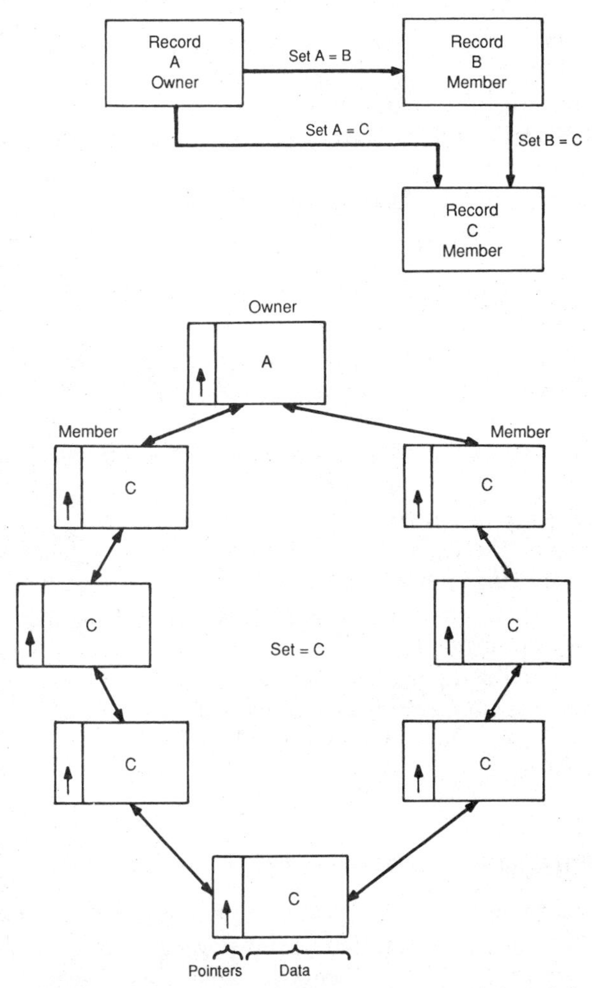

Figure 7.2 Logical and physical views of the network model.

have many different records containing unique identifiers, each of which acts as an entry point into the record structure. Record types are grouped into sets of two, one or both of which can in turn be part of another set of two record types. Within a given set, one record type is said to be the owner record and one is said to be the member record. Access to a set is always accomplished by first locating the specific owner record and then following the chain of pointers to the member records of the set. The network can be traversed or navigated by moving from set to set. Various different data structures can be constructed by selecting sets of records and excluding others.

Each record type is depicted only once in this type of data model and the relationship between record types is indicated by a line between them. The line joining the two records contains the name of the set. Within a set a record can have only one owner, but multiple owner member sets can be constructed using the same two record types.

The network model has no explicit hierarchy and no explicit entry point. Whereas the hierarchic model has several different hierarchic structures, the network model employs a single master network or model, which when completed looks like a web of records. As new data is required, records are added to the network and joined to existing sets.

The relational model

The relational model (Figure 7.3), unlike the network or the hierarchic models, does not rely on pointers to connect and chooses to view individual records in sets regardless of the subject occurrence they are associated with. This is in contrast to the other models which seek to depict the relationships between record types. In the network model records are portrayed as residing in tables with no physical pointer between these tables. Each table is thus portrayed independently from each other table. This makes the data model itself a model of simplicity, but it in turn makes the visualization of all the records associated with a particular subject somewhat difficult.

Data records are connected using logic and by using that data that is redundantly stored in each table. Records on a given subject occurrence could be selected from multiple tables by matching the contents of these redundantly stored data fields.

The Impact of Data Management Systems

The use of these products to manage data introduced a new set of tasks for the data analysis personnel. In addition to developing record layouts, they also had the new task of determining how these records should be structured, or arranged and joined by pointer structures.

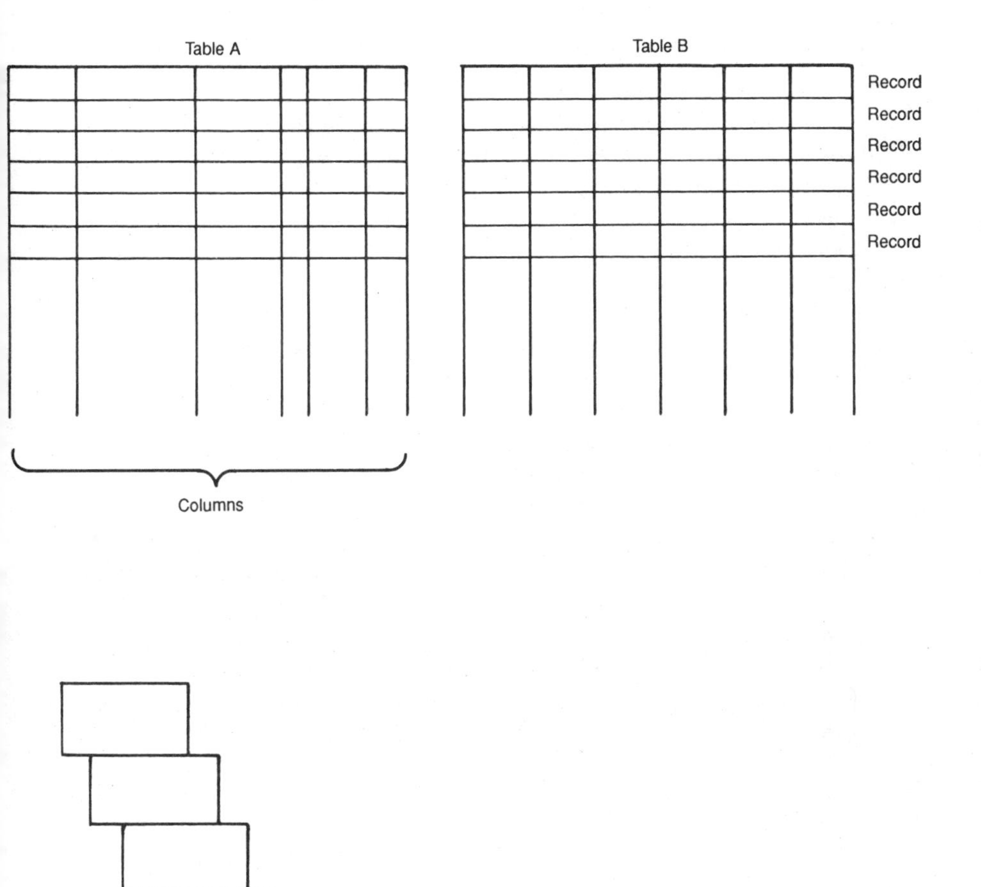

Figure 7.3 Logical and physical views of the relational model.

Once those decisions were made they had to be conveyed to the members of the implementation team. The hierarchic and network models were necessary because without them the occurrence sequences and the record-to-record relationships designed into the files could not be adequately portrayed. Although the relational "model" design choices also needed to be conveyed to the implementation team, the relational model was always depicted in much the same format as standard record layouts, and any other access- or navigation-related information could be conveyed in narrative form.

Data as a Corporate Resource

One additional concept was introduced during the period when these new file management systems were being developed—the concept that data was a corporate resource. The implications of this concept were that data belonged to the corporation as a whole and not to individual user areas. This implied that data should somehow be shared, or used in common by all members of the firm.

Data sharing required data planning. Data had to be organized, sized, and formatted to facilitate use by all who needed it. This concept of data sharing was diametrically opposed to the application orientation where data records and data files were designed for, and data owned by, the application and the users of that application.

This concept also introduced a new set of participants in the data analysis process and a new set of users of the data models. These new people were business area personnel who were now drawn into the data analysis process. The data record models which had sufficed for the data processing personnel no longer conveyed either the right information nor information with the correct perspective to be meaningful for these new participants.

The primary method of data planning is the development of the data model. Many of the early data planning was accomplished within the context of the schematics used by the design team to describe the data management file structures. These models were used as analysis and requirements tools, and as such were moderately effective. They were limited in one respect, that being that organizations tended to use the implementation model, which also contained information about pointer use, navigation information, or in the case of the network models, owner-member set information, access choice information and other information which was important to the data processing implementation team, but not terribly relevant to the user.

Normalization

Concurrent with the introduction of the relational data model another concept was introduced—that of normalization. Although it was introduced in the early 1970s its full impact did not begin to be felt until almost a decade later, and even today its concepts are not well understood. The various record models gave the designer a way of presenting to the user not only the record layout but also the connections between the data records, in a sense allowing the designer to show the user what data could be accessed with what other data. Determination of record content however was not addressed in any methodical manner. Data elements were collect into records in a somewhat haphazard manner.

That is, there was no rationale or predetermined reason why one data element was placed in the same record as another. Nor was there any need to do so since the physical pointers between records prevented data on one subject from being confused with data about another, even at the occurrence level.

The relational model however lacked these pointers and relied on logic to assemble a complete set of data from its tables. Because it was logic driven (based upon mathematics) the notion was proposed that placement of data elements in records could also be guided by a set of rules. If followed, these rules would eliminate many of the design mistakes which arose from the meaning of data being inadvertently changed due to totally unrelated changes. It also set forth rules which if followed would arrange the data within the records and within the files more logically and more consistently.

Previously data analysts, file and record designers, relied on intuition and experience to construct record layouts. As the design progressed, data was moved from record to record, records were split and others combined until the final model was pleasing, relatively efficient, and satisfied the processing needs of the application that needed the data that these models represented. Normalization offered the hope that the process of record layout, and thus model development, could be more procedurally driven, more rule driven such that relatively inexperienced users could also participate in the process. It was also hoped that these rules would also assist the experienced designer and eliminate some of the iterations, and thus make the process more efficient.

The first rule of normalization was that data should depend (or be collected) by key. That is, data should be organized by subject, as opposed to previous methods which collected data by application or system. This notion was obvious to hierarchic model users, whose models inherently followed this principle, but was somewhat foreign and novel to network model developers where the aggregation of data about a data subject was not as commonplace.

This notion of subject-organized data led to the development of non-DBMS–oriented data models.

The Entity-Relationship Model

While the record data models served many purposes for the system designers, these models had little meaning or relevance to the user community. Moreover, much of the information the users needed to evaluate the effectiveness of the design was missing. Several alternative data model formats were introduced to fill this void. These models attempted to model data in a different manner. Rather than look at data from a record perspective, they began to look at the entities or subjects about which data was being collected and maintained. They also realized that the relationship between these data subjects was also an area that needed to be modeled and subjected to user scrutiny. These relationships were important because in many respects they reflected the business rules under which the firm operated. This modeling of relationships was particularly important when relational data management systems were being used because the relationship between the data tables was not explicitly stated, and the design team required some method for describing those relationships to the user.

As we shall see later on, the entity-relationship model has one other important advantage. In as much as it is non-DBMS specific, and is in fact not a DBMS model at all, data models can be developed by the design team without first having to make a choice as to which DBMS to use. In those firms where multiple data management systems are both in use and available, this is a critical advantage in the design process.

Chapter

8

Overview of the Entity-Relationship Approach

Background and Origins

Almost all data modeling as practiced today uses some form or variation of the entity-relationship analysis. Almost all CASE tools are either based on entity-relationship models, or support the creation of entity-relationship models. The various forms of information engineering all use some form of the entity-relationship data model for their data side activities. The entity-relationship (ER) approach consists of both an analytical and design method and a modeling technique.

The ER approach was first described by Dr. Peter Chen in the March 1976 issue of the ACM publication *Transactions on Database Systems* (Volume 1, Number 1). Since that time it has evolved into one of the most important tools in the data analysis and systems design tool kit. Today there are many practitioners of entity-relationship analysis and modeling, and many books and articles on design methodology and technique routinely include at least some mention of it in their work.

Prior to the introduction and use of this approach, most data analysis activities focused either on determining data requirements as a by-product of analyzing the processes to be performed, or on data elements presumed to be needed by the user. Some concentrated on trying to fit lists of data elements into one of the data structure models which can be implemented by a DBMS, others on designing from reports, screens, and files, still others on following trails of transactions through their various processing stages. From these processes, flows, data elements, and/or outputs they attempt to re-create the real world. Many attempt to re-create the processes from the desired results.

Today many designers and data analysts attempt to combine both old and new by developing record mode entity-relationship models and then switching to older analysis methods to populate those models with data elements derived from lists of elements gleaned from their analysis documentation and from user requirements interviews. This approach not only results in ineffective data design choices and decisions, but fails to use the full power of the entity-relationship approach.

What contributes to the notable lack of success in following this path is the failure to realize that concentrating record structures and following formula rules for the placement of data elements in records ignores the inherent meaning of data as a means of describing things and of recording information about things. Without a proper understanding of those things themselves, neither the system designer nor the data analyst can make reasoned decisions as to what data was needed about those things.

In the business environment, examining only transactions, or processes, or outputs, or data flows, or even a combination of all four produces a picture, which is correct as far as it goes, but which does not reflect a true or complete picture of the environment. Business environments are populated by people, using things, and both people and things are located in places. Any business description must not only include these people, places, and things, but it must also start with them. These people, places, and things are called entities.

These people, either individually or in groups, work with things, or provide services, for other people. Since both the people and the things are real (they physically exist) they can be described, and they must be located somewhere (in some place). Additionally, relationships which exist between people and things, people and places, things and places, and between different types of things, different types of places, and different types of people themselves must be described.

Processes are the actions which people entities (or their mechanical or electromechanical surrogates) perform with other people entities and with other thing entities in place entities. Transactions and reports are mechanisms for recording those processes or for communicating between entities, and data flows are the paths that these transactions, reports, etc., take between and among the people entities and the location entities where such records are stored.

These entities may be well defined, in that the firm may know a great number of things about them, or vaguely defined, in that the firm may know very little about them. In some cases, such as with either prospective customers or employees, the firm may only know or suspect that they exist, but not who they are, or where they are.

These entities may exist in large homogeneous groups where all members are capable of being described in the same manner, or they may be fragmented into many different subtypes, each with descriptions which are either slightly different, or in some cases radically different, from the other members of the same group.

The relationships that exist between these entities are real. And as with the entities these relationships themselves may be well defined, in that the firm may know a great number of things about them, or vaguely defined, in that the firm may know very little about them, again as little as knowledge or suspicion of their existence.

The power of the ER approach lies in its ability to focus on describing these entities of the real world of the business, and the relationships between them. By describing these real-world entities through the identification and definition and assignment of attributes to them, and their relationships, the designer is describing how the business should operate.

Although the business itself may change, sometimes dramatically, these types of changes occur much less frequently than changes in the routine processes and activities. Regardless of the business changes, the entities of the business rarely change. What may change, however, is the firm's perception of which attributes of those entities are currently of interest. Some relationships between these business entities may also change but even these relationship changes occur infrequently. Thus by understanding and properly describing these entities and the relationships between them, the designer can form a very stable foundation for understanding and redesigning the business itself, and for properly recording the results of, or changes caused by, the processes of the business.

Constraints on the ER Approach

As with any analytical method, the effectiveness of the ER approach is limited, or constrained, by three factors, all of which have to do with the designer's understanding of the business environment. These closely related factors are (1) entity identification and definition, (2) entity description, and (3) business context.

Entity identification and definition consists of recognizing the various entities, determining why they are of interest to the firm, and naming them. The identification and definition process must specify the entity at the exact level of precision which ensures that it is not so general as to be meaningless, and yet not so specific that it fragments into too many subsets. For example, "people" as an entity would be too general since it includes both customers and employees, among others. On the other hand, "full-time employees" and "part-time employees" would be too specific since both are employees and "full-time" and "part-time" are attributes of employee and a person can alternate between the two states, and still be the same employee.

Entity description consists of identifying which attributes of the identified entities are needed by the firm, and why those attributes are of interest. For example, is the firm interested in the attribute "hobbies" or "clothing sizes" for the employees? If the firm is a sporting goods firm, the answer to the former might be yes. If on the other hand the firm provides uniforms for its employees, the answer to the latter might be yes.

Business context involves identifying and defining the relationships which exist between the identified and defined entities, and their relative importance to the firm as a whole, and to each specific part of the firm. Business context also involves identifying and defining the use or role of each of the entities within the firm. An entity's appearance, role, or use in one firm may be entirely different in another firm, and yet the entity itself is the same.

Just as an entity may have different roles or uses between firms, so also, each part of the firm may have a different perspective on the business, and each part of the firm may have a different perspective on the entities of the firm. This perspective does not change the fact of the entity's existence, only the attributes and relationships of those entities which are of interest to that portion of the firm and their role or use in that firm.

The specific description of these entities and their relationships with other entities within the firm are relevant only within the context of that firm and are totally dependent upon the attributes of the entities which are of interest to the firm. An entity within one firm may be only an attribute of an entity within another firm, and vice versa.

Entities, Relationships, and Attributes

The importance of identification and definition, description, and context can be seen when one looks at the formal definitions of the three key elements (Figure 8.1) which form the heart of the ER approach. These definitions form the basis for both the data analysis method and the data modeling technique of the entity-relationship approach.

1. An *entity* is defined as a person, place, or thing which is (*a*) of interest to the corporation, (*b*) capable of being described in real terms, and (*c*) relevant within the context of the specific environment of the firm.
2. An *attribute* is any aspect, quality, characteristic, or descriptor of either an entity or a relationship. An attribute must also be (*a*) of in-

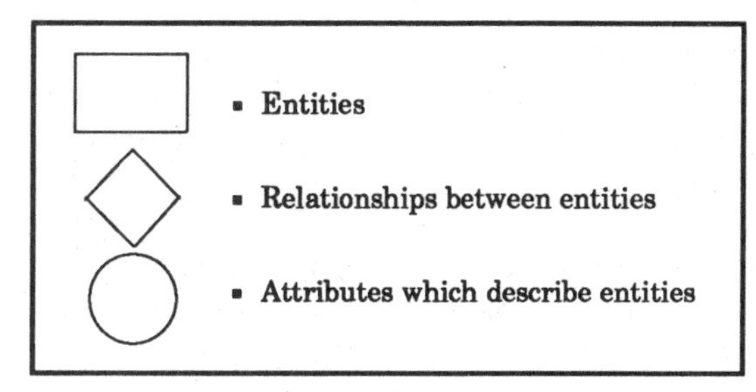

Figure 8.1 Major components of the ER approach.

terest to the corporation, (*b*) capable of being described in real terms, and (*c*) relevant within the context of the specific environment of the firm.

An attribute must be capable of being defined in terms of words or numbers. That is, the attribute must have one or more data elements associated with it. An attribute may be the name of the entity or relationship. It may describe what the entity looks like, where it is located, how old it is, how much it weighs, etc. An attribute also may describe why a relationship exists, how long it has existed, how long it will exist, or under what conditions it exists.

3. A *relationship* is any association, linkage, or connection between the entities of interest to the corporation. These relationships must also be (*a*) of interest to the corporation, (*b*) capable of being described in real terms, and (*c*) relevant within the context of the specific environment of the firm.

It is important to note at this point that relationships exist only between entities, not between attributes of entities.

To illustrate:

The entity "person" could be anyone.

When the attributes *name, age,* and *sex* are added, we can identify men from women, adults from children, and one person from another.

When the relationships *married to, parent of, child of, member of,* and *works for* are added, we know whether we are talking about a group of unrelated people, a family, or a corporation.

To describe the entity, we must describe it in terms of its attributes and its relationships with other entities. An entity description consists of a series of statements which complete a phrase such as "the entity is . . .," "the entity has . . .," "the entity contains . . .," or "the entity does. . . ." Each attribute relates to the entity in hierarchic terms, that is, all attributes of the entity are fully dependent upon the entity itself because individually and together they are the entity.

The question can still be asked, however, "How can we begin to identify these entities?" Is, for example, the entity identified as customer (representing all customers), or is it the specific types of customer (such as mail order, or retail), or is it a single customer? The answer is that it can be all of these, none of these, or more than these.

The specific identification and definition of the entity has meaning only within the context of that firm. However, most businesses can be described using a fairly restricted set of generic entity types such as customer, product, machine, employee, location, organizational unit, etc.

An entity (Figure 8.2) is whatever the business defines it to be, and that definition must make sense within the context of the firm. Thus, an entity in one firm may be a subset of entities included in the entity definition of another firm, or may be the global definition of the entity used within another firm. These differences in identification and definition can be illustrated by the following example:

> A town planning board, with responsibility for community planning and zoning, would describe that community in terms of each of its buildings, and further subdefine those buildings into residential, office, stores, warehouses, and factories. The board might be interested in which people or which firms occupied or owned those buildings, but for their purposes that information would be an attribute of the building, just as the size of the building, the number of floors, the number of windows and doors, and the cost of the building were attributes.
>
> On the other hand, the local chamber of commerce doing a census, or community directory, would be interested in the people and the firms who lived, worked, or were located in the community. In that case they would be interested in the names of the people, their incomes, length of residence, amount of taxes paid, and where within the community they lived

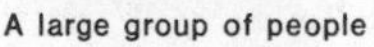

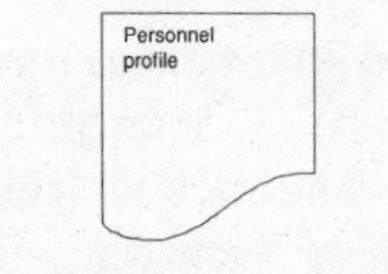

Figure 8.2 An entity can be many things.

- A fact of existence—Something that exists
- The existence of something apart from its attributes
- Thus:
- An entity in and of itself has no attributes and exists only as a label

Figure 8.3 What is an entity?

or were located (the buildings). Here the buildings become attributes of the people.

Neither the buildings nor the people have changed. Both still exist, physically unchanged. The perspective, however, has changed and the things which are of interest about those buildings and people have changed.

The perspective of the town council would need to know all the information about both the people and the buildings, along with information about roads, utilities, etc. In this case, both the buildings and the people become entities in their own right, along with the relationships between them (who lives or works where, who owns what, etc.).

This need for both attributes and relationships is consistent with the accepted dictionary definition (Figure 8.3) of an entity which defines it as "the fact of existence; being. The existence of something considered apart from its properties." Thus although the entity exists, its true form and role is only apparent after its attributes are added.

Without attributes all we know about the entity (Figure 8.4) is that it exists. The distinction between the entity and its attributes, and the relationship between the entity and its attributes, is so important, that the ER diagram distinguishes between the entity and its attributes by using different symbols for each.

The attributes of an entity could be contained in a single record, or it may take a large collection of records where each contains the data elements of a single attribute. Either way, an entity should not be equated to a record, a logical data record, or a table. Records and logical data records are the means for storing related items of data in the data processing environment.

- An entity is a real world person, place or thing, or a conceptual (logical) person, place or thing, of significant interest to the firm, and about which the firm must collect and maintain data
- Under special circumstances an event may also be considered to be an entity

Figure 8.4 Definition of an entity.

ER Models versus Data Structure Models

Records hold individual data elements or groups of data elements. Logical data records are representations as to how selected groups of record types are logically and physically connected. Table rows may also be viewed as records from a data processing viewpoint.

Logical data records, also called logical data models, fall into three main formats: hierarchic, network, and relational. These traditional data models represent implementations, specifically data base management system (DBMS) implementations, of logical data records.

Each one models a different view of the structure of data and in that light they are more properly *data structure models*. The data structure models are creatures of data processing. The real world, when it considers data, does not look at data structures, but rather it looks at things (usually paper things) which contain data.

The entity-relationship model represents a conceptual view of the world, which incorporates all three data models, is independent of any DBMS or data processing considerations, and is a representation of the business environment. The ER model contains the major aspects of all three structural models.

Although we speak of entities as if they were singular, an entity is in reality that set of persons, places, or things all of which have a common name, a common definition, and a common set of descriptors (properties or attributes). This conforms to the relational model and is equivalent to placing all attributes in the third form of the normalization process Third Normal Form (3NF).

The entity representation in the model, while it may represent a single instance, usually represents numerous people, places, or things all of which have a common name and common descriptors and thus can be treated as a set, again in conformance with the relational model.

These entities interact (relate) with other entities. These interactions form a complex set of named discrete, relationships as in the network model.

An entity, although it exists physically, only has physical substance when it is described in terms of what it looks like, where it is, what it does, and how it relates to other entities. Each component of that description is a property or an attribute of the entity. The sum of the properties is the entity. This association of attributes to entities, if diagrammed hierarchically, would appear as a flat (two-level) structure, with the root being no more than an anchor which names and types, or subtypes, the entity. In a network diagram it would appear as a key-only owner record, with multiple set relationships. In relational form, the entity would be the name of the primary relation, and the attributes might be subsumed in that relation or might be separate secondary relations.

Since the entity-relationship model incorporates all three data structure models, it can view data in a more complete and realistic manner. The ER model, although it can be translated quickly and easily into any or all of the data structure models, is not a data structure model, but instead seeks to identify and describe things and how they relate, rather than just data (used to describe those things) and how it can be stored.

The meld of the three data structure models within the ER model reflects the fact that each of these models reflects a portion of the way in which those real-world things actually occur. These entities are physically real and their real properties can be described, these people perform actions, using and transforming both things and information (which is contained on things as data). The common characteristic between all entities is that they can all be described, and the medium we use for that description are words and numbers. These words and numbers, collectively, are data, and individually are data elements.

The fact that entities, especially in the data processing environment, are described by data, does not make them data objects, nor is every collection of data elements an entity.

Some writers have suggested that data entities are built from collections of data elements in the same manner that a car is built from a collection of parts. In fact, an ER model can be complete and meaningful with no traditional data elements at all. The parts of a car were specifically chosen because each contributes something to the overall design of the vehicle. Any number of different sets of parts could be assembled and would result in a car, but a specific car can only be built from a specific set of parts.

A car is a thing, it is a subtype of the larger group of things called vehicles, and part of another subtype called self-powered vehicles for transporting people and things. Just as there are many different types of vehicles not all of which are cars (some may be boats, planes, or trains), so too there are many different types of entities.

A final type of attribute needs to be discussed, and they are, attributes which do not describe the thing itself, but what it does, or how it is used, or why it is used. These things that an entity does are called activities, and collectively they are called processes. The attributes which describe these are called *processing-related attributes.*

The processes, or activities, of the business are in reality the actions that people take with respect to things or places, or other people. These actions usually result in some change in the physical appearance, state, or condition of one or more other entities, or sometimes in the creation of a new entity itself.

We can use the entity called car as an example:

> The physical characteristics of the car—its size, weight, year, make and model, color, and parts list—represent the car itself. What ever happens to it, so long as it remains a car, these characteristics (except for possibly

color) will never change. Whether or not it is owned by anyone, whether or not it is new or used, in good repair or falling apart, driven 1 mile or 100,000 miles does not change these facts of its existence.

However, the fact that that car exists is meaningless unless we put it in some context which tells us why the firm is interested in it.

If we were a new and used car dealer, or a company fleet manager, we might want to know other things about it, such as ownership, use and usage, options and accessories, etc. We might also want to know how many miles it was driven, how much gas it uses, how many times it was maintained, what was done to it at each maintenance, how many times it was in an accident, how many different people have driven it, what it cost new, what it costs now, how much it costs to maintain, etc. These latter attributes are really process attributes. They are part of the description of the car, in some cases even part of the physical description, but these attributes tell us about what was done to or with the car, not about the car as a thing.

If we were an auto parts dealer, we might be interested in the parts of the car themselves, both new and used, in which case both the year, make, model, and color of the car become attributes of the part, along with its usage characteristics (if it is not a new part), its cost, size, shape, weight, how many are used in a specific year, make and model, etc.

A specific part could be an elemental part such as a bolt, tire rim, windshield, etc., or it could be a complex subassembly such as a transmission, radio, motor, etc. It could fit one year, make, and model of car, or any car. By combining several of these parts into a subassembly we have in effect created a new "part."

All entities and most relationships have these types of process attributes associated with them. In many cases, these process attributes tell us why the firm is interested in this entity. In other cases, they help to define how the firm distinguishes between different classes of the entity, or why the firm is interested in some instances of the entity and not in others. These attributes also assist in determining when the firm first becomes interested in an entity, or ceases to be interested in the entity.

These process attributes are variable in that their values change frequently, and these changes usually involve the participation of some other entity. Thus, since they relate what one entity did to another, or where or how many of one entity are contained in another entity, they are normally descriptive of the relationship between the two, rather than descriptive of one entity or the other, although obviously they could be.

The processes of identification and definition, description, and contextual placement of the entities are vital to any understanding of the business, and to any effort directed at either application development or file design. Processes like data normalization (a much discussed concept) can not be meaningful unless we know what those entities are, what the difference is between an entity and an attribute of an entity, and, further, what relationships exist between those entities.

Chapter

9

Classification Overview

Categorization Is a Fundamental Process

Categorizing or classifying things is a fundamental process of human existence. The world we live in, business or personal, real or conceptual, is composed of myriads of things. Some of these things have very real differences between them, others are somewhat similar, and still others are highly similar to each other. The differences or similarities between many of these things are sometimes more artificial than real. Distinctions are made between groups of things because it is clearer to do so than it is to refer to ungrouped things. One reason for making distinctions between things is to put them into groups which are easily manageable or understandable.

In almost every case some common characteristic of these things is used to make those distinctions. Sometimes, several characteristics are required in order to make those distinctions. Because things in the real world have many characteristics, any set of characteristics they have in common can be used to make these distinctions, or to group the things. For purposes of illustration only, let us take one of the largest group of things which we deal with, people.

Obviously the world is full of people and it would be impossible to deal with or discuss people in general in any meaningful manner. There are just too many different kinds of people. There are only a few things that you can say about people in general without excluding some of them.

Once you start adding obvious physical characteristics such as age, sex, race, height, weight, color of hair, color of eyes, etc., you start to place people into groups which are smaller than the whole (people). The more characteristics you use the smaller the number of members in each group, and the more different combinations of characteristics you can use to make up each group. Once you start using characteristics (or values of characteristics) to group things, you are categorizing or classifying them.

However, using additional characteristics to take a large group and divide it into smaller groups is only part of how classification works. Characteristics also can be used to help define vague or complex ideas. For instance, ideas such as quality and utility have long eluded definition. In many companies the concept of a customer, or in some cases a product, is equally elusive.

Definition. To *classify* is to organize or arrange according to class or category. A *class* is a set, group, collection, or configuration containing members having or believed to have at least one attribute or characteristic in common.

A major process of data modeling is to determine how data required by the firm to describe each entity of interest to the firm must be grouped for optimal efficiency, accessibility, and usefulness.

Classification techniques are an invaluable method for assisting the data modeler in constructing those groupings. Classification techniques can also assist the data modeler in determining the dependency relationships between those data groups, and conversely in determining which data groups are independent of each other. Classification is also the preferred method and the most accurate method for handling that most difficult of data model chores, the modeling of roles.

Classification of Entities

An entity is a fact of being. Everything that exists in reality, or in the perception of reality is an entity. Because entities are devoid of attributes it is not possible to classify or group them. However we can state that since everything is an entity, and everything consists of persons, places, things, concepts, or events, then those things are entities by definition.

Although the definition of an entity for data modeling purposes distinguishes them into five groups, even these groups are too general to work with.

For the purposes of developing a business system design, and in particular the data models that are an integral part of those designs, each of these five classes must be divided into two, more restrictive, classes, one class containing those people, places, things, concepts, and events our firm is interested in and one containing those in which it is not interested.

Normally, data models do not include entities the firm is not interested in and thus they are discarded after identification. The remaining members (Figure 9.1) of each of the five now restricted classes can be further classified into two still further restrictive classes, those the firm must collect data about and those it does not have to collect data about. In this case however many models do not discard those entities about which the firm does not collect data. In those cases they are used for consistency purposes and to provide context for the remainder of the model.

We can see from this discussion that the term entity (the highest grouping in the data model) already represents three levels of categorization or grouping before we begin.

Returning to the people illustration, we now have a group called people, more specifically people the firm is interested in (for whatever reason) and more specifically people the firm is interested in and about which the firm must collect data or maintain records (for whatever reason).

This is still a fairly large group, because we are interested in different groups of people for different reasons (Figure 9.2), and each of those different reasons usually dictates that we need to collect specific kinds of data about each group. However since they are all part of a larger group called people they must obviously have certain characteristics in common.

Just as we group entities into people, places, things, etc., and because entity was too large and too general to handle in a meaningful way, so too we categorize each of those groups into smaller groups, i.e., kinds of people, for ease of handling. These grouping categories may be based upon what the entities are, what they look like, what they do, what purpose they serve, how they are used, etc.

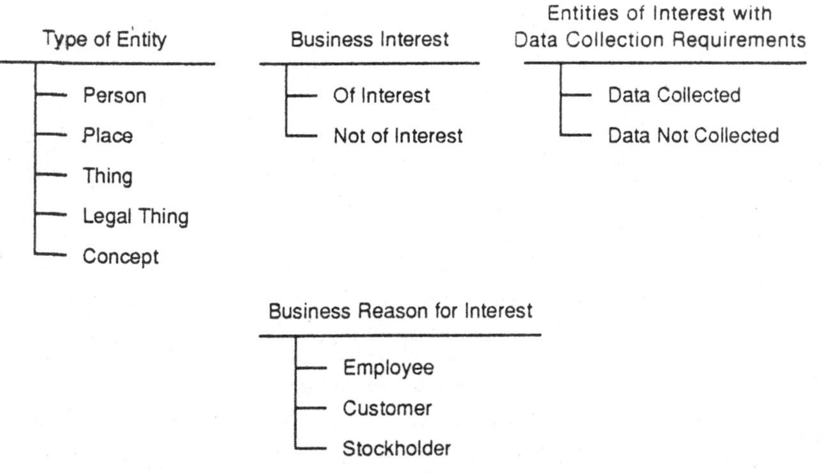

Figure 9.1 Characteristics of an entity—from its definition.

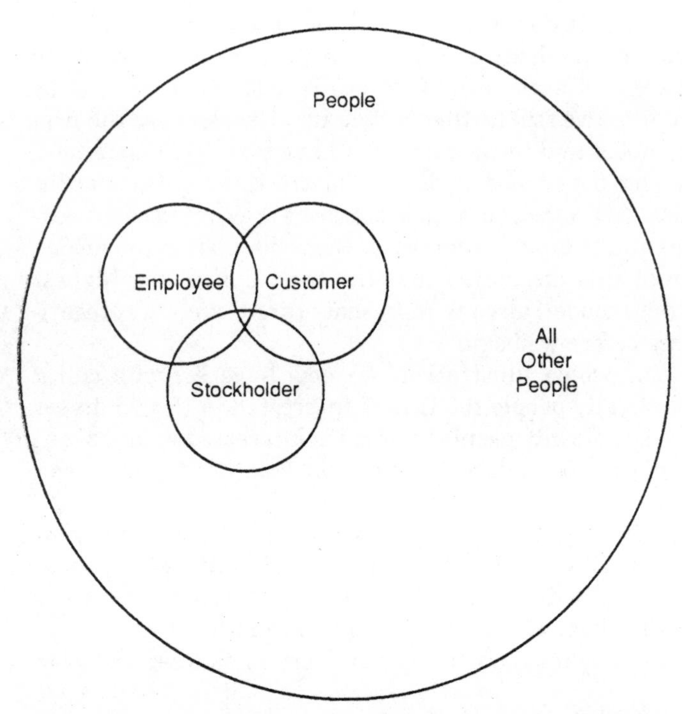

Figure 9.2 Isolation of some people from the general category people.

Once the classification scheme is known, at various times during the design process the designer can use each of these categorizations or classifications for purposes of discussion, analysis, or usage, recognizing that however they decide to group them for a particular purpose, the base population remains the same.

A given population may also be grouped or categorized for various uses by the values of characteristics selected for that purpose.

When producing a real-world business model, entities may be concurrently grouped by what they do, by the purpose they serve, how they are used, sometimes by what they look like, and sometimes by what they are. It is this ability to and need to concurrently group things in more than one way that distinguishes classification-based data models.

It is easier to view these smaller groups of the larger population by group name than it is by naming the individuals which comprise the group. Group names are used because although each member of the group is different and uniquely identifiable, the group's members are similarly described, act the same way, or are used for the same purpose. The group names tend to reflect these actions or usages. The group name is in many cases identical to the characteristic used to distinguish the members of the group.

The more general the statement of purpose, the description of the actions or usage, or the characteristic, the more members the group will contain. Conversely, as these statements of purpose, description of action or usage become more and more restrictive, the narrower the group becomes and the smaller the number of potential members.

Similarly, in the data model, as the definition of the characteristics becomes more and more general the group which can be included under that definition becomes larger. The more specific the characteristic definition or the more extensive the list of characteristics, the smaller the group that can be constructed.

Types, Subtypes, and Groups

In many data modeling texts the terms type and subtype are used. A type is a group. There are broadly defined groups and narrowly defined groups. If a type is a broad group, then a subtype is a narrow group within the broad group. However both broad and narrow groups, groups and subgroups, types and subtypes are all still groups.

Each group, broad or narrow, large or small, has some number of entities which have a set of characteristics in common. The characteristics may be very general or inclusive, or very specific or exclusive, or some combination of both.

Each entity of any given group may have many characteristics but only share some in common with other members of the group. The number of potential groups which can be formed is determined by the number of identifiable characteristics, the number of characteristics selected, and the number of meaningful combinations of characteristics for each number selected.

Entity Families

In the real-world entity model and in the data entity model, we attempt to use the most general, yet most meaningful, classification or categorization possible. These broad classifications of entities are called families. A real-world entity family (Figure 9.3) represents a general class or group consisting of all members who share some minimum set of characteristics in common. A data entity family represents a general class of highly intrarelated data about

1. All the members of the family
2. Each characteristic which distinguishes each group of members from each other group of members at each level of categorization
3. The progression from general to specific, of the characteristic sequence or string for each of the lowest level groups (those with the

most characteristics needed to distinguish them from all their siblings and cousins)

4. The attributes about the members of the group, over and above the characteristics used to form the group (remembering the inheritance of characteristics, and attributes)

In developing entity models, we seek to identify the broad real-world entity groups (or families) that populate the internal and external environment of the business (Figure 9.4). Some of the entities will concern us and some will not. They all have one thing in common, they were derived ultimately from the statements of mission, goals, objectives, etc., which were used to define the strategic and tactical direction of the company and its business processing rules and determinants.

Real-world entity reference and usage are within the context of the business and its concomitant actions. For representational reasons, ease and clarity of definition, and ease of handling and discussion, they are segregated into subsets or groups, but all are nothing more than some aspect of the whole, and therefore unified, entity.

Active versus Passive Entities

There are two additional ways in which to classify data entities, as either active or passive. Active data entities are the data entities which change over time, which do things or cause things to be done.

The other category of data entities are of interest, more so because they describe and/or relate entities. These are passive data entities. These data entities are usually fixed in data content, come about full blown, or exist more conceptually than in reality. Some examples of these are job requisitions, job or other related skills, education, locations, organizational units, sales territories, sales offices, and job de-

- A set of objects which share one or more characteristics
- A characteristic is some property or attribute that distinguishes one thing from another

Figure 9.3 Entity family is . . .

- The largest group which can be constructed is called the entity family
- Within the family are groups
- Each group within the family share a characteristic common to that group and all the characteristics of the family as a whole.

Figure 9.4 Entity families.

scriptions, to name a few. These passive entities have static data content, and no meaningful life cycle of their own.

These data entities are describable, but in narrative terms, or as lists of other items, rather than physical things. They are carriers of a concept or an idea. Again, there is overlap between active and passive entities, mostly dependent upon viewpoint. There are no hard and fast rules, but it is important to recognize their existence. It is important in the data modeling portion of systems design to identify both active data (nonstatic) entities and passive (static) ones. From a business systems design standpoint they behave differently and are used differently.

Process Control Entities

There is one final class or family of data entity which appears in many data models. The family has no name and thus can be called by any name. We will call it the process control family. Its members are used to remember sequences of data events and to guide processes, and later data events, within the organization.

If we scan all the documentation collected and generated from the analysis phase, we would probably have a myriad of entity groups, and probably only a few entity families and no definitive way to tell which is which. Entity class, entity set, and entity family are interchangeable terms within this context.

An entity family consists of all individual and groups of member entities which behave the same way in our organization. All entities which have the same role in the organization or which relate to the environment in the same way usually belong to the same family. Thus the entity family customer contains all entities who fill the role of customers, that is, who order, receive, and or pay for the products or services of the company. This family may also include both past customers, present customers, and potential customers, and these may be both active and passive.

Entity Definition

For each entity (family or otherwise) identified by the design team, a definition must also be created. These definitions will provide valuable insight into where the entity belongs and what level of generalization it represents. For an entity family, the definition should be broad or general enough to include all members of the family. We must describe the role that the members of this family play. We must define as completely as possible, who and what are the members of this family, or more succinctly, what is the universe of this family. The definition should also permit the determination of who are and are not members of the family.

This is usually stated in the form of tests or characteristics. The definitions of groups within a family will always be more restrictive than the family.

Entity Family versus Entity Group Reference

All entity references throughout the system design will either be to a family as a whole, some group of members (Figure 9.5) within some family, or to some individual member. All relationships are expressed in terms of an entity relating to another entity. In the business system design models, we assume that because entities relate to the environment, either explicitly or implicitly, they relate to each other as well. These relationships may be strong or weak, active or passive, and in some cases may be of no interest to the company.

Relationships can be viewed in two ways, entity family to entity family (interfamily), and entity to entity or entity group to entity group (intrafamily). These relationships, both inter- and intrafamily, are another manner in which the classification scheme may be represented. To illustrate:

> A person may be on the faculty of, be a student of, may be an alumnus of, a trustee of, and a contributor to an educational institution. Each relationship represents a separate, distinct, noteworthy, and more importantly definable characteristic.
>
> Likewise, a person may be a depositor of, a lender to and a borrower from, a mortgagee of, etc., a bank.

Each of these ideas may be represented by either a characteristic used to form an entity group, or by a relationship. These relationships may be direct or through some intermediary entity, such as an account entity.

Thus each group (Figure 9.6) is defined in terms of its relationship to some member of another family, rather than through shared characteristics. In this representation however the characteristic is transferred to the relationship. The model's descriptions must explain as fully as possible

1. Each of these intra- and interfamily relationships
2. The conditions under which each relationship exists

- Are constructed of objects which share one or more common characteristics
- Are constructed of objects which can all conform to the same definition

Figure 9.5 Entity groups.

- Share the same characteristics
- Share the characteristics of the family
- Inherit the characteristics of its immediate parent up the chain to the family root

Figure 9.6 Entity groups . . .

3. The group or entity within each entity family which participates in that relationship

Since the majority of activity within an organization can be expressed in terms of the relationships between entity and entity, or between entity and company (also an entity, by the way), we can expect that there will be a large number of intrafamily relationships in the structure and that relationships between entities, both intra- and interfamily, will be multiple, conditional, and complex.

Distinguishing between Entities (Entity Roles)

Entity groups, at the family level and below, are primarily developed from the role which the members of each group play in the organization. In some instances however, an entity can play multiple roles. For instance, a company can be a supplier and a customer. While these roles are distinct they are not mutually exclusive. A bank's customer can be a borrower for a car, a depositor, and a mortgagee. Again, non–mutually exclusive. The following are general recommendations for entity class, or entity family, identification, recommendations which also govern whether similar entities can, or should be merged into a single family.

1. If the roles are mutually exclusive, i.e., if the entities can play one role in the organization and not any other, define separate entity families.

   The attributes needed about each role will probably be different with little in common between roles. There should be no duplication of individual members in another family.
2. If the roles are distinct, but *not* mutually exclusive, merge the entities into a single entity family.

To illustrate:

1. School rules state that no faculty member may be a student of the school. Although similar in most respects and relationships, these are mutually exclusive entities.

2. The above school restriction does not apply. The faculty entity and student entity may be merged.

A third alternative is also possible. This states that there are entities who play one role exclusively, but there are some which can play both. This can be handled in the following manner.

Each different role entity is defined into a different family. For each entity that is a member of both families:

1. Define it completely in one family and create a "skeleton" or pseudoentity in the other. This pseudoentity would be related to the real entity. The pseudoentity would have all the characteristics of the second role which are not defined for the first role.
2. The entity member can be fully defined in both entity families, with a relationship and/or indicator in each which notes that the other exists and must be kept synchronized.

Entities are assigned to a class, or family, according to the role they play in the company environment. Care must be exercised to restrict the definition of those roles. All entities in the family or class play the same role within the organization. The entities within each family or class are different in specifics, just as people are different in specifics, but alike in their general nature and description.

As with the real world, each entity is unique in that it has its own distinct set of physical attributes (descriptors), operational attributes, and relationships. Thus the assumption cannot be made that all data elements within a given attribute of the entity family will be present or active for any given member group of the entity family. Overall however, those elements are needed to describe the entities in the family. Since the description of the family can only be in terms of its family members, the design team must assume that any given entity family member may have any and thus all possible attributes and relationships.

Just as entities are treated as families, so too the entity attributes are developed for the family. For instance, the demographic data for a doctor and a teacher are different (Figure 9.7). These in turn are different from the demographics of a school which in turn is different from those of a hospital. However, all of the above have some demographic data which we want to record.

The classification of attributes into descriptive, operational, or relational is vague at best. The categorization of any given attribute might easily change depending upon usage. Generally speaking descriptive data is more stable and infrequently changed, operational data is more volatile, and connective data describes relationships. The categorization does not affect the usage or structure per se, but assists in the pro-

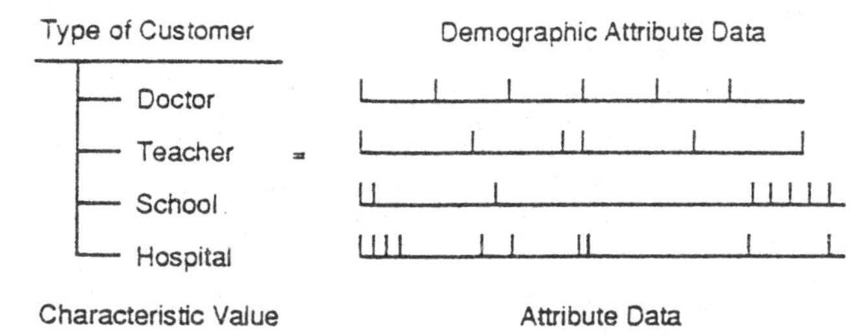

Figure 9.7 Different demographic attribute data for each kind of customer.

cess of identification, segmentation, partitioning, and combination. We try to combine entities with like data characteristics. Each characteristic of data should be such that it is the only place we have to reference to obtain data on that aspect of the entity. If all data characteristics are such that they could participate in the entity equation, then they are properly placed. If the characteristic of data can appear in the function equation of more than one entity, then it should be isolated.

Exception Attributes

There is a special category of data characteristics which constitute an exception to this general rule. Generally speaking, they can be termed transient exception data.

To illustrate: The customer family members contain standard ship-to data and instructions. On a given order the customer can request a special nonstandard, ship-to address or instructions. This special data applies to and overrides the standard data, and is used only for this one order. In this case, the customer can override the standard or default information for a particular order, thus the value of that attribute is dependent on a specific order and must be recorded as order operational data as well. As each order is processed the order override must be tested for contents, and in the absence of override data, the customer standard may be used.

The definitions of each characteristic describe their function, or role—descriptive or operational. The definitions answer the questions: What role does the characteristic play in describing the entity, its actions, or our actions against it? What data would we expect to find in this characteristic, if we assume that this, and only this, characteristic described that aspect of the entity? What is the definition of this aspect of the entity? Why is that particular data characteristic needed?

Data Acquisition and Retention

Acquisition and retention of the data must also be addressed. If a characteristic is needed for a given entity, where and how is that characteristic acquired?

The narratives for operational characteristics must address the questions—What is the minimum level of data necessary to support the function? How does the function relate to the entity? If data characteristics relate to multiple functions, or multiple data events, what are the identifiers necessary to distinguish a characteristic from its siblings? If this is a repeating characteristic of data, what identifiers do we need, real or internal, to distinguish its twins, its multiple parts? How many multiples may there be?

The design team should at this point be capable of creating a structure or schematic which gives pictorial representation to the entity families, groups of entities within each family, and the various facets of classifications of those groups within each family. They have separated out all the common data and created separate characteristics which reflect data which can be used commonly to describe both the family in general, and each group within the family. For these families they should have defined relationships or structures such that they can relate both the family members to each other, and members of different families to each other.

Some of these new characteristics may themselves be described in terms of other descriptive characteristics, which are common to still larger groups. It is a general characteristic of many of these families of entities that their description is more narrative than elemental. That is, they are conceptual in nature and can only be described by narrative.

Describing Process Control Entities

The final family of entity is one which we term the process control entity family. Within this family are members that are kinds of events, or time-sequenced things.

Within any functioning system, with randomly occurring events, there is a need to "remember" the order in which things happened, or to store the results of actions such that later actions can be taken against them. There is a need to record the results of decisions, or actions which determine which process is to be taken. There is a need to remember the results of tests which, once made, govern future actions and which would be tedious to make again. In some cases randomly occurring events must be processed at some later date in a certain order. Our process control entity serves this function of "remembering" time or ordering time. In essence this entity remembers sequences of occurrences by recording lists of trigger identifiers, or entity identifiers.

To illustrate: A process consideration calls for randomly received orders to be arranged in a priority sequence based upon a set of variables and for orders to be filled, or attempted to be filled, based upon FIFO (first in, first out) sequence, by priority. A member would be established for each priority and order identifiers recorded as occurrences of that member according to arrival time and priority. When orders are filled, the member occurrences are accessed and identifiers selected to identify the appropriate orders.

To further illustrate, as orders are processed against inventory, they can be filled and be ready to ship, partially filled and partially back-ordered, or completely back-ordered. As this determination is made, order identifier occurrences are created and used to populate the appropriate members. As changes occur or as conditions change, occurrences can be transferred from member to member. In this manner, action decisions can be passed simply and easily through the system. Appropriate functions can be performed simply by examining the relevant member and taking the action indicated. Sequential and conditional activities can be taken or not depending upon whether there are any occurrences of a particular member

This conceptual family of members can be used for system and operational status checks, work allocation, process control, and procedural control.

Chapter

10

Data Modeling Problems and Constraints

As the use of data modeling moved from an implementation tool of the physical file designers to a design tool of the systems analysts, systems designers, and more importantly the user, many of the problems inherent in the process began to become apparent.

The meaning of the record data model as a representation of the physical file design was apparent. It represented a schematic of record interconnections that could readily be translated into code which instructed the DBMS how to construct the files. Data record content was determined by the analyst and designer and only they needed to understand the logic behind the placement of data in specific records. The model was a tool of physical file design and a method of communicating design decisions between the designer and the implementation team.

The use of the analysis data model during the design phase as a communication mechanism between designer and user was less effective. Its meaning was also less apparent than that of the record model. The analysis model attempted to address the notion that data from the user perspective were descriptors (attributes) of things (entities), and that by identifying those things, their attributes and their relationships one would be identifying the subjects of data required by the corporation. The activities to produce these new models were positioned at the beginning of the development life cycle before the beginning of the data element identification process and well before the steps of assembling those elements into records.

Until the introduction of these models any data analysis activities that were performed attempted to develop the file and record designs by going from the detail (elements) to the general (records and files).

The new models took a general to specific approach and added a new component to the model—the concept of data subjects. This allowed the designer to proceed with the design logically, beginning with identification of subjects, then developing conceptual data groupings, populating those groupings with data elements, and then taking the resultant model and translating it into physical records and files. The specific record layouts and file structures would be dependent upon the specific DBMS or data management technique chosen for implementation.

Areas of Difficulty

The differences between the record models and the ER models stemmed from their content, from their perspective (what they were intended to represent), from their method of construction, and from their use. Differences also arose from the terminology used by each. The following is a summary of these areas of difference.

1. Changes in perspective

The first area of difference arose from the change in perspective of the modelers. Prior to the analysis model, data file design tended to follow the pattern set by the forms that preceded them. That is, the files were designed to contain data obtained from earlier forms. These forms tended to be utilitarian and rather restrictive or limited in the amount, kind, and variety of data they collected. They were also highly standardized. A given form was designed to collect a certain kind of data, for a certain purpose. Any data not anticipated in that form was not intended to be included. Where unanticipated data was added to existing forms, or where form fields designated for one kind of data was used for another kind, confusion occurred and miscommunication resulted.

The data collected by the forms and later by the automated files that replaced them did not allow for variation. Data was strictly formatted, strictly coded, and all data indicated on the form had to be collected. Because forms represented the data to be collected for a specific purpose, the data was codified for that purpose and rarely for any other. Customer information on an account-opening form was rarely of much use to the marketing department, since it was usually designed by the sales department, sometimes in consultation with the credit department, to determine the creditworthiness of the client and to determine what kind of account was to be opened for that customer.

2. Changes in content assumptions

The record models assumed that all data represented by the model had to be collected, although some variation was allowed. Another major assumption of these models was that each occurrence or entry in the file, each set of records, was relatively uniform. These types of models allowed for few variations in the kinds of subjects their data represented. They also assumed that for the most part all occurrences would be processed in a similar manner.

There was one additional assumption which was key to the record model. Each symbol on the model represented a collection of data elements (segment, row, or record) and each line (where they were used) represented the physical address or pointers which connected the records to each other. The only additional information contained on these models (in most cases) represented whether a given record occurred once or more than once within a "logical" set of records.

3. Changes in terminology

Each of the many different types of data model, both record and conceptual, introduced terminology and definitions intended to explain the concepts inherent in these models, and in some respects to differentiate the model from all other models. Each model had proponents who explained, clarified, and extended the model beyond its original scope. Many of these models also engendered large groups of practitioners who met regularly to exchange ideas and experience. From these meetings originated more new terminology and concepts. Because the models were used primarily for DBMS file construction, and because most companies tended to standardize on a single DBMS, practitioners tended to be well versed in the terms and concepts of their particular model but relatively ignorant of the terms and concepts of any other model.

As firms began to use more than one DBMS, the terminology became confusing, because the same words meant different things for each. Records, segments, rows, or tuples were all terms used to represent how the DBMS "saw" the data, but in reality they all represented a set of data items from the designer's perspective, although not always from the programmer or user's perspective.

This difference between what the designer built and what was presented to the programmer or user led to the rise of a distinction between the "physical" records and the "logical" records, between "physical" data base and "logical" data base.

The conceptual, analytical, or logical models shifted the focus of the designers and analysts from the question "how should the data be grouped and stored?" to the question "what information does the business require and what data must be collected and maintained to provide that information?"

During design, the analyst and user attempt to solidify concepts and business rules into data requirements and to represent those data requirements in some form which could ultimately become the physical file design.

The analytic model became a tool for stimulating ideas, identifying requirements, and organizing those requirements in a coherent fashion. This use of the model however introduced many new concepts and perspectives which were only vaguely understood, and directed the analysis into areas which were equally vague and ill-understood. Further confusion was introduced when designers attempted to translate concepts from the record models into the analytic models. The analytic models, because they portrayed concepts, became vague and muddled. This was because in most cases the concepts themselves were vague and muddled. The intent of the model was no longer clear nor was it clear in many cases what the model was trying to communicate.

The primary form of the new or analytic models was the entity-relationship model. As originally proposed it was to be a link between the real-world things that the user worked with and the record models that the automated system implementation teams worked with. It was intended to be DBMS independent, and focused on things about which data was collected rather than on how data about things was to be stored. These new models were part of a new approach to design, an approach from the user perspective. These models depicted business entities and their relationship with each other.

The concept was stark in its simplicity. All business data is collected and maintained about people, places, things, or concepts of interest to the firm. Thus if we model those things we have a strong foundation for determining what data is needed about these things. This new approach however developed still another set of terms to describe its components and to explain its concepts. It was strongly grounded in the relational model, and incorporated many of the concepts of normalization associated with the relational model.

Although data is collected about people, places, things, and concepts files are created about groups or collections of people, places, things, and concepts. Since it is cumbersome to repeat the phrase people, places, things, or concepts each time when talking about these groups in general, data modelers use the term generalized entity. Thus an entity is any group of persons, places, things, or concepts about which the firm must collect and maintain records (records in this sense are business records).

Many of the analysts and designers familiar with the record models saw the new models as a new way to portray the record relationships, rather than as a different kind of model. The developers of the CASE tools, also used the ER model in a similar manner. Unlike the record model where the symbols or model components represented a record, which was a representation of a group of data elements, the ER model symbols, or components, represented entities. The term *entity* as defined in the dictionary means the fact of being, existence. There is no representation, implied or otherwise, as to the subject of that existence. In other words, without further detailed explanation, the term entity means absolutely nothing.

Even if the ER models were limited to people, places, and things they would probably have not been easy to build and understand. The greatest difficulty however is engendered by the inclusion of concepts in the definition. First, by including concepts (and sometimes even events) within the definition of the term entity, we have in effect made an entity equate to anything we want it to be, since the span of the definitions includes everything within our perception. Thus, not only can records become entities, but also roles, and even entities themselves can become part of what is being modeled by the ER models. The latter can be seen most clearly in data dictionary (also called repositories and encyclopedias) models when data processing personnel attempt to create entry types to document entities from their analytic models. The inclusion of concepts and events in the definition caused many modelers to find themselves in the curious position of having to discuss the "entity entity."

4. Intermediate versus final products

Another difference between record model and analytic model also caused confusion. The record model described a record structure. It was implicit in the model that each structure or schematic of records represented the data about a given subject and that each iteration of the structure, or each iteration of records, represented data about a given instance. The record model however was the final product, it did not decompose into any other type of model, nor did the records described decompose into different kinds of records.

The entity-relationship model is a decomposition model. That is, it is not intended to be used as a final form, but as an intermediate product. It was a transition product in much the same manner that the requirements documentation of the procedural analysis was not a final product but a reference point for the analysis phase and the starting point for the detail design phase.

5. Semantic versus structural models

The entity-relationship model however was also substantially different from all other models then in use in the analysis and development cycle. That difference arose from the fact that all other models were either schematic (such as the data record models) or strict decomposition models such as the functional and process decomposition models of the analysis and design processes. It was also different from the flow models as typified by the data flow diagrams used by structured analysis advocates. The difference was that the ER model was what was called a *semantic* model. Semantics is defined as pertaining to meaning, as in language. The semantic model attempted to translate the meaning of the words used in requirements statements into pictorial representations for analysis. Specifically the semantic modelers attempted to translate the business rules which governed how, when, and why the objects of business interest (entities) related to each other.

Previous data models looked at data record relationships, and portrayed the paths that had to be established between one set of records and another. These paths were analogous to the indexes and cross references established between sets of paper form files. They attempted to automate the means of associating data in one file with data in another file.

The new models were an attempt to step back from the record models and look not at the data about things, but at the things about which the data was collected, and the relationships that had to exist between them based upon the statements of business requirements.

6. Conceptual ambiguity

This step back forced both analyst and user to look at and clearly define those things, those entities. The development of the ER models was begun at a higher level and from a different perspective than most previous models. The higher level took it outside a specific business area, outside most operational areas and into the realm of the managerial, and sometimes even into the strategic levels of the firm. The focus shifted from ascertaining the data content of forms to trying to understand or come to some common agreement about some of the fundamental concepts of the firm—those of product, customer, location, and sometimes even function and process. The new models highlighted many areas of ambiguity, misunderstanding and sometimes disagreement, problems which were masked by lower-level models because they did not have to deal with them.

These models also highlighted hidden redundancy of concept and data by looking at the business rules which were the foundation of the business processing. In many cases these business rules were never clearly defined, or were defined in several different ways. The models also highlighted another and perhaps more disturbing problem, that of conceptual inaccuracy. Many employees, in most cases highly experienced employees, did not have an accurate understanding of those business rules, nor of the legislative and regulatory rules under which the firm must operate. In still other cases, the models highlighted objects of business interest about which data was not being collected, or for which data was being collected in an incorrect manner. These omissions could, if not detected, severely handicap data collection activities and impede management's visibility into the firm's operations.

7. The meaning of relationships

Another problem area could be viewed as technical rather than analytical. Record models, because they were built to support the construction of DBMS files, conformed to DBMS rules. One of those rules was that the DBMS could not support what were known as "many-to-many" relationships. A given record could be related to many other records, or to one other record, or even to no other records. However, the DBMS could not support the concept of many records being related to many other records. In building record models, great care was used to avoid or remove these many-to-many relationships. The ER model had no such restrictions, because the real world had no such restrictions.

Another relationship-related problem had to do with the number of relationships portrayed by the model. In the record model, the relationships that were incorporated into the model were record-to-record relationships and represented, for the most part, pointers or record address relationships. For the most part, although a given record could be related to multiple other records (particularly in the network models) there tended to be only a single, or at most two, relationships between a given pair of records. In the real world, and in the ER model which portrayed the real world, multiple, independent relationships can exist, and often do exist, between any two entities.

Again, in the record model a relationship means only one thing, two records are related. Because these relationships represent pointers or record addresses, there was no data associated with them. Only in the case where the designer must resolve (eliminate) many-to-many relationships is a data record created to take the place of the relationship, and even in those cases these created records are related to their parent records by pointers. In the ER model, relationships represent business rules, and even one-to-one relationships may have data associated with them.

The concept of the relationship name is familiar to the network modeler (called set names in that model) but is alien to the hierarchic and relational modeler. This concept is integral to the ER model.

8. The introduction of roles

As mentioned previously, the ER model is not, strictly speaking, a decomposition model. However, the level-to-level model creation is based upon the principles of decomposition. The process of decomposing entities when going from level to level usually involves the separation of role entities from the base entity. This separation causes another "entity" to be created. This new entity may be real or not, depending on how important the role is to the firm. If the new role entity was completely independent from the original entity there would probably be no difficulty, however in most cases there is a strong overlap, complicated by the fact that the people, places, and things represented by the entities play multiple simultaneous roles, and the firm must deal with them somehow. This is sometimes portrayed in ER models as the "is-a" relationship, as in the employee also *is a* customer. This treatment of the problem probably causes as much confusion as it resolves.

Part of this confusion stems from the fact that record models decompose according to different rules. When a record is decomposed two or more new records are produced and the old record disappears. There is no need to maintain the identity with the parent record. In the ER model there is a strong need to maintain this identity, and in fact the parent entity may and often does remain in the model along with its offspring.

9. The empty box

Designers and analysts familiar with the record models know that the box on the schematic represented some number of data elements, even if those data elements had not yet been assigned. The box on the ER model represents an idea or a concept, even when the label on the box is something familiar, such as customer.

This notion of boxes in data models without data is disturbing and many modelers, and most CASE tools, make the assumption that the box does in fact represent data elements. They also treat the relationships between those boxes more like the pointer indicators in the record model than as representations of a business rule.

10. The meaning of the term entity

The definition of an entity itself has caused several problems for modelers attempting to use the ER models. Among them are that in unqualified form, the term "entity"

a. Can be used as both a group and singular term, sometimes within the same context. Models must be consistent. The symbols represent concepts and the concepts must be clearly understood. If a box is labeled people then it represents many people and must be treated as if it represents the group. If the model is labeled person, then it represents a single individual. Since the ER models are semantic models, each pair of entities and each relationship represent the basic components of a simple sentence, subject and object (the entities) and verb (the relationship).

Just as we would not intentionally switch from singular to plural when speaking about the same thing we should also not switch from singular to plural when discussing the entities or using the entities in the model.

b. Can be used to refer to the whole group and a portion of the same group, sometimes within the same context. This is particularly important when we deal with roles and decomposition of the entities. An entity called employee can also be split into temporary and regular. Since these are mutually exclusive groups (an employee cannot be both at the same time) one group has become two by adding a qualifier. However, when employee is split into manager and employee it is not so simple, because managers are also employees, and managers are managed by other managers. Thus portraying manager and employee in the same model is confusing at best.

c. Can be used as a general term when it is impractical or cumbersome to use the phrase "person, place, thing, or concept. . . ." The term entity is the most general term we can use when referring to something. It includes things, and even objects. In fact, it includes everything. When we refer to entities in our models we are in effect saying that the term can be replaced by any other term and still mean the same thing. In most cases, this is not true, since we are usually referring to something more specific.

d. Can be used to refer to many different levels of aggregation and to conceptually different components at the various design levels (conceptual, logical, physical). Employee as an entity in one model refers to all employees, whereas in another model we may be referring to a specific employee. This is of particular importance when we begin to discuss relationships. The reference "some," or "all," as part of the relationship statement must be included just as the terms "sometimes" and "always" must be included. Although it is rarely used, the term "never" is also a possibility in a relationship statement.

When multiple levels of model are produced, it is the designer's option to repeat the entities from one level to the next. In most cases this is not done, but the same names are carried forward when the entity does not change from level to level. An entity at the conceptual level—representing the perspective of the firm—may not be the same entity at the logical level—representing the perspective of a specific business area even though the same name may be used. At the physical or record level the entity becomes a record which is dissimilar from the entities at each of the other levels, and yet they are all referred to as entities.

e. Has been borrowed and used by physical designers and by CASE tool vendors to refer to the records in the data base structure models. Even though entities represent people, places, and things, and records are collections of data, the CASE vendors borrowed both the term and the form when they provided data modeling capabilities with their tools. Although it is possible to produce a standard ER model, when one looks at the definition of the entity it is replete with data elements as part of its description.

Within the ER model the term *attribute* is used when discussing a property of the entity. The entity, strictly speaking, is nothing more than the label of something, devoid of properties or attributes. An attribute is a property, aspect, descriptor, identifier, or characteristic of either an entity or a relationship. The entity is in fact the sum of its attributes. Entities are described in terms of their attributes. The term attribute has also been used as the name for data elements and data groups.

The difficulties with this definition are that these terms are not synonymous and thus the term "attribute"

a. Is used as both a group and singular form, sometimes within the same context

b. Is used to refer to a group of data elements, a portion of a group of elements, or a single element, sometimes within the same context

c. Is used to refer to many different levels of aggregation and to conceptually different components at the various design levels (conceptual, logical, physical)

d. Has been borrowed and used by physical designers and by CASE tool vendors to refer to the data elements in the data base structure models

e. Is used to refer to the properties (descriptors) and the characteristics of entities and of data elements

In some data models attributes have been elevated to the status of entities. Many models and most CASE tools have only two constructs, the entity and the attribute. An attribute is a single data element, and an entity is anything that has more than one attribute.

Because of these differences in concept, different terms should be used. In later chapters, we will introduce some new terms (at least new to data modeling) and will suggest how they should be used, and why.

Part

2

Data Analysis and Building the Real-World Entity Model

Classification helps people think by organizing the subjects of their thoughts and facilitating their understanding of commonality and differences. If the scheme that organizes those thoughts is muddled and ambiguous, so will the thoughts be. If the scheme provides more than one approach to a subject or more than one way to categorize it, you can be assured that it will fail to communicate a single, consistent message to its users.

SOURCE UNKNOWN

Chapter 11

Semantic Analysis and Data Analysis

Semantics is the study of meaning in language. It is also, and perhaps as important, the study of the relationships between signs and symbols and what they represent.

A model is a narrative and/or graphic representation of a physical or conceptual environment. A model must identify the major components of the environment, describe those components in terms of their major attributes, and depict the relationships between the components and the conditions under which the components exist and interact with each other. A model may also represent an idea, or be a graphic expression of some concept or other expression.

A model is constructed from signs and symbols. In order for the model to accurately portray the ideas of the model developers, that developer must have a clear and precise understanding of what those ideas are. This is especially true when the model is attempting to depict a conceptual environment.

Communication is the exchange of ideas, or at minimum the presentation of ideas. At minimum, because while ideas may be presented, words may be transmitted, they must be received and understood for communication to occur. Word are the mechanism for the transmission of ideas.

The Importance of Precise Communication

We use both words and symbols to communicate ideas. The most common form of symbols is mathematical. If we wish to extend the point even further we can look at words themselves and even the letters used to form the words as symbols. The effectiveness of the communication is due in a large part to its precision. That is, how precisely the symbols express the idea and how precisely both parties understand that expression.

Even a mathematical formula composed of basic symbols, numbers, and operators (plus, minus, equal, etc.) can express a very precise idea only if the meaning of each symbol is understood. More complex mathematical ideas employ still more symbols, and the most complex mathematics employ symbols known only to those who have had advanced training. In some cases, ideas are so complex that new symbols are invented to express them.

In mathematics however, each symbol has one and only one meaning or use. If that were not so, the foundations of mathematics and of mathematically based sciences would flounder and generally be rendered ineffective.

Mathematics can be used imprecisely, in that numbers can be chosen which represent only partial truths, or in other cases numbers can be chosen and used in ways that they were not meant to be used. Statistics is a science which uses numbers to prove various hypotheses, and by selecting the right numbers anything can be proven. There is a cliché which is used frequently when referring to statistics which states that figures don't lie but liars figure.

This is not to imply that statistics is inherently inaccurate, nor that we cannot use statistics effectively. It does however imply that the explanations of statistical evidence, and the manner in which those numbers are generated and extrapolated, is open to interpretation. If we count the males and females in a room we can get precise figures. If we use those numbers for any other purpose, we are extrapolating and the conclusions are less precise than if we looked at the original numbers.

The difference in meaning is derived from the fact that we have placed interpretation on the numbers. We have changed their meaning.

Communication using Words versus Numbers

Words, unlike numbers and mathematical symbols, have no precise meaning. Most words in fact have multiple meanings and the correct (or sometimes approximate) meaning is derived only because the words are placed in context, or in juxtaposition with other words. Frequently words are made up to represent an idea (a frequent occurrence in scientific and high-tech circles) and in others words are borrowed from other contexts and given new meanings.

Many words are used as if they have a precise meaning. For instance, in the previous paragraph I used the word "frequently." Frequently means often. Now we have one imprecise word defined by another imprecise word, which according to the dictionary I am using is defined as frequent. In other words we have a circular definition, one word used to define another which defines the first. How many is frequently? And yet the word is used in documentation to describe how many times something happens. How often have we used the word high-tech? We all know what it means, but how precisely can we define it. Exactly what does high-tech mean?

Words are symbols—symbols which represent both things and ideas, and which in turn are used to describe other things and ideas.

Words have multiple meanings and are used as a communication vehicle, relying on context and other words to make communication clear.

Models may be more or less precise than words. When we use pictures in our models it is usually clear as to what the picture represents, a house, a tree, a car, etc. When we use shapes with labels it becomes less clear, and the fewer the words we use in the label, the less clear the meaning.

Models are a representation of reality. Graphs and charts (bar charts, pie charts, etc.) represent mathematical ideas. However they only are meaningful to the extent that the numbers are present, the context are clearly identified, and the components are clearly labeled. Imagine, if you will, the effectiveness of a pie chart with no numbers associated with the slices. The chart conveys a vague, but imprecise message, much less precise than if the percentages or raw numbers were presented as well. Without numbers we could not tell exactly how big a slice we were looking at, however we could draw some conclusions from its relative size.

A bar chart or line chart without the axes clearly labeled again gives a general impression, but no precision. How much of a difference is there between a line graph where the horizontal scale is clearly marked as starting at zero and one with no scale notation at all?

Data Processing Models

Data processing professionals use many different types of models, with many different types of symbols. These models represent a wide variety of concepts which themselves are not clearly defined. In many cases these models are not accompanied by any explanation as to the meaning of those symbols, nor even definitions of the concepts themselves.

A frequently used model is the functional decomposition model. This usually begins with a single function which is decomposed into more elemental functions. The iterative decomposition is complete when the functions have been decomposed to the point where processes have been identified. These processes are in turn decomposed to the point where activities or tasks have been identified.

The models look impressive, and yet they are extremely imprecise. To begin with, rarely is the term or concept of a function defined, much less the individual functions themselves. If decomposition is the process of separating into component parts, then a given function must be described in such a manner that we know what the component parts are. How else can we decompose a function into subfunctions? In addition a function must have identifiable components that are in fact separable.

A picture is worth a thousand words. Pictures and models clarify words by providing an alternative means of expression. The use of both words and pictures or diagrams in documentation is for precisely that reason. They provide the reader, in our case the user, with alternative ways of looking at a problem, or a solution. In some cases however it is difficult to communicate an idea with words alone, and the pictures or diagrams take the place of, or augment, the words.

Words and Data

Much has been written about data dictionaries and their capacity to store definitions about all the components and elements of a data processing system. Dictionary entries are described by a combination of fixed items (size, format, program use, file name, value ranges, etc.) and narrative definitions. These entries are intended to serve two purposes. First, they provide the developer, the programmer, with the specifications of the data. These specifications describe what the data must look like, and how it must be described to the computer programs which must operate on it. Second, they provide a definition for the users of that data which explains what that particular element or component means or what it represents, how it was derived, how it is to be used, and why it is important. The definition may provide other information but these are the most critical to the user.

But it must be remembered that we are not describing the content of data items but the container of that data.

Data is nothing more than words and numbers to which we have attributed meaning. Data derives its meaning not from what it is but from how it is used. Data is one or more words or numbers, that have a label (data items always has a name) and a meaning assigned to it. Without a label an element of data cannot be referenced, and without a definition or meaning assigned to it, we do not know what it represents. Some data has meaning which appears obvious. A person's last name is more or less obvious. However, that word which represents the last name can be a person's last name, the name of a store, the name of a street, the name of a city or town, or anything. For instance the word

"Pontiac" is the name of a make of automobile and an Indian chief, it is also the name of towns in both the state of Michigan and the state of Illinois. What the word means at any given time is obviously dependent on context and usage.

With numbers, the assignment of meaning is even more critical. A given number can represent just about anything. The number 98.6 could be the normal temperature of the human body, the frequency of my favorite radio station, part of a set of map coordinates (latitude or longitude), or the call number for a book in my library. Without meaning it could be anything.

Symbols and the Real World

All around us are myriads of things. We use our senses to perceive them. If we want to recall what we saw at a later date we can use pictures (photographs). We can also describe what we see using words. These pictures and words are symbols for the real things. They are not the things themselves. We choose what goes into the picture and we choose the words we use to describe the things. The pictures and words are never a substitute for the real thing. We have translated our perception into symbols. Data elements are symbols which we use to describe reality on forms, machine readable or otherwise. We describe those data elements to machines, not so that the machines may also perceive them, but to instruct the machines how to store those elements. We document those descriptions so that we may store the data consistently.

In the course of analyzing and designing business systems many different models will be developed and many narratives will be written. In the beginning the models are general and vague. They begin in most cases (those that employ a top-down approach) with concepts. These concepts are incorporated into models which attempt to concentrate a view of reality into charts and graphs so that the participants in the design team—users and developers—can describe, discuss, and agree to a common vision of reality. These charts and graphs, these models, depict all the components of reality as the modelers understand it.

The descriptions of reality are usually as vague and general as the models. Successive iterations of the design process refine the models and provide more detail. They add more and more components, but in many cases the original definitions remain as vague as when they began.

The building of various kinds of models is a foundation for identifying the firm's requirements for data. The models themselves however do not describe the data. They describe the things the firm must collect data about, and they describe how the data elements must be grouped for processing and storage. In most cases they do not describe why that data must be collected, how it must be collected, nor even provide justification for collecting it at all.

The data analysis must describe all these things if the requirements statements are to be complete. They must also describe how the business requirements are translated into data and data storage rules.

All these descriptions are narrative. Narratives use words and words have meanings. Narratives explain the meaning behind the data model symbols and the meaning behind the data elements chosen to describe the objects of interest to the firm.

The data analysis process is iterative. It begins with the identification of the people, places, and things of interest to the firm. It also identifies the concepts of interest. It must develop a clear understanding of those things before it can continue. Once those things, those entities, are clearly identified, from all relevant perspectives, their relationships must be examined, identified, and documented. The firm must determine why it is interested in those entities and what information it must maintain about them.

The process of building models and developing narratives is one of translation. We translate our perception of reality into symbols. Each model uses different symbols, from boxes and lines on diagrams, through data element lists. Each time we build a different type of model we translate from one set of symbols to another. In order for those translations to be successful we must ensure that the meaning of each symbol is clear and that we understand and are clear as to what we are trying to depict. Entities are not reality. They are symbols however for real things. For the entities to have meaning the real things must be understood. We assign attributes to entities in an attempt to describe them. We assign data elements to attributes to describe the attributes. We assign properties to data elements in order to describe them. Each time we create a different model, using different symbols, and we translate the contents of one model into another. In effect, we move from translation to translation. Each time we use a different set of symbols and try to describe the real things differently. The symbols however cannot adequately describe the things or even the symbols from the preceding model if we do not ensure that adequate meaning is associated with each symbol.

The Meaning of Models

Each model is developed to describe something or some aspect of the environment. The model is not just a collection of symbols, but is rather a story told without words. Models should be "read" and "readable" in a manner similar to narratives. The model should make sense and should be consistent. The models should tell the reader what the modeler intended to say. In other words, models are a form of communication. The development of models is a method of communication between developer and user. If both do not understand the meaning of the model, than the model has failed in its role. Models are not developed for the sake of drawing pictures. We build models because they should be able to express our ideas in a clearer and more meaningful manner than words.

In some cases we build models because the things we are trying to depict have no reality that can be perceived. We cannot adequately depict a company, nor a student, nor a customer, nor even a vendor. At least we cannot when we are trying to describe the concept of a vendor. To be sure we can describe one student, but are we describing "studentness" or are we describing the person that is the student. We must be clear in what we are describing for it is easy to confuse the thing with the role it plays. It is also easy to associate attributes with things which are mere concepts, such as a company. In some cases we may confuse the thing with its actions, or its representation, or even with the records we keep of it. Is the customer a person or is the customer a set of order records? Is the contractor a person or is it a document describing an agreement between two parties?

We shall see that in most cases we are modeling concepts—companies, customers, contractors, vendors, etc. We shall also see that concepts are not easily modeled, nor even easy to describe. We use concepts and words in many cases without really thinking about what they really mean. The process of data analysis is in part the process of clarifying these concepts to a point that we can accurately and precisely determine what data we need to describe them.

Semantics and Classification

Understanding the meaning of the concepts we are trying to model is critical to the success of the effort. Using terminology with precise meaning to discuss the model components and the model constructs is equally critical. Several concepts must be presented before we can begin to discuss the development of the various kinds of data models.

Categorizing or classifying things is a fundamental process of human existence. The world we live in, business or personal, real or conceptual, is composed of myriads of things. Some of these things have very real differences between them, others are somewhat similar, and still others are highly similar to each other. The differences and/or similarities between many of these things are sometimes more artificial than real. Distinctions are made between groups of things because it is clearer to do so than it is to refer to nongrouped things. One reason for making distinctions between things is to put them into groups which are easily manageable or understandable.

We can see from the above discussion that classification is used for two purposes: to group like things and to separate unlike things.

Definition. To *classify* is to organize, arrange, or group things according to family, class, or category.

The terms *family, class,* etc., are biological terms and refer to various levels of specificity or generality when discussing sets, groups, or collections containing members having some characteristics in common. These terms are used in taxonomic charts for biology (where modern classification began) when categorizing flora and fauna and are used in a general to specific sequence. That is, the most general term covers the broadest group of things and the most specific term covers the most specific group of things. The level of specificity of the group is determined by the number of characteristics the members of the group have in common.

Since the term entity must always be qualified by some adjective or noun, and since the data model must distinguish between groups of entities in the same general to specific manner, and since we must distinguish between a whole group and a portion of that group, we will use the term *entity family* to refer to the largest, most general group, the term *entity group* to refer to a subdivision of the entity family, and the term *entity occurrence* to refer to a single entity.

The terms class, type, subtype, etc., are frequently, and interchangeably, used to the point where people talk about types, subtypes, subsubtypes, etc. Although the taxonomic terms of class, order, etc., could have been borrowed as well, they all refer to groups, general groups, specific groups, large groups, small groups, groups within groups, but groups nonetheless. As we shall see later, data classification is not just a general to specific decomposition, and thus it would have been misleading to use terms which implied that it was. Since these terms also refer to level of specificity and commonality of characteristic, and have specific meanings when used in relation to each other, they were discarded in favor of the simple term entity group.

The term family, although below class in the taxonomy charts, has no current usage within data modeling and was chosen primarily for that reason. Thus we now have a set of terms which allow us to identify the whole group, one member of the group, and that which is in-between.

The use of the terms family, group, and occurrence (Figure 11.1), as we shall illustrate later, is more significant since the terms class, type, and subtype, etc., imply a hierarchic decomposition of an entity in much the same context as the hierarchic decomposition of function and process. In reality although the data model concentrates on the identification of groups within groups (decomposition) it must also account for

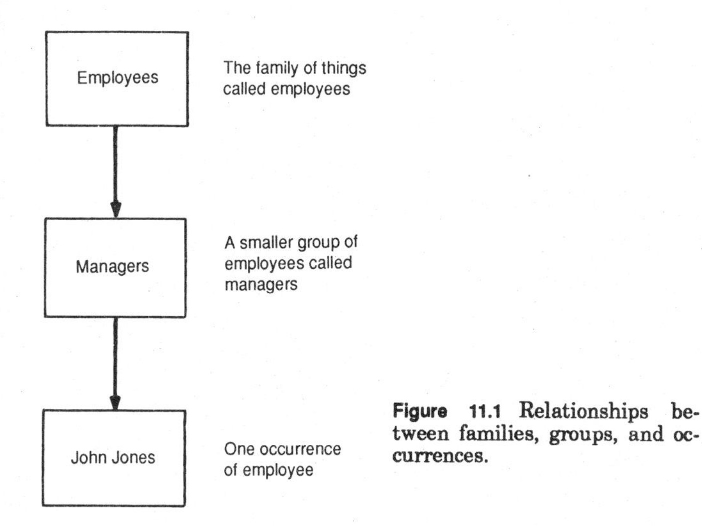

Figure 11.1 Relationships between families, groups, and occurrences.

overlapping groups and multiple groups decomposed from the same population but using differing characteristics.

Entity Families versus Entity Groups

An entity family is that group of entities with the fewest characteristics in common. The fewer the characteristics that the members of a group have in common, the more members the group can potentially have. Thus an entity family is that group of entities with the largest possible membership since it uses the fewest characteristics as criteria for membership. Entity families are identified in the first phase (usually called the enterprise or conceptual phase) of data model construction and form the components of the conceptual or highest-level data model.

In the vast majority of cases the entity families in the data models become the subjects of subject area data bases (or entity data bases, files, or just data bases). That is, the data about these subject entities are found in the data base which corresponds to that subject entity. In this case, where there is a one-to-one correspondence between entity family and subject area data base, the term subject entity is another name for an entity family.

These entity families are general groups of things which are in many cases only loosely related. Because the business processes of the firm usually only deal with selected (or specific) entity groups and need both general (familywide) data and (group) specific data, the identification of both family and group and the relationship between the two is critical to the effectiveness of the data model.

A data entity family represents a collection of highly interrelated data common to all the members of the family. For each distinct entity group within the family, and for each business user perspective, it also includes

1. The characteristics which distinguish each entity group from each other entity group, at each level of categorization
2. The progression from general to specific of the characteristic sequence or string for each characteristic of the entity group
3. The attributes of interest of the entity group, over and above the characteristics used to form the group

Chapter

12

Entity Identification

Data modeling has two major objectives—first, to identify the data requirements of the business and second, to organize and arrange that data for efficient processing and storage. Processing in this context means collecting and preparing that data for processing, processing the data, and preparing reports from that data. The sources of business data are both internal, within the firm, and external to the firm. Internal data predominantly reflects the activities of the employees of the firm as they interact with each other to produce the products and services of the firm, or as they record the results of their actions for either management use or for future reference.

External data predominantly reflects information collected about the people, places, and things that the firm's employees interact with, events that take place, or records of business transactions which initiate internal activities of the firm.

For all firms (public and private, government and commercial), the normal course of doing business (regardless of the actual business itself) results in the generation of a vast number of forms and other business records. These records reflect the business transactions that transpired, the actions of firm personnel, and the information collected and stored for current and future reference. The collective data and information contained in these records constitute the data base of the firm.

The sheer number, complexity and interrelated nature of these business records, if not properly and consistently organized and cross referenced, could easily inundate the firm. All firms have therefore created systems for organizing, categorizing, classifying, and storing business records in a manner such that they can be retrieved for later reference and use. All systems begin with a scheme for segregating the records by major category or group. These data-organizing activities hold true for all firms regardless of whether their business records are stored manually, electronically, or some combination of both.

In most firms the majority of the systems or schemes used for organizing these business records were developed using a personal, or local, perspective, and in other areas of the firm, and in other areas a common, centralized or partially centralized perspective was used. Thus, with a firm, any given set of records may be used by a relatively small group of persons, or a relatively large group of persons. Rarely, however, can the same set of records be used by all personnel within the firm.

Firms today are attempting to reduce data and information acquisition, maintenance and storage costs, to improve productivity, and to improve information access by centralizing storage of commonly used records such as those contained in central account files and those used for central reference, etc., such that the same set of records can service the largest population of persons. This process is made more difficult by the need to accommodate the many diverse business perspectives and data retrieval needs of large populations with differing need for the same records.

Business data modeling and the models which result from that process attempt to develop a categorization, classification, and data storage scheme for the firm based upon an analysis of the firm's data, requirements, the characteristics of the firm's data, and on the integration of the various views and perspectives of the functional areas of the firm which collect, maintain, or rely on that data. This classification and categorization, however, depends upon first having developed a clear understanding of those things the firm must collect data about.

Beginning the Data Model

Data analysis and data modeling are not separate processes. Nor is one the result of the other. The data model is both the product of the data analysis effort and the primary method by which the data analysis is performed. Data analysis is a process of continuous refinement of concept, description, and definition which begins with business concepts and ends when the analysis team has determined the actual data elements needed to describe those concepts and the specific organization of those data elements for processing and storage.

The data analysis process will produce the specifications of one or more data files, each of which contains one or more records. These records contain reference material about the people, places, and things of interest to the firm, and they contain the records of actions taken by and against those people, places, and things. Whether these records are manual or automated, on a large corporate computer or a desktop personal computer, each record must be uniquely identifiable so that the data contained within it can be distinguished from all other records in that same file. The method of identification may be a single data item (such as a purchase order number) or multiple data items (such as a customer's name, address, and telephone number). This implies that each person, place, thing, or concept occurrence is identifiable and is capable of having an identifier assigned to it. This in turn implies that we are able to distinguish one occurrence from another. This ability to distinguish one occurrence from another is relatively easy when we are dealing with tangible items, and much more difficult when we are dealing with concepts. In many cases concepts exist only as a description or text and have no descriptive attributes.

Any filing system is only as good as its retrieval capability. That is, we can develop data filing systems that can store tremendous amounts of information but if we cannot retrieve specific information for a specific purpose, those systems are useless. Moreover, we should also be able to rely on the accuracy and completeness of that information and on the timeliness of the information and its consistency.

Certain rules and procedures have been established and certain methods have been developed which, if followed, will ensure that we achieve these goals. The first rule is that each file, and thus each record in each file, should reflect data about a specific subject. Conversely, all data about a specific subject should be in one and only one file. Each record within a given file should reflect information about a specific occurrence of that subject. To illustrate: All data about the firm's employees should be in a single file, and the information about a given employee should be in one and only one record. This permits us to go to one and only one place when we want information about that employee.

Thus the first task of the data analysis process is to identify the subjects of that analysis. The first step of identification is to name these subjects. Using the above illustration we have a file of information about employees and therefore our subject is employee.

The second step, that of developing a definition for each subject, usually reveals that most firms do not have a clear understanding of who and what these commonly used terms represent. It is not enough to design a file to contain information about a subject, and to design records to contain information about instances of that subject. We must have sufficient information about that subject to determine when we have identified a candidate for entry into the file. In other words, we must be able to recognize an employee, or a competitor, or a customer, or a technology when we see one, so that we can record information about it into the files. It is during the definition step that most of the problems arise, and that most of the mistakes are made. In addition, to ensure that our record-keeping system is as robust as possible, and that it is as flexible as possible, we must ensure that we have accurately identified the scope of each of the groups represented by the labels. To extend our illustration, we must determine what kinds of people (or things) our file will have to keep records about.

What Is an Entity?

Before we continue with the process of identification and definition, we must understand some of the concepts which underlie the data modeling task. Specifically we must understand the concept of an entity, and in particular how that concept is used within the data modeling framework. We have used and will continue to use the term entity when discussing the major component of our models. For this discussion it does not much matter whether we are talking about entity families, groups, or occurrences. Just what is an entity? As we have stated several times previously, the term entity literally means a fact of existence. The existence of something apart from its attributes. In other words, an entity is a term we use when we either have not yet assigned another name or when we are dealing with a group of undefined objects.

We do not model entities as such. Entities are stand-ins for other things. They are place holders. Entities are empty boxes. They are nothing in and of themselves. An entity is a void. We could have called them objects, or things, or blobs. The term entity is nothing more than a name we apply when we refer to an indeterminate and undefined concept. All that can be said of an entity is that it exists (Figure 12.1). Strictly speaking then, once we place a name in that empty box, we have ceased to model entities and we have begun to model something else. That something else is the something that is represented by the label we attached to it. Thus the entity is the starting point of our data model. However the term entity is also used as a general term when referring to these objects of business interest and is used almost synonymously with the terms object, thing, something, etc. The term entity is used as a nonspecific term when we do not wish to be more specific, or when we cannot be more specific.

The assignment of a label, or a name, to an entity, to this empty box,

- A very large group of loosely related objects
- A smaller group of more closely related objects
- A small group of very closely related objects

Figure 12.1 Entities can be . . .

- Identified
- Defined
- Described
- Placed in the appropriate business context

Figure 12.2 Entities must be . . .

is the beginning of the process of data modeling. We still have not necessarily expanded our knowledge of that something. Because data analysis is, in part, the process of file design, and more specifically record design, we can make certain assumptions. The something (we shall continue to call it an entity for convenience) represents a collection or group of instances all of which can be referred to by the same label. We have not said anything about what those somethings look like, or whether they are all the same or they are all different (Figure 12.2). We also have not said anything about how they will be described, or how they must be described.

The identification of an entity (Figure 12.3) does not make any representations as to whether the occurrences within the group are highly similar or highly dissimilar. It only means that the label we have used can be applied to each occurrence within the group equally.

We have not even made any representations as to whether the firm is interested in these somethings, or why it is interested. We have not even determined whether the firm is interested in all the occurrences or just some of the occurrences. In other words by giving a label to a group of somethings, entities, we have made no representations as to the size of the group, nor have we made any representations as to the composition of that group. We do not know what kind of things make up the population of the group, and without that knowledge, we cannot effectively make any decisions as to what we need to identify or describe the members of that group (Figure 12.4).

Without knowing the extent of the group or its composition we cannot even determine the kind of identifier which can be used to distinguish one member of the group from another, nor can we determine whether

- Recognition
- Determining level of interest
- Determining why they are of interest
- Determining the proper label (name)

Figure 12.3 Entity identification.

- We must know something more about it
- At a minimum we must have a definition
- That definition must tell us
  1. why we are interested in the entity
  2. how we can distinguish this entity from all other types of entities

Figure 12.4 Thus to understand the entity . . .

all members of the group can be identified at all. In the data modeling context however we have added to the definition of an entity several qualifiers, first that it must be of interest to the firm and second that we will be able to collect and maintain data about each instance in the group. Therefore we can make the assumption that these entities are of interest and that we can collect data about them, and thus our task is to determine why the firm is interested in the entity, what kind of data it requires about the entity, and later on we must determine how much of the data that is required can actually be collected.

In its first stages, entity analysis concentrates on the population of the overall group or entity family. The members of the entity family are the subjects of the file that ultimately must be constructed and the records of that file are records which describe and provide information on those members. Until the members of the family have been determined, no determination can be made as to what records are needed, or what those records must look like. That is, no determination can be made as to which data items they must contain.

Identifying the entity family requires that we determine and document what criteria can and must be used to determine when a member is part of the group. That is, if we have decided that one of our entities is called "employees" then we must be able to determine, without ambiguity, when a particular person is, or is not, an employee. We must be able to state with a high degree of confidence that a given person is an employee because that person meets a given set of criteria. This is a binary condition, it either meets the criteria or it does not. This binary condition holds true for all entity definitions. Without that information we would not know when to create a record about something, or whether that something belongs in our file, or which file it belongs in.

The end result of the processing of data analysis and the production of the data models is the creation of a set of files each containing a set of records on each instance, each individual, defined as a subject of each of the files. The data modeling process thus is twofold—first to determine the scope and membership of the group or population of subjects which are to be contained in the file (Figure 12.5) and second, to deter-

Figure 12.5 Entities can be completely separate.

mine the kinds of records and the content of each of the records to be developed and maintained about each of the entries in that file. It should be obvious, then, that before we can design a record about something we must first know what that something is, and we must also determine how many, and what kinds of, variations there are about those somethings (Figure 12.6).

To illustrate: Before we can begin to design the records for a file of information about employees, we must first determine what an employee is, and we must also determine how many different kinds of information we need about those employees (Figure 12.7).

In addition, the analysis team must clearly define when the record-keeping process begins for each employee and when it ends, that is, at what point does the firm begin to maintain records about an employee.

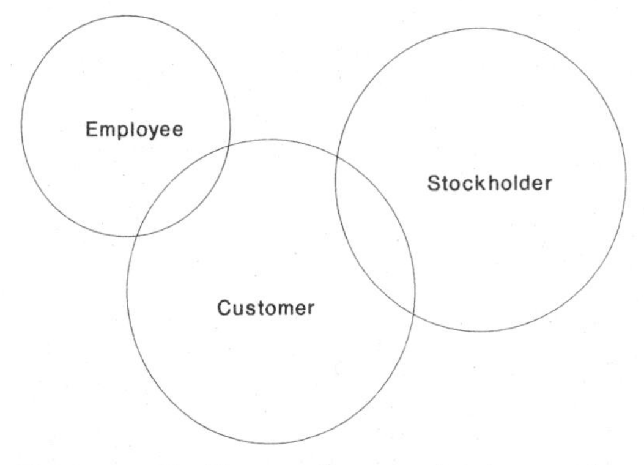

Figure 12.6 Entities can have overlapping membership.

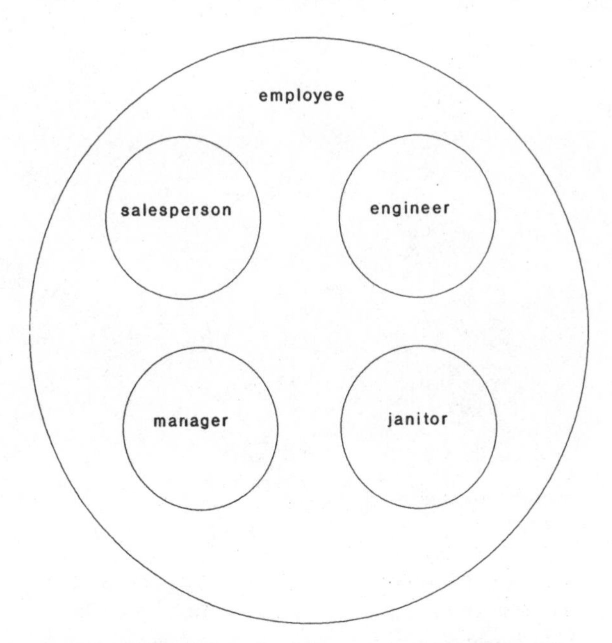

Figure 12.7 Entities can be fully contained in other entities.

That determination is governed by the rules, procedures and policies of the firm, and by the laws and regulations which govern those types of records. These rules, etc., determine how widely or how narrowly we define the subject of the file. This determination also determines how many different files we maintain and how those files must be cross referenced. Within a given file these rules also determine the kinds of records that must be maintained, and the content of those records.

The terms file and entity have been used interchangeably in the preceding discussion. Data analysis and data modeling always result in the creation of at least one file per entity. There are several exceptions to this statement, which will be discussed in more detail in later chapters but for now we will present some of the salient points.

The entities used in the data analysis and modeling process are understood to be sets or groups of people, places, or things. In the earlier phases of the analysis these groups are fairly large and not well defined. In almost all cases these large groups can be divided into smaller, more well-defined groups. This process of division and regrouping is a natural product of the analysis.

Throughout the analysis and design phases, the entities never change. The analysts may shift their focus from the family to the groups within the family, to the individual members of the family or a group, but the entity remains one or more persons, places, things, or concepts.

The records which result from the models of the final phases are not entities, rather they are descriptors of entities. They represent the attributes used to describe the entities. They are to the entity, what the employee application is to the employee—a set of records, a collection of information used to record items of interest about the entity itself.

The final product of the analysis is a set of records designed to contain the information about each member of these sets, and the records are designed such that any variations in description, or information requirement, can be accommodated.

The analysis team must always remember that regardless of the size of the group, groups are composed of individual members or instances. Although many filing systems have been devised which contain duplicate records of occurrences which can be filed in multiple files, to maintain an effective system of records, any given person, place, or thing should have a single place, or file, within which the records about it are kept. This is made more difficult in cases where someone or something plays multiple roles simultaneously, such as when a person is an employee, a customer, and a stockholder all at the same time. By recording the information only once, the firm can make a change to the information about that person once and only once. A single set of records about a given occurrence has the effect of eliminating redundancy and inconsistency of information. This maintains data integrity, but makes the design process much more difficult. These statements notwithstanding, the firm may not always know when these multiple file resident conditions exist, but they can identify the potential for their existence. The firm must decide how it wishes to handle it, and it must know the consequences of each alternative. If the choice is to duplicate information, then the firm must resolve the issues associated with maintaining synchronization between the various records, in the various files, on the same occurrence.

Single file residency allows the firm to assign a single identifier to each individual. Since each file should have a unique identifier, multiple file residence means that a given occurrence must have multiple identifiers and that those identifiers must be known in order to maintain linkage between the various sets of records.

Development of the Data Entity Time Line

Each entity of interest to the firm can be described in terms of its life line or time line. This line begins when the firm first recognizes the entity and ends when the firm ceases to be interested in the entity. Although the start of this line is usually a relatively fixed point in time, and can be identified with a specific event such as receipt of the order or the identification of an employee candidate, the end of the line is usually much less defined. In many cases the firm may not have identified a specific event where interest ceases and the file for some of the entities may continue indefinitely. Between beginning and end, start and finish, other events happen randomly.

The entities themselves are dynamic. The information about them is constantly changing. These changes occur randomly. Changes may originate within the firm as it does something to the entity or it may originate outside the firm when the entity itself or some other entity does something which changes some aspect of the entity.

The definition and understanding of the entity life line however is critical during the analysis of the entity. Most entities, most people, places and things, do not exist in a single state or single role. They pass through many states during their life. Life in the context of this use begins when the firm first recognizes the entity and ends when the firm is no longer interested in it. During its life an entity instance usually has only one role, however in some cases a given entity instance may play multiple roles at the same time. This complicates the analysis since the design must account for this multistate condition.

The life lines will also help the analysis team to understand the various aspects of each entity under study.

Entities of Interest to the Firm

We have used the phrase "entities of interest to the firm" consistently. In order to understand the time-line concept we have to further define what we mean by entities of interest to the firm. Obviously, not all entities are of interest to the firm. The firm is only interested in those entities with which it interacts, or which it uses in the course of its business transactions. Further, the firm is only interested in those instances of those entities to which it is specifically related. In other words the firm is interested in vendors but only those vendors from whom the firm buys items, would like to buy items, or has bought items in the past. In some cases the firm may also be interested in vendors from whom the firm would like to avoid ever buying items.

To continue the example, for each vendor of interest to the firm, there are many things which could be known but there is a limited subset of those things (attributes) which the firm actually wants to know. This subset of "want to know" things, may be further limited by what the firm actually needs to know. The basic design for the new system must include the "need to know" items, should include the "want to know" items, and could include as many of the "would like to know" items as resources permit.

There are many things which can happen to the vendor, which

change it, however the firm is only interested in those changes which relate to its interaction with that vendor.

In many cases, in fact most cases, the firm is interested in a specific entity instance only within a specific time window. Within that time window however the entity may not always be the same, nor act the same. For instance, a person becomes an employee of the firm on the date he or she starts work. The firm however becomes interested in that person at the moment that person is identified as a candidate for employment. From that moment on, the firm begins to collect data about that person. If that candidate is hired, then he or she becomes an employee. At what point does the firm assign an identifier to that person? (Remember that an identifier is always necessary to build an effective system of records.) If that person is not hired, does the firm still need to retain the records it began to build? When that person ceases employment, when that person separates from the firm, does the firm still retain the records?

In other words, are the candidate, the employee, and the terminated employee the same entity or are they different? The answer to that question determines how many named boxes appear on the entity model. The answer to that question also determines how many different sets of records, how many different identifiers, and how many record-keeping systems are necessary. It also raises several questions which must be answered, primary of which is how will the firm maintain the records as the person moves from role to role?

In order to determine the extensional limits of the entity, one useful technique is to construct an entity time line.

Producing a Data Entity Time Line

For each entity of interest (not entity instance) we start with a straight line to represent the entity time line. On this line we indicate each of the states or roles that the entity can play, and each of the states that the entity can exist in during its life. These states and these roles should be indicated on the time line in the sequence in which they occur. If the entity can occupy several roles simultaneously, or move in and out of a given role, the roles should be indicated as parallel time lines. The difference between states and roles is that an entity can occupy only one state at a time, whereas an entity can occupy several roles simultaneously. An entity passes through its possible states in a fixed sequence whereas it can occupy a role randomly.

If we treat the members of the data entity set generically, without regard to their individual idiosyncracies, or differences, we can expect that what can happen to one member of the set can happen to any member of the set and thus can happen to all.

However most entities in the corporate environment are not simple entities. That is, they are not homogeneous in nature, they do not all look, or act, the same, nor are they all treated the same. There are different categories of employees, customers, vendors, products, orders, etc. The people entities may interact with the firm in a series of roles. A person interacting in one role may cause things to happen, or have things happen to it, which could not happen to the same person interacting in a different role. The most common examples of these types of roles are salespersons and management personnel.

The Library Analogy

One complex example of entity identification exists within the public libraries. If we were to build a data model of the library, several entities would be relatively obvious—the library customers, the library shelves, other libraries (for interloan), the suppliers of the things which are loaned, and that which the library loans. The shelves, customers, suppliers, and other libraries are relatively easy to identify and define. That which the library loans is not as easy to identify or define. What single label can we apply to those diverse items. Libraries today loan a wide variety of items ranging from books (paperback and hardcover), records, tapes, CDs, video tapes, periodicals, and in some cases works of art. There is not a single term which applies except perhaps inventory or collection. Each of these things is part of the inventory or collection of the library, and can be defined as inventory or collection, even though the items themselves are substantially different. When we use the collection or inventory as an entity however we must always remember that we are not going to be describing the collection as a whole, but rather the individual components that make it up.

Each of these components has something in common, in that it is something that is loaned out or that can be used within the library itself (as is usually the case for reference works) but each is also different. We can group the collection in several different ways, and we can shelve the items in several different ways but (ignoring duplicates) a particular item has to have one and only one place to be shelved, even though it may belong to several different categories. The designers of library shelving systems have to allow for a patron to locate a particular item by some aspect or characteristic of its content and not just by its name, or shelf number. It is this need to locate by content, even when the identifier is not known, that makes classification and grouping of data such an important part of the data analysis and data modeling process.

The entity family called collection is not made up of a homogeneous group of items and in a sense the entity family is more of an entity cousins club than anything else. The data modeler must analyze this entity and determine how to deal with these loosely coupled groups of things which are different and yet which must be treated the same for certain business processes.

Defining the Entity

The definition of an entity should answer the following questions:

1. Is it a person, place, thing, concept, or event?
2. What distinguishes this entity from all other entities?

The definition statements should follow the form:

> A(n) (*name of entity*) is a (*person, place, thing, concept, or event*) that (*what it is, what it does, and/or how it is used*).

In the preceding form, (*name of entity*) is unique and descriptive of the distinguishing characteristics. It should be a noun or noun phrase. A noun phrase must have a noun and may include adjectives and participles. Prepositions may also be included for clarity, for example,

Paper

Acid-free paper

Recycled acid-free paper

Recycled acid-free paper for archives

The name of an entity is a label for a set of data. Entities may be grouped in families. Unique labels are applied to the family as a whole, to groups of entities within the family, or to individual members of the family. Individual family members are distinguished by separate labels because they have different relationships and/or characteristics.

> A(n) (*name of entity*) has the following distinguishing characteristics: [*characteristic (1), characteristic (2), ..., characteristic (n)*].

In the preceding form a distinguishing characteristic is a feature or property of the entity that sets it apart from its siblings. Siblings are entities that are children of the same parent.

Chapter

13

Entity Analysis

Characteristics and Attributes

Identification and definition depend upon the use of characteristics and attributes. We have used the terms characteristic and attribute without really defining them or the differences between them.

An *attribute* is some aspect or descriptor of an entity. The entity is described in terms of its attributes. An attribute may contain one or more highly interrelated data elements. Attributes have no meaning, existence, or interest to the firm except in terms of the entity they describe.

An attribute may be a very abstract or general category of information, a specific element of data, or a level of aggregation between these two extremes. Most attributes appear as clusters of highly interrelated elements of data which in combination describe some aspect of the entity. The data values of attribute data elements are not critical to the data model and in most cases they are unique to an entity occurrence. The data model must however document the valid ranges of the data, its format, etc.

A *characteristic* is a special multipurpose, single data element attribute whose *discrete values* serve to identify, describe, or otherwise distinguish or set apart one thing or group of things from another. Within the data model, all valid data values of each characteristic must be identified and documented. These values form the basis of entity classification, which controls processing, data grouping, and entity identification. Since both the characteristic name and its values are of interest, and since as we shall see later, attempting to diagram the hierarchy, or rather polyhierarchy, represented by these characteristics is difficult and misleading, characteristics are diagrammed as a "T-list."

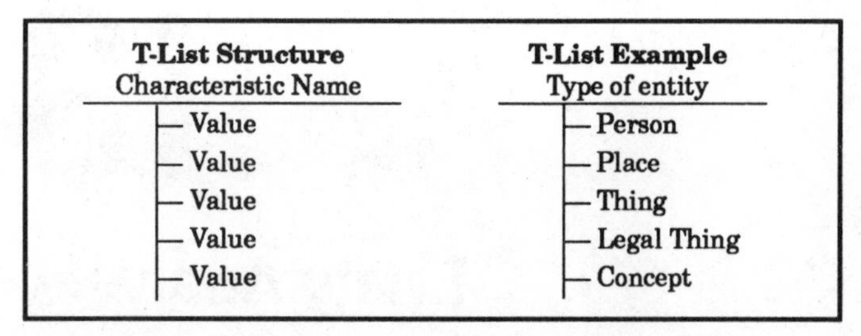

Figure 13.1 Diagramming characteristics using T-lists.

The standard form of the T-list and an example are illustrated in Figure 13.1.

The most definitive characteristic is the identifier (or key) whose values distinguish one member from another, or put another way, the unique range of values of the identifier characteristic creates the smallest most restrictive group—a group with only one member.

Both the entity family and entity group characteristic are mandatory, and each occurrence of a characteristic must have a valid value for correct identification, processing, and data grouping.

Kinds of Characteristics

Classification science uses the characteristics of things as a means for grouping them. Data modeling uses attributes for describing things and characteristics for grouping both entities and attributes.

There are two kinds of characteristics—extensional and intensional—each has its use and each has its own type of analysis. *Extensional* characteristics are developed from corporate policy, corporate business rules, and the corporate perception of the entities it deals with. Extensional characteristics are largely fixed by policy and are subjective in that they are what the firm says they are. Extensional characteristics determine the criteria for entity family creation and entity family membership. In other words, corporate policy determines what groups of entities are treated as if they are the same and how to identify what those groups of entities are.

Extensional characteristics must be single-value characteristics. All members of a given entity family will have the same extensional characteristics since possession of those characteristics is the criteria for family membership.

Extensional characteristics are used to determine how large the group will be. They are used to complete the statement—an employee is someone (or something) that. . . .

Intensional characteristics are used to determine the differences between members of a family, how they are to be grouped, for purposes of processing. All members of a given group within an entity family will have the same intensional characteristics. Intensional characteristics determine the various kinds of members, their identifiers, and their relationship to each other. Intensional characteristics form the bulk of the characteristics of interest to the firm. It is the intensional characteristics which are used to construct the entity family model. Unless otherwise noted all characteristics discussed in the remainder of this book are intensional. Intensional characteristics are used to describe and categorize the different kinds of entities within a family (Figure 13.2).

Dependent and Independent Characteristics

Intensional characteristics may in turn be either dependent or independent. *Independent* characteristics are independent of each other. All characteristics between chains, and at the first level (below the family) within a chain, must be independent of each other. Examples of characteristics that are *independent* are

Contract price terms (fixed price, variable price)

Contract payment type (lump sum, installment)

Note the form of the above statement. The characteristic named "contract price terms" was immediately followed by the exhaustive list of legal values. We will attempt to follow this form whenever we are discussing specific characteristics.

Dependent characteristics are those whose values further qualify the values of another characteristic. In other words, a dependent characteristic is value dependent upon another characteristic for its definition and use. At a given level dependent characteristics must be independent of each other. An example of a characteristic that is *dependent* is

> Type of price variability (incentive, discount, indexed, etc.) which is dependent upon the value *variable price* of the characteristic contract price terms.

A characteristic *chain* is similar to but not identical to a leg of a hierarchy. A chain is a sequence of values, not of data fields. More specifically, a chain is a sequence of characteristic values, each headed by a value of an independent characteristic and followed by one value each from each of its dependent characteristics. It is important to note that the extensional characteristics which identify the family and distinguish its members from other members of other families are also intrinsic or intensional characteristics to the entity. When extensional characteristics are used as intensional characteristics all applications and uses of intensional characteristics apply, including chain heading. Figure 13.3 illustrates the classification of the contract entity by the characteristic price terms, the further classification of price terms by type of price variability, and one of the characteristic chains resulting from that classification.

For purposes of grammatical correctness, chains are read upward rather than downward. For example, the following chains are formed from the illustration

Contracts
  Fixed-price contracts
  Variable-price contracts
    Incentive variable-price contracts
    Discount variable-price contracts
    Indexed variable-price contracts

Each of the above chains is formed by the use of one or more characteristics, and each indentation level of each chain names a group of contracts or kinds of contracts. Each level of indentation indicates a set of more restrictive groups formed from the group at the preceding level of indentation.

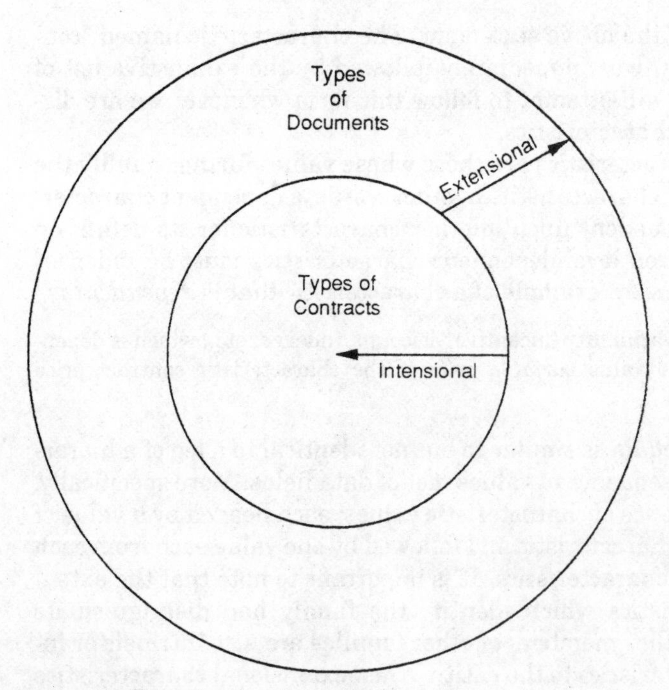

Figure 13.2 Extensional vs. intensional.

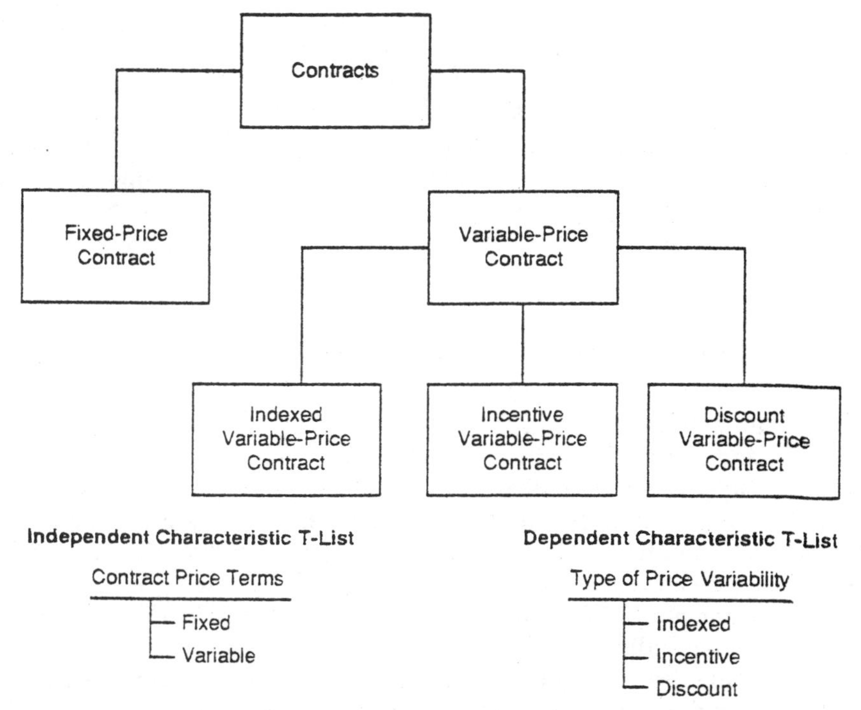

Figure 13.3 Dependent vs. independent characteristics.

A characteristic can have multiple dependent characteristics each of which is independent of each other, however these are still dependent characteristics. Each chain of characteristics from the base begins with an independent characteristic followed by one or more dependent characteristics.

Characteristic Levels

We have and will continue to refer to characteristics by level. A first-level characteristic must be capable of grouping all members of the entity family population independently of any other grouping of the same population. Second- and succeeding-level characteristics are dependent in that they can only group within a first-level characteristic. It is this representation of qualification levels (length of qualifier chain) and the entity groups which are determined by those qualification levels that gives rise to the notion of entity decomposition or the notion that entities can somehow be decomposed in the same manner that the activities of a functional area can be decomposed.

To continue our employee example, both *employee type* (full-time, part-time) and *pay status* (nonexempt, exempt) are independent first-level characteristics, since all employees will be either full-time or part-time and will be either exempt or nonexempt.

If, for the sake of illustration, all part-time employees were paid weekly, but full-time employees had a choice of pay cycle, then *pay cycle* (weekly, biweekly, semimonthly, or monthly) would be dependent only on the value full-time. Figure 13.4 illustrates the concurrent classification of the employee entity by both employee type and pay status.

Rules Governing Characteristics

The values of a characteristic must be *exhaustive* and *mutually exclusive.* That is, the values of a characteristic must cover all possible conditions, and two values of the same characteristic can not apply to the same entity. Each entity occurrence of an entity group must have one and only one value from the list of values, each entity must have a value, and no entity within the group may be missing a valid value. For instance, the characteristic *sex of employee* (male, female) is both mutually exclusive and exhaustive. The values *both, other, all others,* or *unknown* are not valid values for a characteristic. An individual characteristic value cannot include the connectors *and* or *or.* Characteristic values should wherever possible be a single word, or at worst a two-word phrase.

The list of characteristic values may not have an explicit or implicit *and* between individual terms. On the other hand the list of characteristic values must always have an implicit *or* in its list of terms.

Each intensional characteristic at the first level must completely divide up the entire population of the family. Each value of each intensional characteristic forms the name of one of the divisional groups and heads its own independent chain. The use of additional dependent intensional characteristics further group the members of the value-dependent entity group represented by each chain.

The concept of mutual exclusivity can be illustrated as follows:

> *French language proficiency* (read, write, speak) is exhaustive, but not mutually exclusive, since a person can have proficiency in reading, writing, *and* speaking.

Uses of Characteristics

Characteristics serve a number of distinct purposes. First, their values can be tested to distinguish one entity family from another (using extensional characteristics), and within an entity family, one entity group

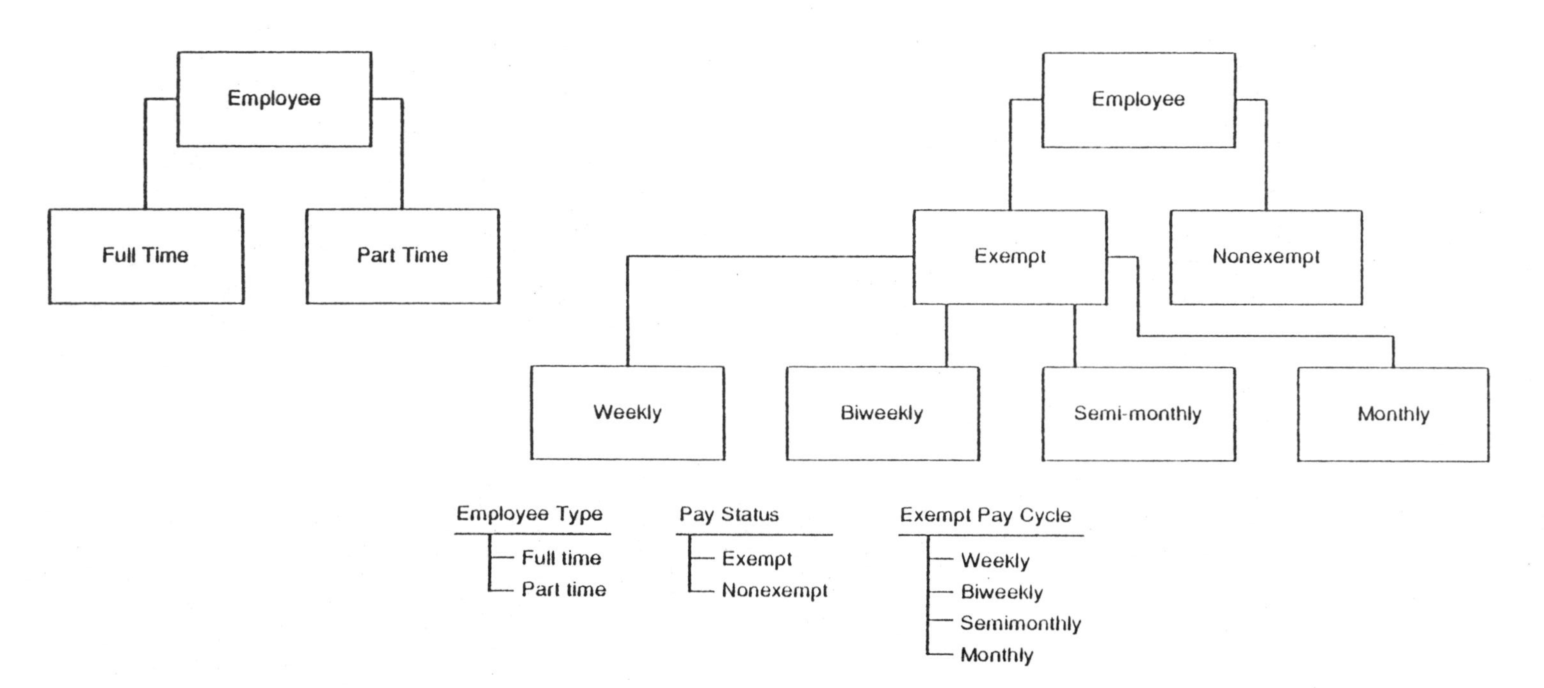

Figure 13.4 Concurrent classification of employee.

from another (using intensional characteristics). We group entities for the following reasons:

1. When each individual value represents a different kind of processing. Whenever conditional processing takes place on some occurrences and not others a characteristic is being tested to determine which occurrence gets processed in what way. For instance, the characteristic *pay status* has two values—exempt and nonexempt. Every employee must be one or the other. Those employees who are coded exempt do not get paid for overtime, those coded nonexempt will get paid for overtime.
2. The entire family or a group within the family must be sequenced for reporting purposes based upon the values of one or more characteristics.

Second, although characteristics are usually coded attributes, these codes are surrogates for a condition, state, or test result that has an English language word or phrase associated with it. The English word or phrase associated with each value of a characteristic (alone or in combination with the name of the value of one or more other characteristics) gives us the name of the entity group containing the members who have that value (or those values) of that particular characteristic. In the above example we have two named groups—exempt employees and nonexempt employees.

Third, characteristics stand as surrogates for and are usually keys or identifiers of larger groups of data which depend entirely for their existence (existence dependent) on the presence of that characteristic. In many cases, each specific characteristic value implies the need for a specific (unique to it) set of attributes or group of data elements, one specific group of data per characteristic value. These groups of data are called data groups, records, or in the relational context they are called functional dependency groups.

In the example above (and as illustrated in Figure 13.5), the business data about nonexempt employees must include a data group which is used to determine how overtime is to be compensated (agreed-upon work week, agreed-upon work hours per day, agreed-upon work start and end times, rates/overtime hours, rates/shift, etc.). These data groups are based on the value of the characteristic itself, or on a unique sequence of characteristic values, and are in third normal form.

In those cases where these data groups are existence dependent on a specific value of the characteristic, these single-value dependent data groups are in fourth or fifth normal form.

This will be elaborated on later when we address the topic of classification and normalization.

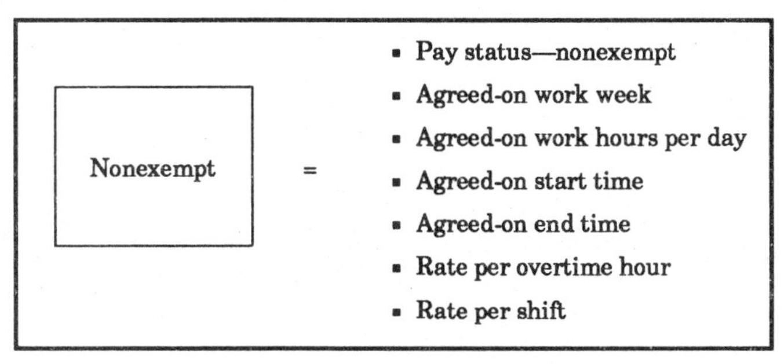

Figure 13.5 Characteristic value used to identify additional data.

Defining Characteristics

The data model uses characteristics to group entities into families and groups within families. Each entity must have some distinguishing characteristic which determines its family and group membership. These characteristics could be used to form a data equation of the form:

$$\text{Entity} = f(\text{characteristic } (1), \text{characteristic } (2), \ldots, \text{characteristic } (n))$$

The definition of each characteristic must describe its function or role in identifying family or group membership, and what particular aspect of the entity it relates to. The definition must also describe why that particular characteristic is used and where its values originate.

The definition of a characteristic should indicate why it is used. A suggested form for the definition of a characteristic is as follows:

> The values of the characteristic (name of characteristic) delineate the (what is being delineated) aspect of the entity (name of entity). The list of values of the characteristic (name of characteristic) are
>
> (1) Code value—English equivalent
> (2) Code value—English equivalent
> (3) Code value—English equivalent
> (4) Code value—English equivalent
> .
> .
> .
> (n). Code value—English equivalent

The following statement should be added when the characteristic is dependent to another characteristic:

> The characteristic (name of characteristic) further qualifies the characteristic (name of characteristic).

where

(*Name of the characteristic*) is the English name of the list of values.

(*What is being delineated*) states what aspect of the entity is being described.

(*Name of entity*) is the name of the entity family.

For example, the values of the characteristic "pay cycle" delineate the frequency of the exempt employee paycheck issuance aspect of the entity employee. The list of values of the characteristic pay cycle are

1. w—weekly paycheck
2. b—biweekly paycheck
3. s—semimonthly paycheck
4. m—monthly paycheck

The characteristic pay cycle further qualifies the characteristic pay status.

The Three Goals of the Data Model

The data modeling process must accomplish several goals. The first goal is to determine the labels of the major families of entities within the firm. A family of entities—or an entity family—is that group of entities whose members share one or more meaningful (to the firm) characteristics that separate those members from all other entities.

The second goal of the data model is to determine the composition of each family and to determine the data the firm must collect about the family members.

The third and final goal of the data model is to determine how the data should be grouped for maximum efficiency and maximum utilization.

The first goal of the data model

The activities associated with the first goal distinguish one family of entities from another. That is, they define the scope and boundaries of each entity family. These activities are *extensional* (entity family outward), or interfamily analysis activities, and use extensional characteristics.

The achievement of this first goal—the identification of these entity families—is the primary product of the conceptual phase. This phase creates a definition of that entity family that describes why the group was formed and why the group is meaningful to the firm.

The model also attempts to identify those groups that are interrelated, that is, those combinations of groups which need to be cross-referenced with each other or which need to be used in combination with each other. For example, the firm must maintain records that reflect where each employee works (a cross reference between the records pertaining to the employee and the records pertaining to a location).

In order to maintain a manageable number of entities, the data model attempts to achieve a balance between entities whose definitions are so abstract that they include entity occurrences that are not of interest to the firm (i.e., all people) and entity definitions that are so discrete or narrow that they cannot be effectively managed or processed since they form a myriad of groups each of which contains a very small population of members. To achieve this balance, the documentation of the firm must be examined and the employees of the firm must be interviewed to determine the labels of the different groups of entities that are used or referred to by the members of the firm in actual practice.

To place this problem in perspective, we can look at the basic form of the entity definition:

> A (label of the entity family) is a (real or logical person, place, thing, concept, or event) that
>
> characteristic (one)
> characteristic (two)
> .
> .
> .
> Characteristic (*n*)
>
> where each characteristic is something the entity must be, or must do. A characteristic must have a range of discrete values which can be tested.

An example of such a definition might be

> A *contract* (the label of the entity family) is a legally binding written statement of agreement (the entity family is a collection of things, in this case documents) between the firm and a customer obligating the firm to provide one or more products and/or services to the customer and obligating the customer to pay for those products and/or services provided (the list of characteristics a contract must have).

The entity family is contract. This definition answers the questions: What is the label of the entity family? What category of entity is it (person, place, thing, etc.)? What are its characteristics, or, in other words, what is a contract?

The answers may be explicit or implicit in the definition. In the above case, a contract must be written (it must be a physical document as opposed to an oral agreement). It must be agreed to by both the firm and its customer, it must be legally binding, and it must have only one customer to a contract. Contracts cover both products and services. Contracts must state the price or prices (and other fees) to be paid for the products and services.

There is another whole group of documents which meet some of the above criteria. They are written, are legally binding, and are statements of agreement. They cover both products and services and state the price or prices and other fees to be paid for those products and/or services to be provided.

The difference between the two groups of documents is that the first is between the firm and its customers (a sales contract) and the second is between the firm and its suppliers (a purchase contract).

This definition allows the design team to know precisely (although many descriptive questions must still be resolved) what kind of documents qualify as a contract (sales contracts do) and what kind of documents do not qualify (purchase contracts do not). Note that both kinds of contracts *must* be documents since under either of the above definitions it must be a written agreement.

Note also that each of these characteristics as stated in the definition can be converted to a test which can be applied to a document to determine whether it is or is not a contract. Note also that a subtle change in wording in the second set of criteria or tests make it appear almost identical to the first set of criteria. The differences is that in the second, no reference is made to either customers or the firm—the parties to the contract—nor who is obligated to do what.

Had the original definition been altered in that manner, both sales and purchase contracts could have been included, since they have a highly similar set of characteristics (both *are* contracts). In that case the entity family would have truly been contract and it would have been composed of two major entity groups—sales contracts and purchase contracts. As written however, contract is limited to sales contract and purchase contract (or whatever it will be called) is segregated to an entirely different entity family. In our example above, it was corporate policy that determined that contracts and purchase contracts were to be treated differently, and it was corporate policy that determined what constituted a contract (its definition).

The definition does not provide the answers (although it could) to the questions: How many different kinds of contracts are there? Are they all treated the same way? and most important, What kind of information does the firm need to capture, maintain, and record about each contract? The answers to these questions are the second goal of the data model.

The second goal of the data model

The traditional definition of an entity includes the requirement that an entity must be something about which the firm must collect and maintain data. The second goal is to determine what data the firm must collect about each entity.

Since the term entity must always be qualified, the entities the firm collects data about are the individual members of each entity family. Since an entity family is composed of many members, and since it would be impractical to collect an individualized set of data about each member, the data model attempts to analyze the member entities to identify that data which is common to all members, and to identify that data which is common to groups of entities within the family. In doing so the process of attribution (determining what data the firm must collect about each entity) is simplified.

The activities associated with the second goal determine how, why, and when the firm must distinguish the members of a given family from each other, in other words, what the major groups are within the entity family. These activities must also determine how the members within each group are to be described. That is, what does the firm need to know about these kinds of entities, and do the differences between them also imply descriptive differences? These activities are intensional (family inward) or intrafamily analysis activities.

These activities are aimed at identifying each, and every, intensional characteristic of interest to the firm, the list of values associated with each characteristic, and the chains of dependent characteristics which would be necessary for correct and efficient processing.

The third goal of the data model

The third goal of the data model is to determine the characteristics which determine the proper grouping of the data which describe the entity family and the entity groups. These three goals are in effect the three levels of the data model—determine the families, determine entity groups within the family, and determine the data group which describe the entities within the family.

In all cases things are grouped together because they are different in some ways from other things (which are also grouped together). In the data model these differences are reflected by differences in data. That is, each characteristic represents or is a surrogate for a collection of data which exists because that characteristic exists. Each characteristic value forms a group because that characteristic also represents a different group of data, or data which must be treated differently because of the characteristic value. These data groups are needed to qualify, support, and expand on the condition or aspect denoted by the characteristic values.

Chapter

14

Relationship Identification

The second major phase of data analysis is the identification and specification of the relationships (Figure 14.1) between the entities of interest to the firm. These relationships serve several purposes. First, they place the entities in context and second, they help to delineate the business rules of the firm with respect to those entities. From the record model perspective, each relationship identifies a relationship or cross reference which must exist between the files which will ultimately be created to contain the data about those entities.

The various data models, both real world and record, are developed in leveled steps beginning first with a model of the real-world entities and concluding with a model or models of the data record entities. Each model portrays a different type of entity, and a different perspective of the entities. Entity types must not be mixed within a given model, however the analysis team must maintain continuity between the various leveled iterations of the models. That is, the team must maintain the relationship between the various components as the models progress from portraying the entity families, through the portrayal of the entity roles and groups through the translation of the real-world entities into sets of data records for final translation into a physical data model for a particular DBMS.

This task is made more difficult when either entity names are changed or when entities are split or combined during the analysis. This process however is identical to the maintenance of continuity between the functional requirements, the system design specifications, program code, and system test cases on the process side of the design. The process continuity is relatively easy since most design efforts use a straightforward decomposition method to translate from one level to another.

- A relationship is any association, linkage, or connection between the entities of interest to the corporation.
- A relationship must be:
  a. Of interest to the corporation
  b. Describable in real terms
  c. Relevant within the context of the corporation as a whole or some specific part of the corporation
- Relationships exist only between entity families, between entity groups within entity families, or between specific entity occurrences.

Figure 14.1 Definition of a relationship.

There are two different sets of data models—real world and record—and several variations of each. Different relationships are portrayed in each model and between these models. Within each model the relationships represent different things and for that reason we will discuss these relationships as they pertain to the specific models. In addition, the process of developing each set of models involves the development of several submodels, or phase models. For instance, the real-world data model begins (Figure 14.2) with the creation of an entity model (Figure 14.3), and successively develops a series of entity-relationship models, each of which in turn is used to create a corresponding entity-relationship-attribute model. Each model is successively more detailed than the previous one, each portrays entities from a slightly different perspective, and each one uses relationships in a slightly different manner. In a like manner the record data model begins with the set of real-world data models and, depending upon the DBMS or file management system chosen, will develop a set of models using as its entities the record sets to be developed to support the real-world model.

The first phase of the development of the data models concentrated on the exploration and definition of the extensional aspects of each entity family. This was accomplished by the selection of a label to be applied to each family and the development of a definition which described as precisely as possible the population of each family. The family populations were described in terms of the characteristics that each member must possess to be considered for membership. Although the term family is recommended for use when dealing with the extensional entity, the entity is more closely analogous to a cousins club where several family groups are joined together because they have in common some ancestral connection, or they are related by marriage. Many cousins clubs bear the surname of the predominant family even though individual members may have other surnames. Entity families are similar in this respect since a larger group is assembled because of

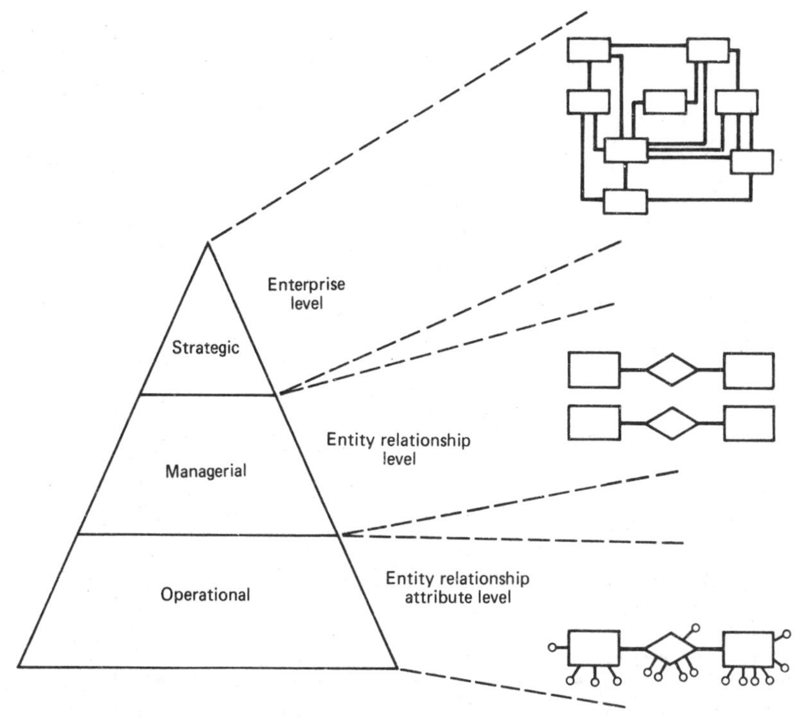

Figure 14.2 The entity-relationship approach models.

selected characteristics even though the qualifications of given individuals might not be obvious. In some cases, as with families and cousins clubs, the selection of the name determines the membership. Had a different name been selected a different membership would have been determined.

Because the membership of an entity is not homogeneous, not uniform in composition throughout, not all members behave in a similar manner. In a like manner that lack of homogeneity also dictates that not all members of the family relate to other entities in the same manner, nor are all members of a family treated by the firm in the same manner. If the members of an entity family are not uniform, are not the same, why then do we work with families? The answer is that we work with entity families to simplify the models, and because in the beginning levels of the data model, it is sufficient to work with families and not smaller groups. The smaller the entity groups that are portrayed in the model, the more groups there will be and the more complex the model will become. At the first levels we attempt to ensure that we have fixed the extensional characteristics of the model. These extensional characteristics include the fixing of the boundaries of each entity fam-

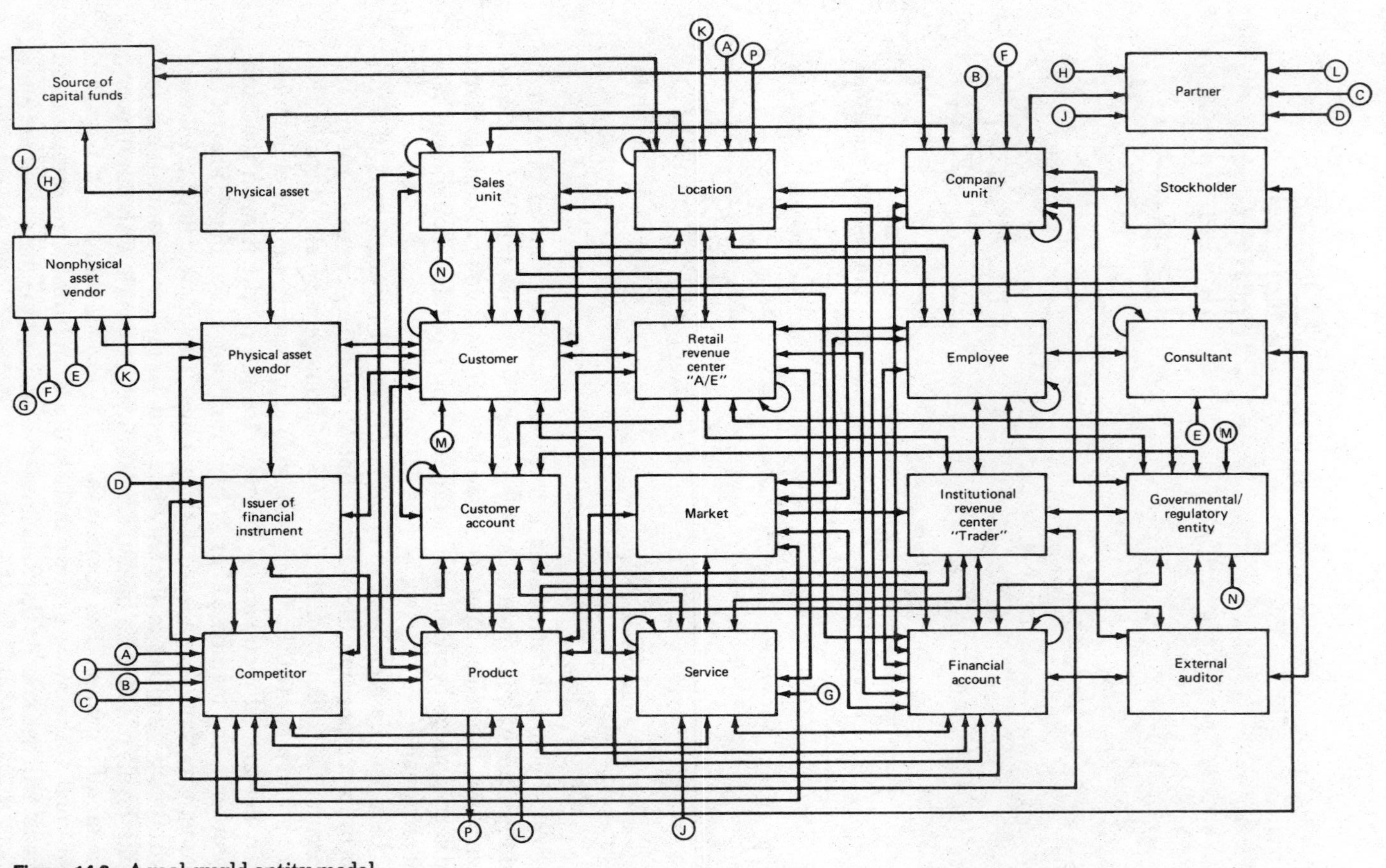

Figure 14.3 A real-world entity model.

ily, and the fixing of the families in the model. After the first level, if the entity is not in the model it is assumed not to be of interest to the firm. Conversely, if the entity is in the model it is assumed to belong to one of the identified families. These families provide the anchor points for the model, for the expansion and decomposition of the model, and for the eventual development of the files of the firm.

N-Nary Relationships

Just as the first levels of the data model define the extensional characteristics of the entity families, so too it defines the extensional relationships. An extensional relationship is a relationship (Figure 14.4) between one entity family and another family. An intensional relationship is the relationship between entities of the same family. Although relationships can have many participants, and can be expressed in many ways, it is easiest to portray them in binary form, that is, the relationship between one family and another.

In its simplest form, a relationship is expressed as a simple sentence, containing a subject (an entity), a verb (a relationship), and an object (an entity). An example of a simple binary relationship might be student (entity) attends (relationship) classes (entity). A more complex relationship can be described such as students (an entity) and faculty (another entity) buy (a relationship) books (an entity). This is an example of a tertiary, or three-way, relationship. This example can be made even more complex if we add the phrase "from the bookstore (an entity)." Obviously such complex relationships are difficult to depict in diagrammatic form, although they are relatively common, and relatively easy to state.

A relationship is defined as any association, linkage, or connection between the entities of interest to the corporation. A relationship must also be (1) of interest to the corporation, (2) capable of being described in real terms, and (3) relevant within the context of the specific environment of the firm. A relationship is any interaction between the entity occurrences of one entity family and the entity occurrences of another entity family. Neither entity families nor entity groups relate to each other. Relationships are between individual entity occurrences.

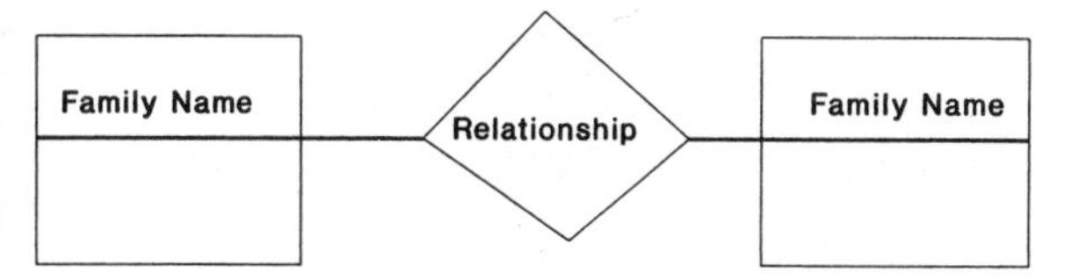

Figure 14.4 Relationships can be family to family.

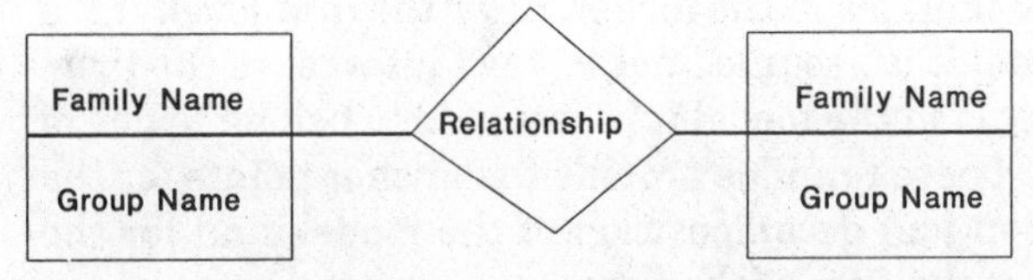

Figure 14.5 A specific group within one family related to a specific group within another.

Intensional versus Extensional Relationships

A given relationship may be either extensional or intensional, but intensional and extensional relationships should not be mixed within the same model. Extensional relationships are defined as those relationships which represent the association between one entity family and another. These relationships depict how the various entity families of interest to the firm interact with each other (Figures 14.5 and 14.6).

A relationship exists when an association is established between two entity occurrences. For example, when it is established that a product is purchased from a specific vendor, the firm has established a relationship between a vendor and a product. This association can be generalized to state that products are purchased from vendors. That is, any given product can be obtained from any given vendor. Since the firm usually has a need to know which product is purchased from which vendor, when the vendor file and the product files are created, provision is made to maintain that association. A given vendor may vend multiple products to the firm, and the firm may purchase a given product from multiple vendors. The relationship however is vendor (an entity) vends (the relationship) product (an entity), or conversely product (an entity) is purchased from (a relationship) vendor. The specific vendor-product pairings will be established when both vendors and products are added to the files, and the implementation may differ depending upon how the

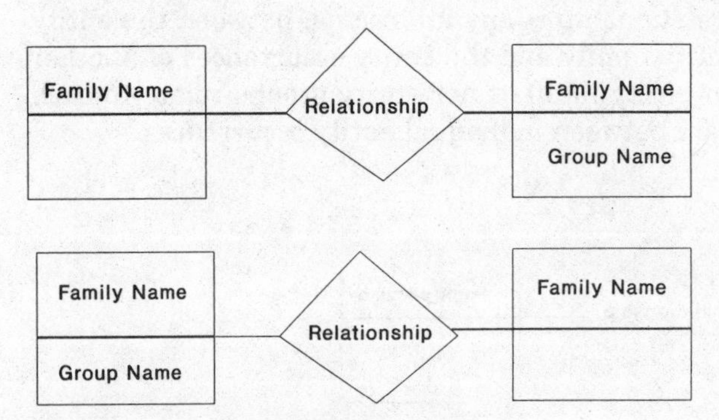

Figure 14.6 Family to group or group to family.

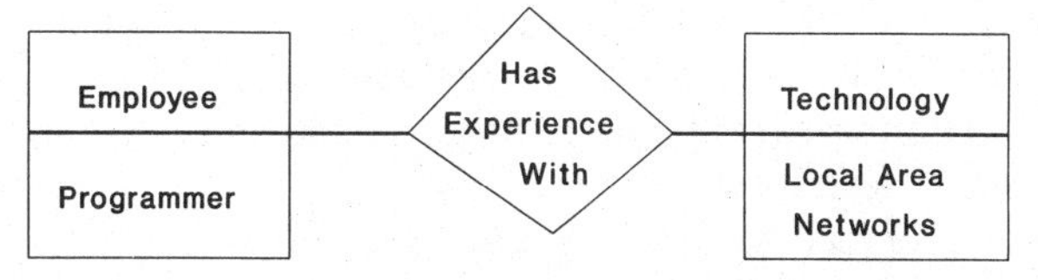

Figure 14.7 Entity group–to–entity group relationships.

files are created, but regardless of implementation, the relationship remains the same.

One of the purposes of the data model is to identify and define the parameters of each of the relationships that are known to exist, that are suspected to exist, or that the firm wishes to create. Because the network of relationships between entities can be extremely complex and because relationship identification and definition are a critical part of good file design, care must be taken to ensure that all relationships of interest to the firm are incorporated into the data model.

The modeling of relationships (Figure 14.7) is thus an integral part of the modeling of data and is built into the process. The data model is composed of a series of discrete, but related submodels, each of which models real-world entities or data records from a different perspective, and models the corresponding relationships from those perspectives as well.

The Importance of Relationship Modeling

Many data modelers pay little if any attention to the modeling of relationships. Those models that do include relationships pay more attention to the properties of the relationships than to the relationships themselves.

Relationships provide the mechanism for associating data from multiple subject files. Each relationship defines the mechanism for taking data from one file and combining it with data from another file. This ability is critical to the ability to edit and validate data in one file, using data in another. Relationships also provide the ability to provide the personnel of the firm, both operational and managerial, with reports combining data from multiple files.

The Enterprise Entity Model

The enterprise model is the first model to be developed. This model is used by the data analysts to identify the major entity families of the firm. The enterprise model is a wholly extensional model. Its purpose is to identify the major entity families and their boundaries. The boundary of an entity family defines the scope of its population. The label assigned to each family and the definition created for each family signify how its population is to be identified. They define what is and what is not within the scope of each family.

The definition of each entity family includes the characteristics which must be common to all members of the family. Since entity families do not exist in a vacuum the enterprise model must also identify the interfamily relationships. Each entity family must relate to at least one other entity family, but does not necessarily have to relate to every other entity family. The enterprise model begins the process of relationship modeling by identifying which entity family pairs are related. A relationship (Figure 14.8) is some association or connection between a member of one group and a member of another group. Relationships are established and maintained at the individual entity occurrence, or family member level. That is, specific instances in one family are related to specific instances in another family for a specific reason. At the enterprise level, because of its global, general nature it is sufficient to identify that one or more relationships exist, although the modeler must always remember that relationships are always implemented between individuals and that each specific relationship must be explicitly identified.

All members of an entity family may relate to all members of another family, or the relationship may be limited to only some members of the other family. From the enterprise perspective how many relationships exist and how those relationships are defined is not material. In fact because the membership of each family is usually so diverse and because the relationships can be so complex, to attempt to model each relationship at this level is usually futile, since many relationships are between members of specific entity groups within the families and not between the families as a whole.

When the enterprise model is drawn, it consists of symbols (usually rectangles or boxes) each of which represents a given entity family, with a line between each pair of related symbols (families). The line carries no other information other than that one or more relationships exist between these two families. Even with this limited amount of information being portrayed, enterprise models can become somewhat complex (Figure 14.4). This complexity is due to the number of families por-

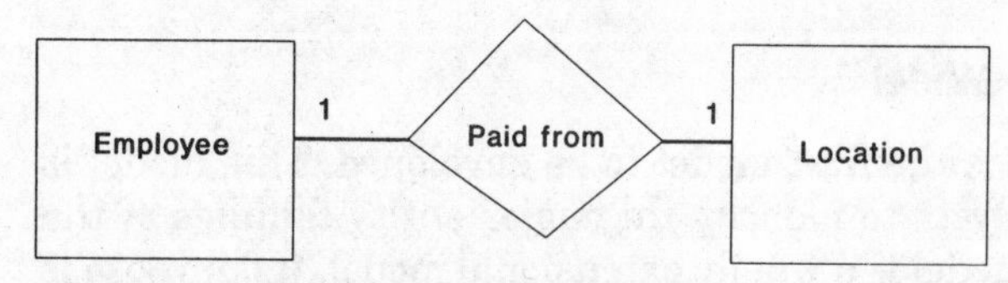

Figure 14.8 Entity-to-entity relationships.

trayed in a given model and therefore the number of families to which a given family can be related.

The entity model provides the broadest view of the data model and thus the broadest view of the data subjects (entities) of the firm. It identifies and places each of the entities about which the firm needs to capture and maintain data in context with each other. If a pair of entities are not related within the enterprise model then there is no business relationship between them that the firm is interested in. Thus in no other model will any member of either family be related, in any manner. If a pair of entities are related through the enterprise model then at least one relationship of interest to the firm exists between one or more members within each family. The model does not carry any information as to the extent or number of the relationships nor the size or complexity of each family.

In some respects the enterprise model is the easiest model to prepare in that it is simple to prepare. In other respects it is extremely difficult to prepare in that it is not complete until all entity families have been appropriately identified, labeled, and defined.

In some instances, depending upon how the family membership has been defined, members of a given family may be related to each other. This is known as a recursive relationship. Some examples of recursive relationships might be the "manages" relationship (one employee manages another employee) or the "owns" relationship (one company owns another company). Recursive relationships (Figure 14.9) are shown as a curved line both ends of which are connected to the family symbol. As with the other relationships portrayed in the enterprise model, the recursive relationship line may represent one or more relationships.

The enterprise model is the first of a series of design and analysis models which begin by describing in real-world terms what the firm requires data about. The series of models is completed when the analysis and design team produces the last record model which describes how the data required by the firm is to be stored. This is sometimes also called the implementation model.

This first model is not strictly speaking a data model, in that it does not describe data. Rather it describes the major subjects about which data will be gathered. Other models will describe the data that must be gathered and maintained about these subjects, how that data is to be

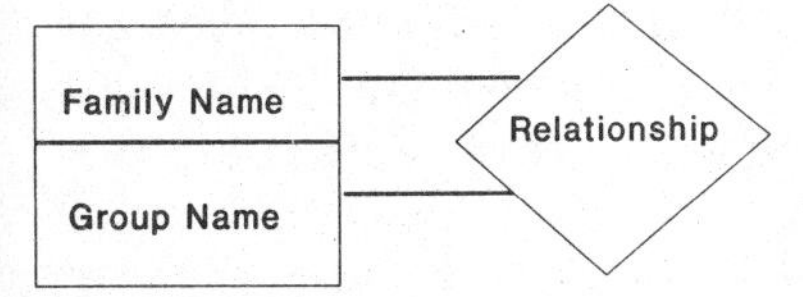

Figure 14.9 A relationship can be within a family as well.

organized into records, and how those records will be organized for storage by a particular data base management system.

Just as each model describes a different aspect of data or its organization, so too each model describes a different aspect of the relationship which must ultimately be maintained by the same DBMS which stores that data. Some of these models will describe the relationships between entity families, others the relationships between entity groups, still others the relationship between the data that describe a specific entity group or family, and still others the relationships between the records used to store that data.

In all but those models which depict how the records are organized for storage within the DBMS, a common set of rules apply. In the record storage models the rules of the particular DBMS must apply and thus a given data model may result in several different types of record storage models depending on which DBMS is used to store which data.

Because there are several different types of data storage models or record models—hierarchic, relational, network being the most common types—and because regardless of which record model is employed each vendor has of necessity implemented their version differently, there are only general rules which can be stated that cover all implementations.

The Entity-Relationship Entity Model

The entity-relationship model represents the first level of decomposition of the data model. In this model each entity family is decomposed into its major entity groups, and each relationship between the groups that is of interest to the firm is identified and defined. The model at this level defines general statements of relationship between each related major group. A general statement of relationship covers a specific relationship between members of one group and the members of another group. A general statement of relationship states that the relationship may exist or must exist, and it identifies the groups that are related but it does not identify which members of each group are related to each other.

The relationship may involve some or all members of each group (Figure 14.10). When the relationship involves all members of a group, it means that each member of the group must participate in that kind of relationship with a member of the other group.

When the relationship involves some members of a group, it means that the relationship is optional for any given member, but at least one member of each group is related in that manner. Relationships are identifiable from several sources. The major source of relationships are the business rules of the firm. These rules, defined primarily through business procedures, specify which relationships are of interest to the

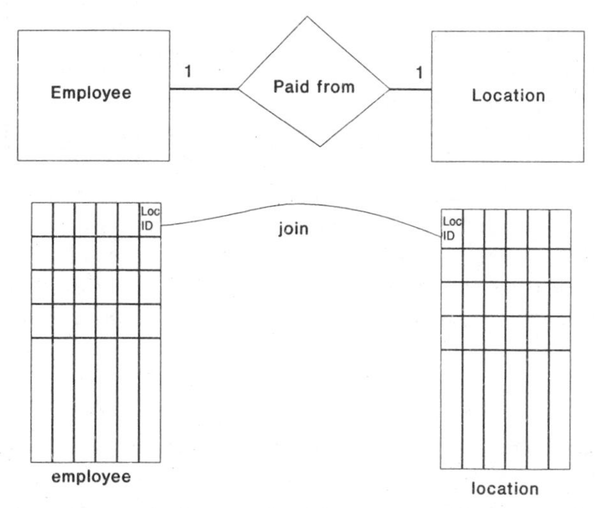

Figure 14.10 Entity-to-entity relationships (physical and logical).

firm, which members of which groups can participate in which relationships, and under what conditions those relationships must (or can) be established and maintained (Figure 14.11). For instance, the rules of the firm might state that the firm must maintain a list of three possible sources for each item it purchases. The rules almost always state that the firm must maintain records about which vendor supplied which items, and when. In most firms the rules also state that records be

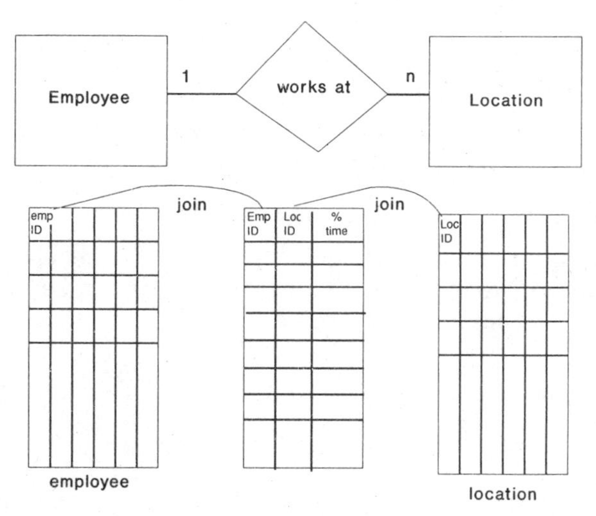

Figure 14.11 Entity-to-entity relationships with additional data.

maintained about which accounts are to be used to pay for each item. Each of these rules represents a relationship which must be captured and maintained by the records of the firm.

In other cases the business rules may state that a relationship is optional. That is, the relationship does not have to exist, but when it does the firm is interested in capturing and maintaining it. For instance, the business rules might state that if an employee is given a piece of office equipment (a personal computer) a record must be kept as to what equipment was given to that employee and when. Obviously those employees that are not given equipment do not participate in that relationship.

We have used the term statement of relationship. A statement of relationship consists of two parts. Each part describes the relationship from the perspective of one of the two groups participating in the relationship.

Although there are many variations in format, there are several general rules which should guide the analyst when drafting a statement of relationship:

First, the definition of a relationship should provide the following information:

1. The names of the two entities which participate in the relationship
2. The business rule(s) that this relationship represents

Second, the definition should be written in the following general form:

1. Each (*name of first entity*) is sometimes or always (*relationship*) (*one or many*) (*name of second entity*).
2. Each (*name of second entity*) is (*sometimes or always*) (*relationship*) (*one or many*) (*name of first entity*).

In the above sample, (*relationship*) must be a valid verb form.

Third, the statement of relationship should enumerate the business rules which are represented by this relationship. These can be included as part of the definition in list form.

1. Business rule (1)
2. Business rule (2)

.

.

.

n. Business rule (*n*)

Fourth, the statement of relationship should include any business rules which provide conditions which limit when the relationship can exist, how many entity occurrences can participate in the relationship, or under what conditions the relationship can be established.

Finally, each statement of relationship should be self-contained and not dependent upon the existence or content of any other statement of relationships or definitions other than those of the entities involved in the relationship, or existence condition statements.

For example, the following are simple statements of relationship:

Each employee is always managed by one employee.

Each manager always manages one employee. A manager sometimes manages many employees.

Each part is always supplied by one vendor. Many vendors may supply each part.

These statements reflect a one-to-one relationship, a one-to-one relationship with an optional one-to-many relationship, and a one-to-one paired with a many-to-one relationship.

Each relationship can thus be viewed, and should be viewed, from both sides of the relationship. Each relationship has two participating entity groups (*A* and *B*, left and right). In order to properly assess and define the relationship statements it must be stated from both sides. In most cases, these left-to-right or right-to-left statements will be complementary, however they should always be stated both ways for clarity.

Consider a slight modification.

Each part may be supplied by many vendors. A vendor may supply many parts. A given part occurrence is always supplied by one vendor.

In this last example, the first two statements define the group-to-group relationships. They also define the conditions under which parts are acquired and under which vendors supply parts.

The third statement delineates a specific case which covers each part, but not each vendor. The words may sometimes identify a conditional relationship, that is, there are times when it may not exist. That is to say, not every entity in each group has to participate. This can be more easily understood if one views the entity groups as separate lists of entries. A relationship statement states that an entry in one list (left hand) is paired with one (or more) entries in the second list (right hand). The relationship does not state which entry in list one is paired with which entry (or entries) in the second list. All it states is that the relationship can or must exist. It is the user procedures and the actual data which the user enters which create or implement the actual relationship pairings.

Most relationships are not complex in that they can be stated using rather simple general statements. However, what makes the relationship model difficult to develop are the following conditions:

1. Any given entity occurrence can be a member of several different entity groups.
2. Any given entity can participate in several different relationships with members of other entity groups, and many times these relationships exist simultaneously.
3. Each relationship while specified on a group-to-group basis can involve one or more entity occurrences from each group.
4. Each relationship may be mandatory or optional from each side of the relationship.
5. The conditions governing optional relationships may and usually are different for each side of the relationship.
6. Any given pair of entity occurrences can participate in several different relationships simultaneously.
7. Each relationship must be supported by a minimum set of data which must include the key of each entity occurrence which participates in the relationship. The business rules and business processing conditions govern which specific entity occurrence keys may or can be used to implement each given relationship.
8. Each relationship must be represented by a set of paired keys (left and right). Conditional relationships may also require additional data elements to define the conditions associated with each relationship (Figure 14.11).

Chapter

15

The Entity Family Model

The entity family is the most general, yet still meaningful, classification, categorization, or group possible within the context of the firm. This broad classification of entities is composed of many smaller more specific, yet similar, groups of entities. A model of an entity family would look somewhat like a hierarchy, in that it would consist of groups dependent upon groups.

An entity family model should be generated reflecting the names of the various entity groups within the family and the various, and sometimes complex, manners in which they are related to each other. That is, the model should depict the derivation of each group. In many respects this is a key-only or identifier-only model, which graphically represents the various characteristic strings which describe and identify the groups within the family (Figure 15.1), since the names of the groups are derived from the values of the characteristics in the identifier string.

The Entity Family Model as a Hierarchy

The entity family model is usually illustrated as a hierarchy showing the familial or decomposition relationship between the larger group (the family) and the smaller groups which comprise it.

This hierarchic representation of an entity family is correct in that classification represents a general-to-specific characteristic tree structure. In such a representation, the entity family hierarchy is usually created by adding one characteristic at each level such that each new characteristic forms the basis for the new groups at that level.

The sum of the characteristics of any given group at any given level must include all the characteristics used to form the more general

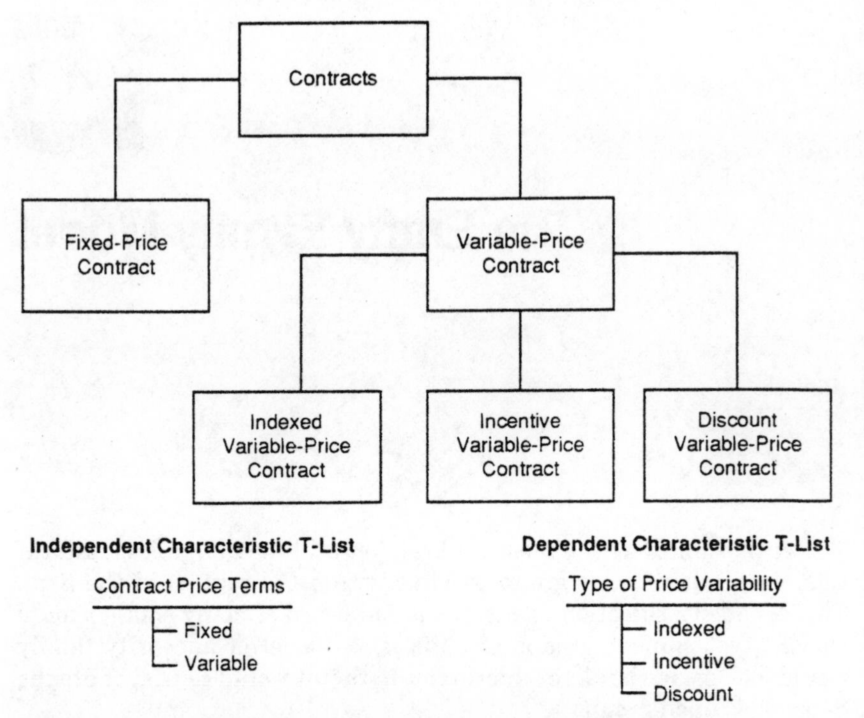

Figure 15.1 A characteristic string within the family contracts.

groups in a direct line to the family root or base. The lineage from ancestor to descendent is called the chain (of characteristics). Since each successively smaller group is formed from the members of the larger group which precedes it in the hierarchy, all members must possess the characteristic which formed the parent group as well as those additional characteristics which were used to create its group and those of its siblings. The children of the parent are said to have inherited the characteristic of the parent.

The development of the entity family models seeks to identify the relationship between the broad real-world entity groups (or families) that populate the internal and external environment of the business, and the narrower groups derived from them.

The Entity Family as a Polyhierarchy

If the members of a given family or the groups within it were each identified by a single value characteristic the family model could be represented by a simple hierarchy. In other words, each group in the hierarchy chart would be the child of a group above it (its parent), and the parent of any number of groups below it. No child would have more than one parent, and its parent would have to be within the same family branch.

The data model is much more complex than that, a complexity that is masked if the concentration is on the characteristic as a data element, rather than in the characteristic as a value list. A characteristic is a multivalue element, each value of which identifies a group. Each value-dependent group is further decomposed into smaller groups by the values of other dependent groups. For a true entity family representation each first-level characteristic should be modeled separately. Under this view the entire population of a family would be decomposed using a single characteristic. Within that model each value of that characteristic should be isolated and treated as a group and head of chain. Each qualifier (characteristic) value is modeled as a separate group derived from the main value group.

There would be as many of these charts as there were first-level characteristics. Because each chart maps the entity family population differently, and because each characteristic applies to the entire family, these models when used together depict the concurrent and overlapping nature of the entity groups within a family. Figure 15.2 illustrates a very simple polyhierarchy which is created by the employee characteristics used in our illustrations.

Much of this graphic representation would appear to be hierarchic in nature. When placed one over another, it forms a network of interlocking, overlapping groups. This complex networklike hierarchy is called a polyhierarchy and may be used to represent any type of complex family relationship pattern. Most entity family models reflect this polyhierarchic structure, as do the relationships between the families themselves.

Entity Family Model Notation

The top of each separate hierarchy is called the *base*. The label of a base entity is the label of the entity family and is the only label that can be applied to any member of the family without exception. A base entity cannot be a kind-of-another entity. There is only one base entity per family.

More specific, characteristic value-dependent groups within less specific groups (group decomposition) formed by the use of additional sets of characteristic values form a *chain* of characteristic values from the most general to the most specific (top-to-bottom). In this case each more specific group is said to represent a *kind-of* or more specifically qualified group of the less specific group from which it was formed. These groups are sometimes called entity *types* and are shown as being re-

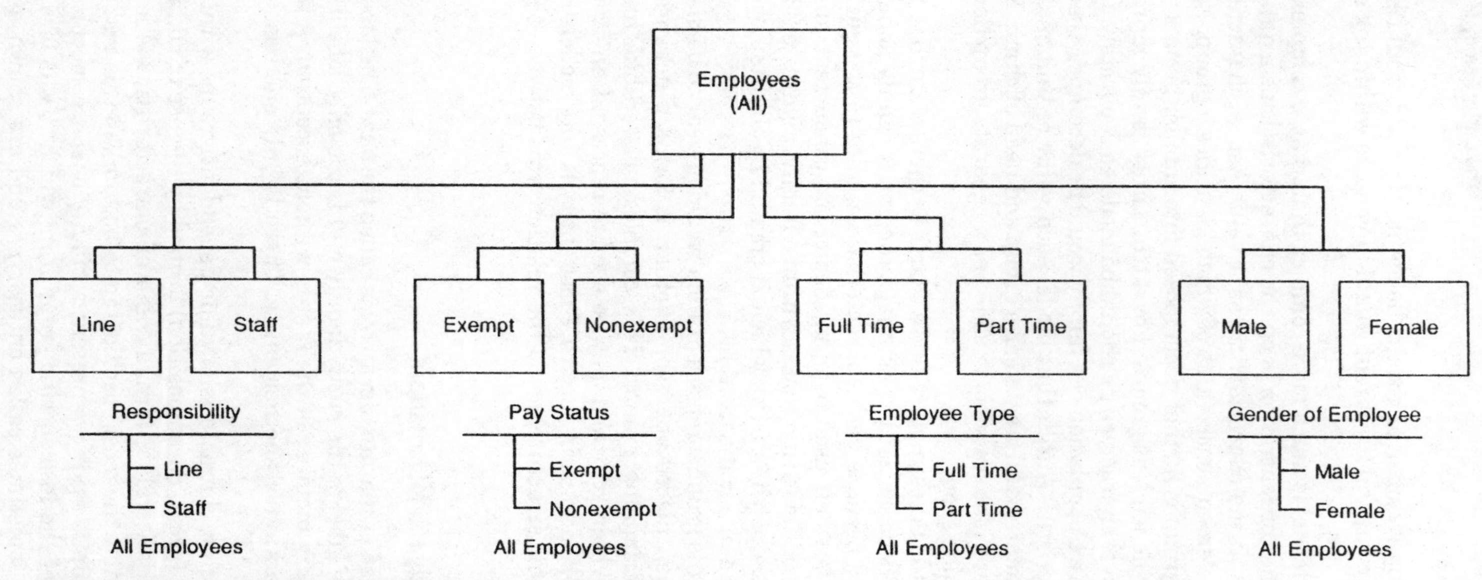

Figure 15.2 Simple polyhierarchy of the entity family employee.

lated to the base entity using a relationship named *is-a.* While this works for first-level characteristics, it becomes confusing and cumbersome when an entire chain must be represented (B is-a A, C is-a B, etc.) and becomes more so when all the values of a characteristic are shown (more so when all values from all the characteristics are shown). This method of representation cannot show the polyhierarchic nature of the entity family model.

In some cases entity groups from different chains at a given level of specificity from the base may be used to form a group at the same level of specificity. That is, some of the value-derived groups within a characteristic model may be grouped across chains for a reason. This composite group is named a *grouping.* For instance, if the characteristic is *country of origin* (United States, Canada, England, France, Spain, India, Republic of China, Egypt,...) and for some purposes we group them as *origin* (United States and foreign), or *region* (North America, Europe, Asia,...), origin and region are groupings of the value-dependent groups of the characteristic country of origin and not necessarily new characteristics.

These terms can be used to describe the various component groups of an entity family structure when documenting them in a dictionary (Figure 15.3). The specific components of an entity family model (as illustrated in Figure 15.4) are:

Base — A composite description that incorporates every characteristic and attribute of every different group and member of the entity family and every relationship enjoyed by any member of the entity family. The label of a *base* entity is the only label that can be applied to any member of the family without exception.

A *base* entity cannot be a *kind-of* another entity. There is only one *base* entity per family.

Kind-of — Is a distinct entity group within an entity family or within another entity group formed by the use of a characteristic value in addition to the values used to form the parent group. Each kind-of group in a chain is always more specific in membership than the group from which it was formed. A group can not be a kind-of group from a different value chain.

Alias — Is another label for an entity group.

Grouping — Is a label for a collection of entity groups at a given level of specificity which otherwise have no explicit common parent, but have a common (but not explicitly used) characteristic that yields the grouping name.

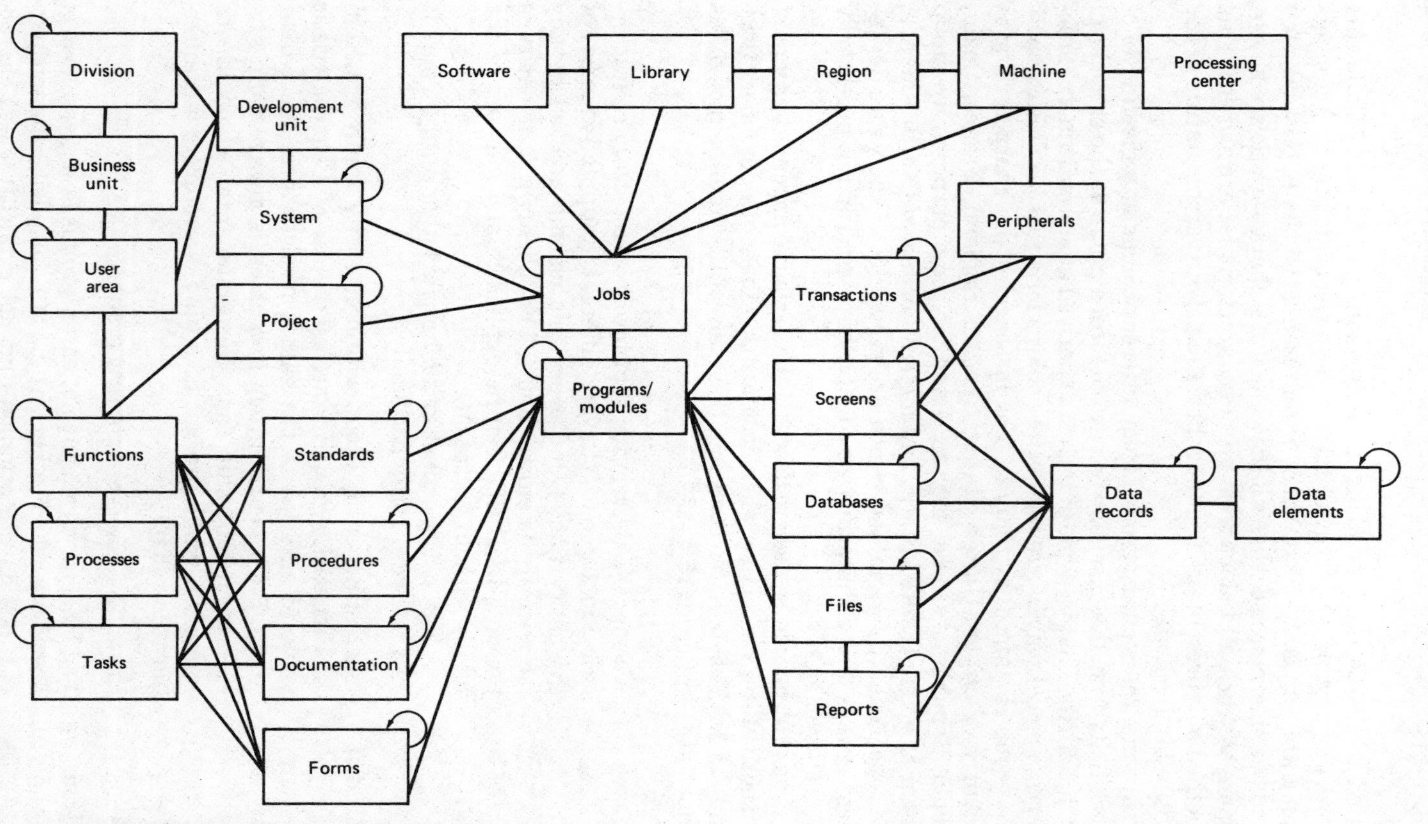

Figure 15.3 Entity families in the dictionary model.

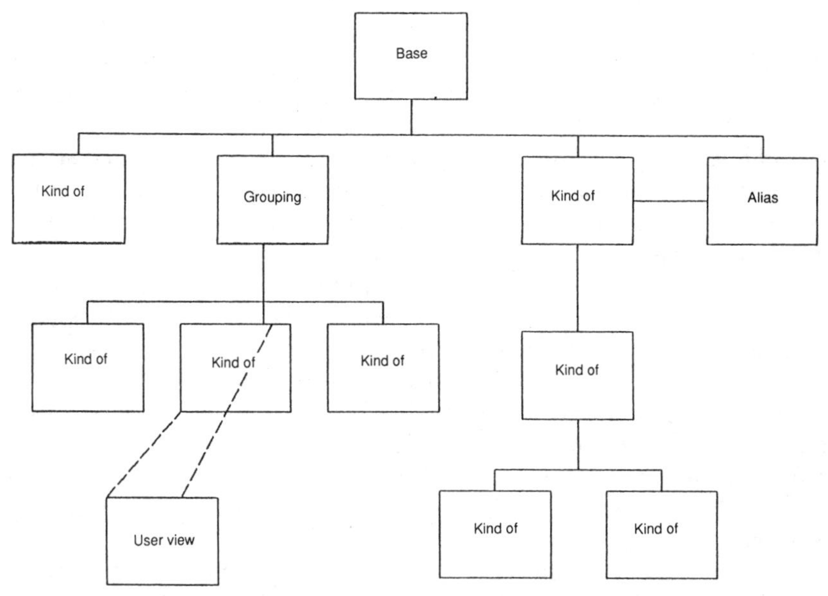

Figure 15.4 Entity family classification model within the dictionary.

Usage Is a view of one or more entity groups within the family formed through the use of a set of relationships and characteristics selected from those groups. [This is not a classification term, but it is used extensively in data modeling. This is sometimes called a *user (usage) view.*]

Entity Classification Issues

The term entity represents an unclassified fact of being or thing. Everything that exists in reality, or in the perception of reality, is an entity. This group being too large and too general to do anything meaningful with, it is usual to break that too general group (phylum in the taxonomic charts) down into four slightly less general groups (classes in the taxonomic charts). In effect we have selected a characteristic of entity—*kind of entity* (people, places, things, and concepts).

Most firms rarely deal with entities at this abstract level, rather they look at smaller more meaningful groups which are more relevant (of more interest) to the business.

The next level of grouping (orders on the taxonomic charts) then is usually based upon the business reason for the firm's interest in each group. This determination is made using the rules of the firm to determine the relevant group names.

The "business reasons for interest" usually correspond to the various roles played by or uses of the members of the groups. This reflects the characteristics which complete the sentence "the firm is interested in the entity because it. . . ." The group names correspond to the labels of those uses or the labels of those roles. However, since each group is also part of a larger group they must obviously have certain characteristics in common. The fact that the firm is not interested in, or is not using, the larger group name is no indication of the firm's interest in the characteristics (and other attributes) inherited from the larger group. In many respects, these characteristics [and other attributes (Figure 15.5)] from the larger group are a critical part of the entity description.

Dependent upon how the entities are grouped within the model and the needs of the firm for data these common characteristics and attributes may be replicated with each specific group, or the model may maintain the common characteristics in the general group, and maintain role and usage specific characteristics in the role and usage groups. The first issue then is related to classification based upon role or usage.

Entity-based data models by definition are restricted to entities that are of interest to the firm, and still further limited to those entities about whom the firm must collect data and maintain records (families on the taxonomic charts). Because no grouping above the level of family interests the firm or is necessary to the firm, most models ignore them, although data modelers must remember that they are there.

It is easier to view these smaller groups of the larger population by group name than it is by naming the individuals which comprise the group or by naming the tests which are made against the group characteristics. Group names are used because, although each member of the group is different and uniquely identifiable, the group's members are

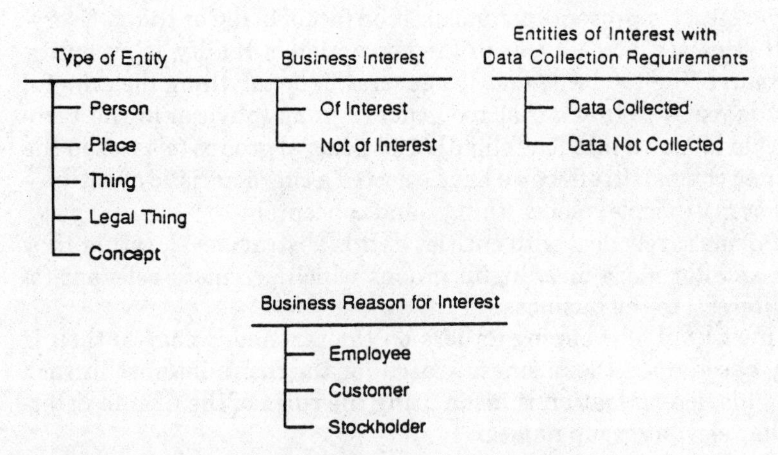

Figure 15.5 Characteristics inherent in the definition of an entity.

similarly described, act the same way, or are processed in the same manner. The group name is in almost all cases identical to the specific characteristic values used to determine the members of the group.

In the data model, as the number of characteristics in the entity family definition decreases, the number and kinds of entities which can be included under that definition increase. As the list of characteristics in the definition becomes more extensive, the number of entities which can qualify for group membership becomes less extensive. The broadest group of entities used within any entity model, regardless of level, is the entity family. However, the entity family and all similar groupings of entities are still a convenience of the data model and as such their definition and population content are highly subjective.

The entities which are collected under the umbrella of the family possess many individual characteristics. These characteristics are extensional, and while the sum of the characteristics of a family determine the family makeup, individual characteristics may be shared across families. That is, the same characteristic may be included in the definition of multiple entity families (that is, written agreement). This characteristic sharing results from the families themselves being derived from larger, more general groups, groups which were not of interest to the firm, or which the business rules or requirements of the firm dictated be separated out into smaller more specific groups. This implies that there is a polyhierarchic relationship between families as well. This separation into families by the characteristic *business reason for interest* (Figure 15.6) is dependent upon adherence to the business rules of the firm which in turn dictates

1. Entity family roles of interest within the firm
2. Entity family relationships of interest to the firm or to other families
3. Identifier differences of interest to the firm
4. Data requirements differences of interest to the firm

Because these separations and distinctions are subjective, their treatment is open to interpretation and debate. Because there are a variety of ways to depict this information within the data model additional areas of judgment and preference are introduced, along with additional areas of debate. In many cases these discussions take on the qualities of religious doctrine with participants defending their own perspective.

Entity Families Determined by Roles

Entity families are almost always developed from the role which the members of the family play in the organization. These roles reflect the

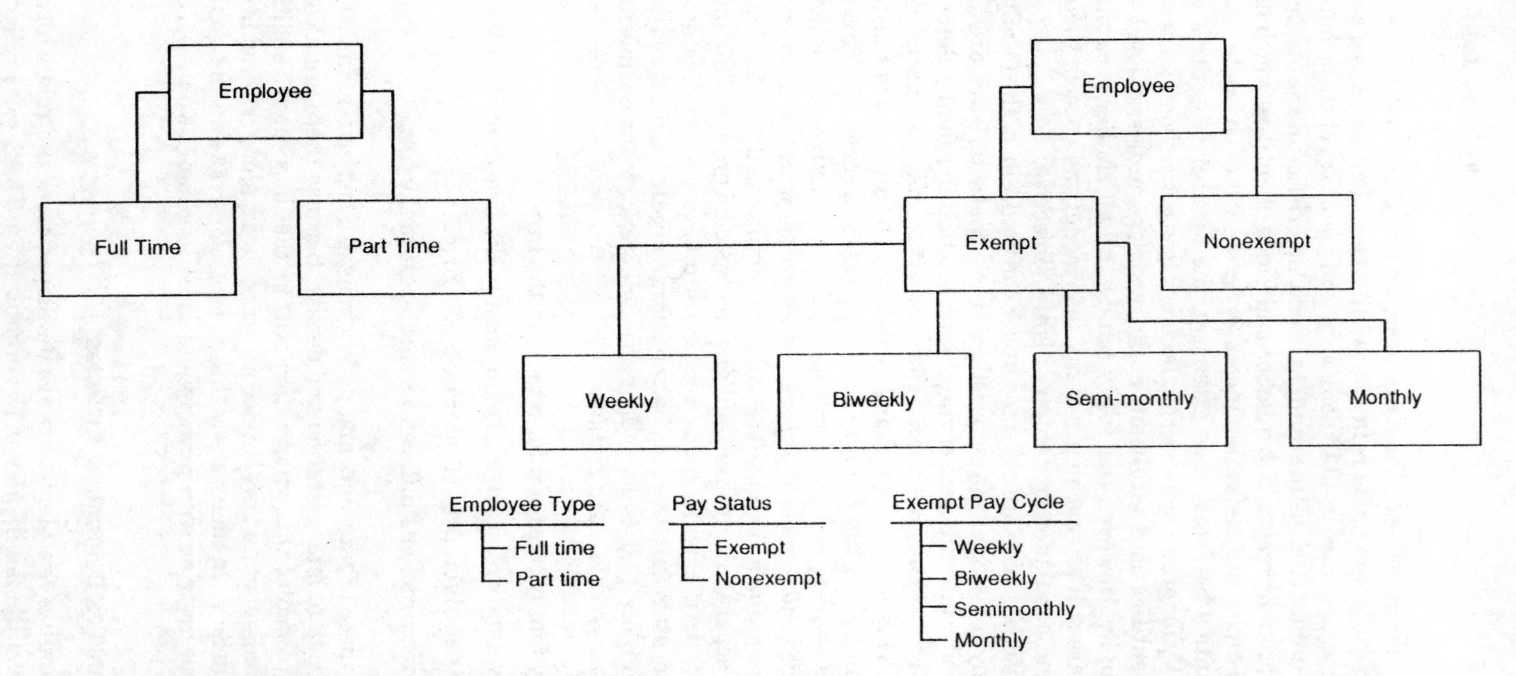

Figure 15.6 Employee family classified by two characteristics.

reason why the firm is interested in the members of that particular group. At the family level, roles are distinct, and an entity occurrence is assigned a role as it is recognized. That role is usually permanent, as are the records that are collected around the role. These records are maintained and retained until the firm is no longer interested in that entity occurrence, in that role.

To illustrate: Many firms have employee stock ownership plans, and many employees avail themselves of that benefit. Once an employee has bought a share of stock in the firm, he or she takes on the additional role of stockholder and joins the membership of the entity family called stockholder. That employee may quit, be fired or retire, but whatever the status of the individual as employee or nonemployee, the individual is still a stockholder, a role independent of employee.

An entity occurrence within the business world may have many different characteristics. One characteristic or combination of characteristics of an entity can be used to place it in a particular group, and another characteristic or combination of characteristics, however, can be used to place it in another group. A given characteristic may be used in combination with others to define many families.

Thus, dependent upon the characteristics selected, and the combinations of characteristics used, a population of entities occurrences may be concurrently grouped into multiple different families by what they do, by the purpose they serve, how they are used, sometimes by what they look like, and sometimes by what they are.

For example, "people," one of the four general kinds of entities, is a very large, unclassified, unorganized group. The firm is not usually interested in all people, but within the large group "people" it is interested in several, more specific groups of people. These groups may be determined by a variety of characteristics, some of which are common to all people and some of which are specific to only one group of people, that is, the values of specific group characteristics.

The firm's interest in different groups of people is usually determined by business reasons that dictate a need to collect specific kinds of data about a specific group based upon the role they play. This could be determined by testing the characteristic *role played* (employee, customer, stockholder). Any given person, however, can be both an employee, a customer, and a stockholder, that is, the roles overlap to the extent that employees are customers, or customers are also employees.

Role characteristics can be both extensional and intensional. That is, roles can separate entities into families or they can separate groups within a family. Roles can also be independent or dependent.

Independent roles are those where the family mutually exclusivity is dictated by business rules but family membership is not. That is, there is no requirement that an occurrence have one role in order to have any other.

To illustrate: Roles are independent when an employee may be a customer, and a customer may be an employee, but

1. There is no business rule that an individual must be both.
2. There is no business rule which states that an individual cannot be both.
3. There is a business rule that says that the records about a customer must be separated from the records about an employee.

All independent roles are extensional by definition since they segregate entity occurrences permanently and independently. Role independence does not preclude role overlap (nor by extension dual-family membership) such that an individual can play more than one role.

Dependent roles are those where an entity occurrence role assignment is dependent upon that entity occurrence already playing another role. To illustrate: An employee may have many *functional roles* (salesperson, engineer, clerk) and many *supervisory roles* (manager, supervisor, executive) but to play either role an entity occurrence must first qualify as an employee.

The role characteristics must be examined with care to ensure that they are mutually exclusive and exhaustive. If the list of roles is not exhaustive, processing conditioned upon role value may be affected, as might data group identification and data content. If the list of roles is not mutually exclusive, then role overlap can occur.

Overlapping Entity Family Membership

Entity family role characteristics are not as clearly definable as entity group characteristics, which leads to fuzzy, and sometimes overlapping entity family definitions. Since entity family roles are extensional, and since all members of the family must possess the same extensional characteristics, the list of family selection characteristics (extensional) are usually confined to the narrative definition of the entity family. Entity family extensional characteristics must always be single valued, thus *role played* (employee, customer, stockholder) would not be valid as an entity family extensional characteristic since it is multivalued.

Multivalued extensional characteristics lead to fuzzy definitions. This fuzziness, and the overlap it implies, can lead to interpretational differences when creating the data model for the family. Figure 15.7 illustrates the overlapping roles within the entity family people.

To illustrate: Let us assume that the entity family definition stated

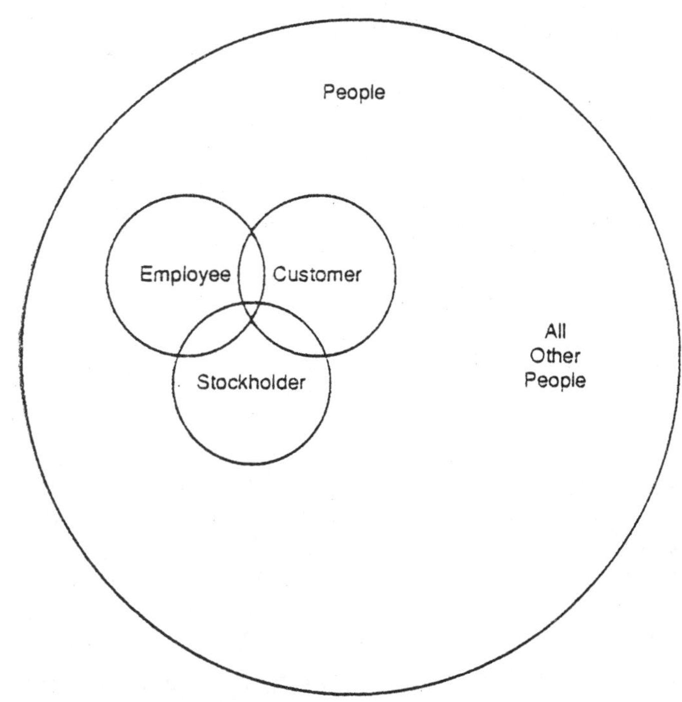

Figure 15.7 Overlapping roles within the entity family people.

that the family consisted of people who could be customers, employees, or stockholders. This would be the same as stating that the family had a characteristic called *role played* (employee, customer, stockholder).

There are at least two possible interpretations of this statement.

1. The family consisted of some number of entity occurrences from each of the three roles and any given member could be any one of the three but not more than one (following the mutually exclusive rule). This would be like saying the family consisted of three entity groups—employees, customers, stockholders. In this case an intensional characteristic has been used as an extensional characteristic.
2. The family consisted of occurrences which were employees, customers and stockholders, concurrently. In this case the implication is that there are families of employees, families of stockholders, and families of customers, and other families which embody the various combinations of the three roles.

In either case the statement is fuzzy which is to say it is ambiguous.

To illustrate further: If the business rules allow it, a person can be an employee and a customer. While these roles are distinct they are not mutually exclusive and the decision as to whether to define one family (employee/customers), two families (employee and customer), or three families (employee, customer, and employee/customers) is left to the judgment of the designers. However if the business rules do not allow it, then they become mutually exclusive and overlap is eliminated.

If the rule is followed that all extensional characteristics must be single-valued then mutual exclusivity is enforced, and overlap cannot occur. Data about each role is collected and maintained independently (but redundantly where the same entity occurrence plays more than one role).

The following summarizes the recommended method for modeling role-based entity families:

1. If the roles are mutually exclusive, that is, if the entities can play one role in the organization or another of the roles, but not both, define separate entity families.

   In this case, there will probably be few attributes in common between roles. There should be no duplication of individual members in another family.

2. If the roles are distinct, but *not* mutually exclusive, that is, if there are some entities who play each role exclusively, but there are some which can play both, the roles should be treated as separate families, as if they were mutually exclusive and the data about dual-family members should be stored redundantly.

3. If the role of an entity occurrence in a family must be explicit and testable, the role characteristic must be used intensionally. If the role of an entity occurrence in a family can be implicit and need not be testable, the role characteristic may be used extensionally.

Because we use the business determinants—statements of mission, charter, goal, objective, strategy, tactic, etc.—and analysis of user interviews and user documentation to identify and label the business entities of the firm and their roles, in practice it is often difficult to determine whether a characteristic value set represents entity families or entity groups within a family. For the same reason, it is difficult to determine with any clarity the characteristics of each family. If we scan all the documentation collected and generated from the analysis phase, we would probably have a myriad of entity characteristics, and thus many entity groups, but probably only a few entity families. Without definitive rules, we have no consistent way to tell which is which. If all the rules for characteristics are followed, much of this difficulty should be eliminated and consistency is increased.

Entity Families and Relationships

An entity family consists of all individuals and groups of member entities which behave the same way in the organization. All entities which have the same role in the organization or which relate to the environment in the same way should belong to the same family.

Entities are grouped into families based upon extensional characteristics. While characteristics determine entity families, characteristics can also indicate relationships. In some cases separate entity families which normally are created based upon the extensional characteristics used must be combined and the required family groupings must be accomplished through relationships. This occurs when business rules or other characteristics of the entity population prevent normal family grouping and segregation techniques from being applied.

Some of the most common conditions when alternative methods must be used are

1. The business rules of the firm dictate that certain role-based entities be aggregated into a single family or group regardless of other factors.
2. When there is a high degree of data commonality which puts pressure on aggregation into a single group.
3. When a high number of dual-family membership is anticipated.

Relationships as Characteristics

In many models, the designer must deal with the condition where a given occurrence plays multiple roles simultaneously. Since characteristic values (the role indicators) must be mutually exclusive and exhaustive, normal grouping cannot be used. Instead a way must be found to handle roles which is both consistent with the general model and in conformance to the rules. One of the most common methods of treating this problem is by transferring the characteristic to relationships. Figure 15.8 illustrates the use of multiple relationships to replace a non–mutually exclusive characteristic value list.

To illustrate:

> A group of people may have multiple simultaneous roles—*role* (faculty, student, alumnus, trustee, contributor)—with respect to a university. For processing and cost efficiency reasons and to develop a more complete profile on the people it deals with, the university has decided to maintain all these people in a single master file. Without these business rule and business reason constraints the population of people would have been represented as separate entity families each named for a single value of the characteristic.

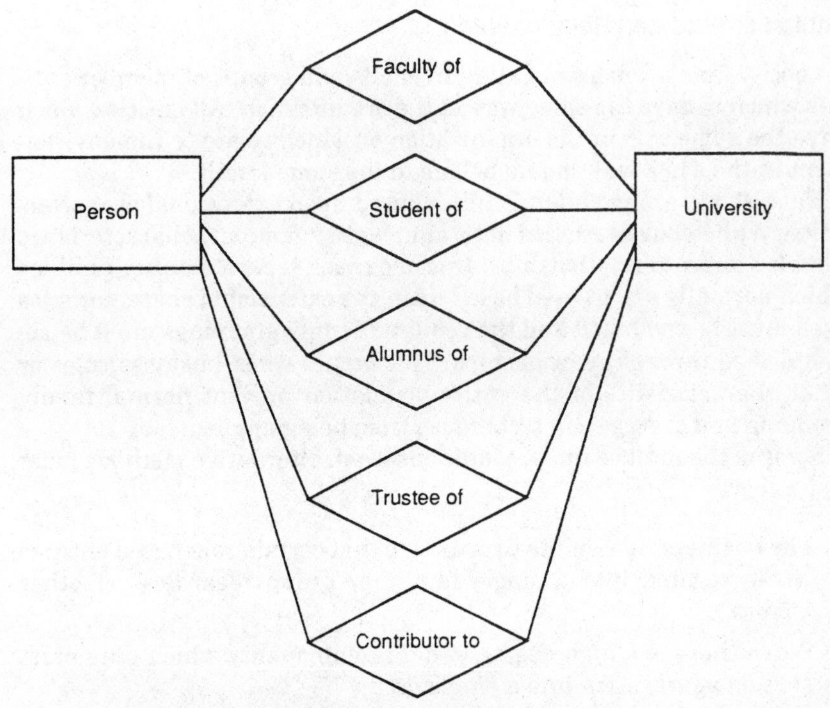

Figure 15.8 Relationships used to replace characteristics.

> However because of the constraints the population has been aggregated into the same family each of whose members may be related to the educational institution in a variety of ways (*relationship names*—on the faculty of, student of, alumnus of, trustee of, contributor to).

The same solution holds true for the person who may be a depositor of, a lender to, a borrower from, a mortgagee of, etc., a bank.

Each of the roles that would normally be represented by an entity family model, is instead represented by a series of relationships to some other entity. These relationships may be direct or through some intermediary entity, such as an account entity.

When relationships are used instead of family groups, the single family group is defined ignoring the role characteristic as a family grouping indicator, and instead the characteristic is defined in terms of a set of relationships to some other family. In this representation the characteristic and the many data groupings which it represents are transferred to the relationship. The model's narrative descriptions must explain as fully as possible

1. Each of these characteristic relationships

2. The reasons (business rules and reasons) why relationships are being used
3. The conditions under which each relationship exists
4. How to identify the entity occurrences within each entity family which participates in each relationship

Since the majority of people-entity processing activities within an organization can be expressed in terms of the role relationships between entity family and entity family, or between entity family and company (also an entity family, by the way), there are usually a large number of interfamily relationships in the data model and those relationships between entity families will be multiple, conditional, and complex.

Chapter

16

Entity-Relationship Attribute Modeling

An *entity* is defined as a person, place, or thing which is (1) of interest to the corporation, (2) capable of being described in real terms, and (3) relevant within the context of the specific environment of the firm. A more precise definition within the context of the classification-based data model should be as follows:

Definition. In a real-world model each *entity* represents a group or family of uniquely identifiable persons, places, things, concepts (that is, logical persons, places, or things), or events of interest to the firm and about which the firm wants or must collect data or keep records. The data or records about each entity describe what they are, what they look like, how they are used, what purpose they serve, what actions they take, or what actions are taken with or against them. Each entity in a real-world model is uniquely differentiated from every other entity by a set of distinguishing characteristics.

For our discussion of entity-relationship attribute models we must use a different definition:

Definition. In a data model, each *entity* is a data representation of a set of uniquely identifiable real-world persons, places, things, concepts (that is, logical persons, places, or things), or events that can be described in an identical or highly similar manner and which behave in an identical or highly similar manner. An entity is represented in the real-world model only if it is of interest to the firm and is something the firm collects and maintains data about. Entities in the data model (or data entities) represent the actual data which must be collected and maintained (Figure 16.1).

The representation of the entity in the data model includes all the characteristics and attributes of the entity, the actual data elements which must be present to fully describe each characteristic and attribute, and a representation of how that data must be grouped, organized, and structured. Although the terms characteristics and attributes are sometimes used interchangeably, attributes are the more general term, and characteristics are special-use attributes.

The definitions of these three terms, attribute, characteristic, and data element, follow.

Definition. An *attribute*

Is any aspect, quality, characteristic, or descriptor of either an entity or a relationship

Is some general grouping of data attributes or data elements that serve to describe an entity

May be a very abstract or general category of information, a specific attribute or element, or level of aggregation between these two extremes

An attribute must also be

1. Of interest to the corporation
2. Capable of being described in real terms
3. Relevant within the context of the specific environment of the firm

An attribute must be capable of being defined in terms of words or numbers. That is, the attribute must have one or more data elements associated with it. An attribute of an entity (Figure 16.2) might be its name or its relationship to another entity. It may describe what the entity

- By identifying its attributes of interest.
- What are attributes of interest?
- Those facts or categories of information about the entity needed by the firm to conduct its business.
- Thus it can be said that:
- An entity is what the firm says it is.

Figure 16.1 How do we describe entities?

- An attribute is any aspect, quality, or characteristic or descriptor of either an entity or a relationship.
- An attribute must also be:
  a. Of interest to the corporation.
  b. Describable in real terms.
  c. Relevant within a general or specific user context within the firm.
- An attribute must have one or more data elements associated with it.

Figure 16.2 Definition of an attribute.

looks like, where it is located, how old it is, how much it weighs, etc. An attribute may describe why a relationship exists, how long it has existed, how long it will exist, or under what conditions it exists.

An attribute (Figure 16.3) is an aspect or quality of an entity which describes it or its actions. An attribute may describe some physical aspect, such as size, weight or color, or an aspect of the entity's location such as place of residence or place of birth. It may be a quality such as the level of a particular skill, educational degree achieved, or the dollar value of the items represented by an order.

Definition. *A characteristic*

Is some general grouping of data elements which serve to identify or otherwise distinguish or set apart one thing or group of things from another. A characteristic is a special form of attribute.

May be a very abstract or general category of information, an element, or level of aggregation between these two extremes.

Is some aspect of the entity that is required to gain a complete understanding of the entity, its general nature, its activities, or its usage.

A data element is the lowest meaningful item of information.

The ability to classify the membership of a set of objects (or in this

- An attribute is a property.
- A property is a characteristic.
- A quality that defines or describes an object (entity).
- Thus:
- An Entity = (property, property, property,..., property).
- Or an entity is the sum of its properties.

Figure 16.3 What is an attribute?

case entities) or to distinguish sets of objects from each other is directly dependent upon the ability to collect data about each member, by which membership in the various classification groups can be assigned. For example, the classification of companies by type of ownership (Figure 16.4) is dependent upon having data about each company which identifies its type of ownership.

The ability to maintain records about an object is dependent upon the ability to identify what must be kept in those records and to subsequently collect that data. The ability to retrieve that data, especially if it is extensive, is dependent upon the ability to classify, organize, or categorize that data into meaningful groupings such that each item of data has a meaningful, logical place, close to data which is closely related to it either by existence dependence or by meaning dependence (the data elements all relate to the same idea, concept or aspect, or action of the entity).

In the real-world model for purposes of clarity we include all entities regardless of their purpose and use. The relationships are the real-world relationships and describe how the entities relate and interact with each other.

The data model by contrast makes a distinction between entities we are interested in because we collect data about them and entities we are interested in because they are carriers of data or forms and documents we use to collect data about other entities. The real-world model describes the relationships between entities by stating that one or more occurrences of this kind of entity must (or may) be related to one or more occurrences of that kind of entity. The data model describes the data we need to know about those relationships, and how we can determine which actual occurrences of one kind of entity are related to which actual occurrences of another kind of entity and under what conditions or subject to what qualifications.

Normally in the data model we ignore document entities which func-

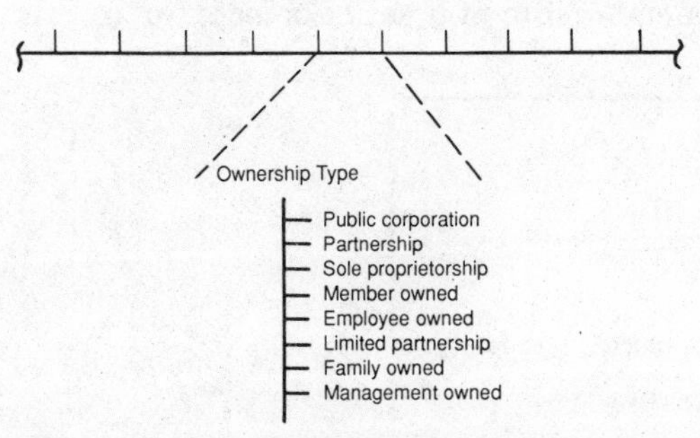

Figure 16.4 Classification of company by type of ownership.

tion purely as carriers of data about other real entities. We instead concentrate on the data they carry and what entities that data describes.

One of the primary techniques for data modeling both in data model development and in procedural development is the entity-relationship model. The first two of the four entity-relationship model levels are used to develop the real-world data model. These were the enterprise level model and the entity-relationship level model and were described in earlier chapters. These models can be used at the real-world level since they can be developed deductively and from empirical evidence.

The remaining two models (the entity-relationship attribute level model and the data element level model) are inductively developed at the detail design level and are dependent on the full description of the entity family classification structure and a complete set of user views for their completion. The user views are necessary since it is only from them that we can develop the composite data model which is the entity family model, and only by examining the complete set can we be sure we have identified every necessary characteristic, and its data content, and every relationship required by every task for data access. All user views are necessary because it is only by examining these that we can determine whether the data we identified deductively (future data needs not currently present, and future relationship needs not currently captured) can be captured and maintained on a practical basis.

Since the data model development at the entity-relationship attribute level is an inductive process and is dependent upon determining the exhaustive set of user views and the exhaustive classification structure of each entity family it must be the last step in the data model development process.

The development of the entity-relationship model is a multilevel process where each level produces a clearer and more well-defined view of the proposed environment. The complete results of this modeling effort results in a series of leveled environmental descriptions, along with a diagrammatic representation of each level. These diagrammatic representations, the ER models, are descriptions of the entities, or real components, of the business environment and how they relate to each other.

On a regular basis the firm deals with customers, products, employees, places, orders, shipments, etc. The firm collects data about these things, these entities, and stores that data in files. With few exceptions, it is the common data resource files of the firms which hold the descriptions of those entities in the form of collections of data items.

The ER models are not data structure models, but data descriptions of the entities of interest to the firm. These data descriptions also correspond to the data contents of the files and thus serve well as a mechanism for developing our data model. Although at their most detailed level they contain and identify data elements, they are not data processing models. They are business models and as such they model business environments and depict business components.

Entity-relationship models consist of representations of the various levels and parts of the organization, from the strategic to the operational levels. Each of these leveled models represent the entities and relationships from the perspective of that level, and within a level the entity-relationship models represent the perspective of one or more particular users at that level.

Although there are numerous variations of the entity-relationship approach model notation, the three basic notational components of the entity-relationship model consist of symbols representing an entity, a relationship between two entities, and the attributes, or descriptors, of either entities or relationships. These symbols are

1. *Rectangles.* Each unique entity type or entity subtype is represented by a rectangle which contains the name of that unique entity type or entity subtype.
2. *Diamonds.* Each relationship which exists between any two different entities or between two occurrences of the same entity is represented by a diamond which contains the name of that relationship.
3. *Circles.* Each unique attribute of either an entity or a relationship is represented by a circle which contains the name of that attribute.

The real-world model depicts real-world families of entities. At this level the entities have the widest possible definition and scope, while still maintaining the general physical and role characteristics of the individual entities which comprise them. These entity sets are treated as if there were no variations in type and as if each of their component entities were defined in a similar manner and behaved in a similar manner.

Just as we use the general term vendor to represent each (and every) kind of vendor and employee to represent each (and every) kind of employee, so too we use an even more general term to represent all the various kinds of people, places, thing, concepts, and events of interest to the firm. Depending upon the model (since a different definition is used for each model—real-world and data) the term, entity, thus represents either any one of the real-world things in the real-world model, or any one of the generalized collections of data we gather, record, and maintain in the data model.

At the real-world level

- Entities are identified and named.
- Relationships are defined as either existing or not existing between any given pair of entities.

- All entities and relationships are viewed from a single perspective.
- Business rules stated are at a strategic or policy level and apply firmwide.
- Business activities are functionally stated.
- Business entities are portrayed at a family, class, or universal level. There is no differentiation between the various subtypes of a given entity, unless those differences have meaning at a firmwide and a functional level.

In the classification model

- The polyhierarchic structure of each entity family is defined.
- Each relationship between the different kinds of entities or entity groups are identified and named.
- Entity groups, kinds of groupings, aliases, parent-child, cousin-to-cousin and generation-to-generation relationships as identified in the structure may be firmwide or viewed from a variety of business unit, divisional, or other organizational perspectives. These perspectives may cross functional or business unit boundaries.
- Business rules represented by this classification structure are tactical and may apply firmwide or to a specific unit or set of units.
- The classification structure(s) within each family must represent all needs of the firm and may be based on external and thus real-world structural views, or internal and based upon firmwide, functional, or user views.
- Business entity groupings and hierarchic and polyhierarchic lineages may be portrayed at a global or universal level or may be differentiated into more restrictive subtypes which relate to the particular business unit

Entity-Relationship Attribute Level

The analysis at the third, or entity-relationship attribute, level combines the work of the real-world level with that of the classification model and the data entity time lines by adding characteristic groupings determined inductively into a classification structure determined deductively, and by adding characteristics and or attributes to both the entities and the relationships. A characteristic or attribute is represented by a circle attached directly to the entity or the relationship which it describes. The circle contains the name of the attribute. Attributes might be identification information, residence information, physical description, inventory status, packaging information, hobbies, clothing sizes, etc.

The attribute names for an employee entity might be very similar to the section or item headings on an employment application, or the section or item headings on the permanent employee record form. For a customer, they might be very similar to the section headings on a new account opening form, or on the customer record form.

For an entity, each attribute represents some grouping of data which is necessary, from a business perspective, to describe a physical or logical characteristic of the entity, or to describe some activity of the entity. For a relationship, each attribute represents some grouping of data which is necessary, from a business perspective, to describe, qualify, or maintain the named relationship between two entities.

The entity-relationship attribute model is an expansion of the entity-relationship model. Until this point the models have only identified the entities and relationships by name and context. For a given entity or relationship little is known about them other than their name, the obvious fact of their existence, and the fact that the firm is interested in them.

At the entity-relationship attribute level, entities and relationships are described in terms of their attributes or characteristics. In other words, beyond knowing that the entity exists, we must also know what the entity looks like, how it is identified, and what it does. These descriptors or characteristics are called attributes. An attribute is thus any distinct aspect of the entity or relationship that is necessary to describe the entity or to qualify the relationship. The full description of an entity or relationship consists of the full set of attributes which describe that entity or relationship.

For an entity attribute to be significant it must relate directly to the entity, be completely dependent on the entity for its existence and meaning, and be definable in terms of one or more data elements. It is immaterial as to whether there are one or more data elements in an attribute, as long as the attribute applies to all instances of the entity being represented. Seen another way, an attribute is some distinct category of mutually related data, the sum of which describes something of interest about the entity. The identifiers (unique or otherwise) of an entity (Figure 16.5) are a special form of attribute.

- Each entity family must have at least one attribute which represents a unique identifier for each entity occurrence within the family

Figure 16.5 Entity attributes.

Entity attributes (Figure 16.6) represent

- A physical characteristic of that entity—size, shape, weight, or color
- A historical attribute—date of birth or date of hire
- A locational attribute—place of residence, place of work, or place of birth
- A nonphysical characteristic—price
- An identifier—name or title
- An occupational characteristic—current position, skill possessed, training received, educational courses, etc.
- The intermediate or final results of some processing activities related to the entity

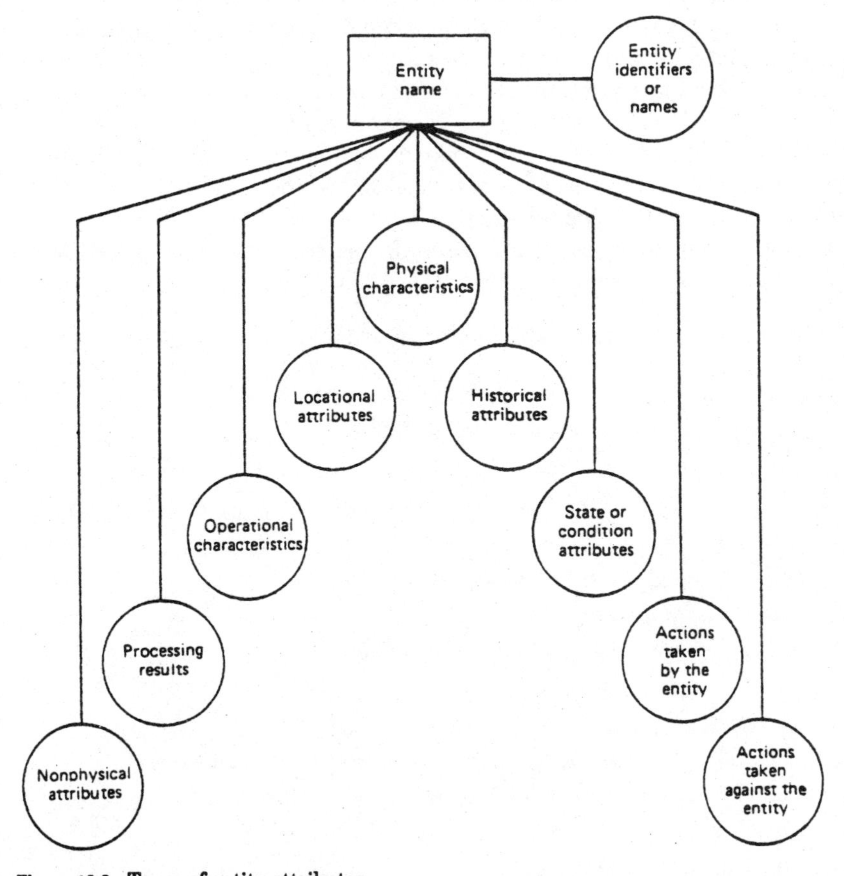

Figure 16.6 Types of entity attributes.

- A relationship must have a minimum of two attributes one representing an identifier or other attribute

Figure 16.7 Relationship attributes.

- Data which relates to some current state or condition of the entity, or to some past or future state or condition of the entity
- Data which relates to some current action taken by or against the entity, or to some past or future action taken by or against the entity

For a relationship attribute (Figure 16.7) to be significant it must relate directly to the relationship, be completely dependent on the relationship for its existence and meaning, and be definable in terms of one or more data elements. It is immaterial as to whether there are one or more data elements in an attribute, as long as the attribute applies to all instances of the entity or relationship being represented.

Seen another way, an attribute is some distinct category of mutually related data, the sum of which describes something of interest, or some qualifier about the relationship between two entities. A relationship attribute must be dependent upon the connection between both entities and should be incapable of existence in the absence of that relationship. The minimum attributes of a relationship are the necessary identifiers of each entity of the related pair.

Relationship attributes (Figure 16.8) represent some descriptor or qualifier of the relationship such as

- A historical attribute—date of marriage, date of sale, or date of storage.

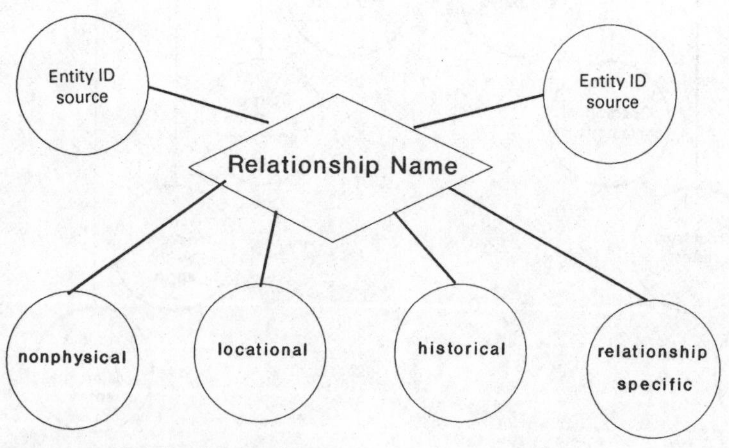

Figure 16.8 Relationship attributes.

- A location attribute—place of storage, place of work, or place of birth.
- A nonphysical characteristic—price at time of sale, discount at time of sale, grade in course.
- Some meaningful data which is not an attribute of either entity participating in the relationship, but pertains only to the relationship between them. This data is sometimes called intersection data.

It is possible for the same named attribute to be used to describe many different entities and relationships. Identifier attributes in particular describe both the entities and the relationships between them.

Entity-Relationship Attribute Level Model

The creation of an entity-relationship attribute model is a multiple-step process. This level produces the most detailed model. Step one extracts each entity from the entity-relationship model and places it at the top of a separate page. Each distinct relationship between each pair of related entities is extracted from the entity-relationship model and placed at the top of a separate page.

Step two identifies, names, and defines each attribute of each entity. Each attribute, represented by an attribute symbol, is drawn below the entity symbol and is connected to the entity by a single line (Figure 16.9). As each attribute symbol is drawn, the attribute name should be placed within it. Although not a requirement, as each attribute is identified and named it is helpful to annotate it with a discrete number or "*n*" (denoting some unknown number more than one) to indicate how many occurrences of this attribute (Figure 16.10) would be necessary to describe the entity.

Step three identifies, names, and defines each attribute of each relationship. The attributes of a relationship are those categories of data which are necessary to qualify the relationship, describe when and

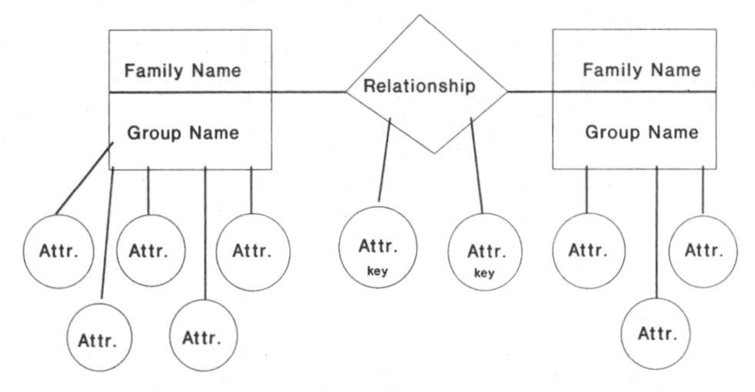

Figure 16.9 Entities and relationships must each have attributes.

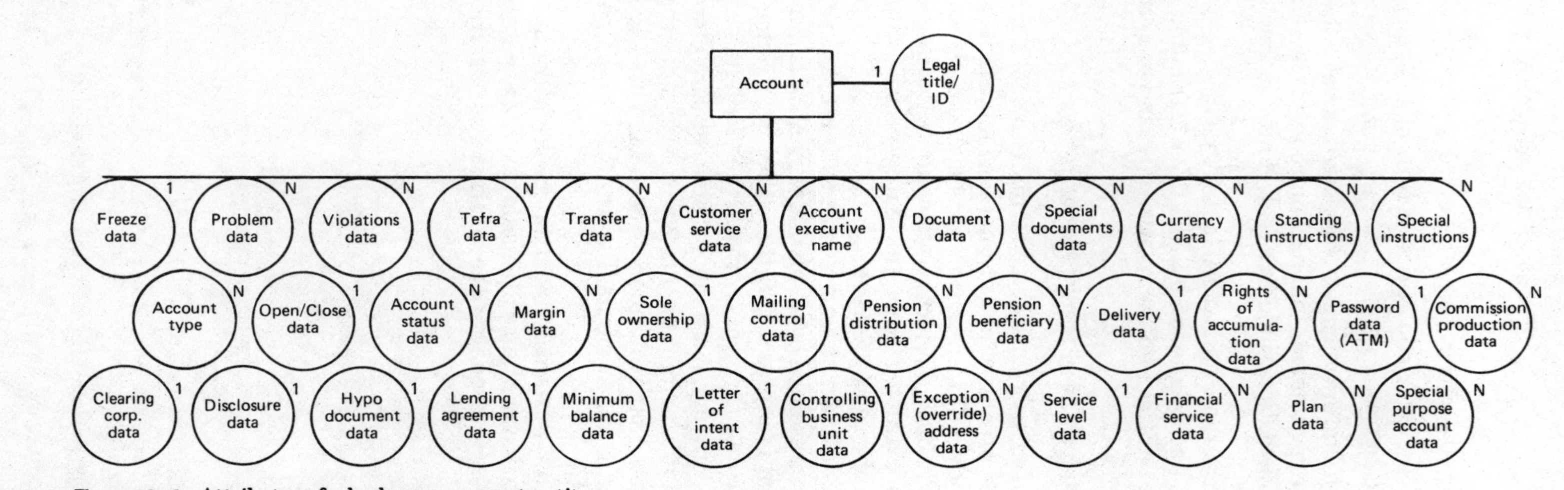

Figure 16.10 Attributes of a brokerage account entity.

under what conditions it occurs, and describe any other information which relates only to the connection between the entities and not to either entity independently. The relationship attributes should include all attributes necessary to clearly and completely identify any qualifications of that particular relationship between the two entities and the conditions under which the relationship exists (Figure 16.11).

As each attribute is identified and named, it is to be drawn below the relationship symbol and connected to the relationship by a single line. As with the attributes of entities, it is helpful to annotate the attribute with a discrete number or with "*n*," to identify the number of occurrences of this particular attribute which are necessary to fully describe or qualify the relationship.

As the attributes of each relationship are modeled, the relevant attributes of each of the entities of the related pair, which are of interest within the context of the relationship, should be extracted from the attributed entity model and added to the entity symbols of the relationship model (Figure 16.12).

In data processing terms, and in a very general sense, the attributes within this model can be considered to be the identification and definition of the record types (or record groupings) which will ultimately contain the data elements. It must be noted that each attribute at either the entity or relationship level represents a mutually exclusive and mutually independent category of data. However, an attribute may or may not represent an actual record type.

In the logical data structure models, created at a later date from these entity-relationship attribute models, attributes may be combined

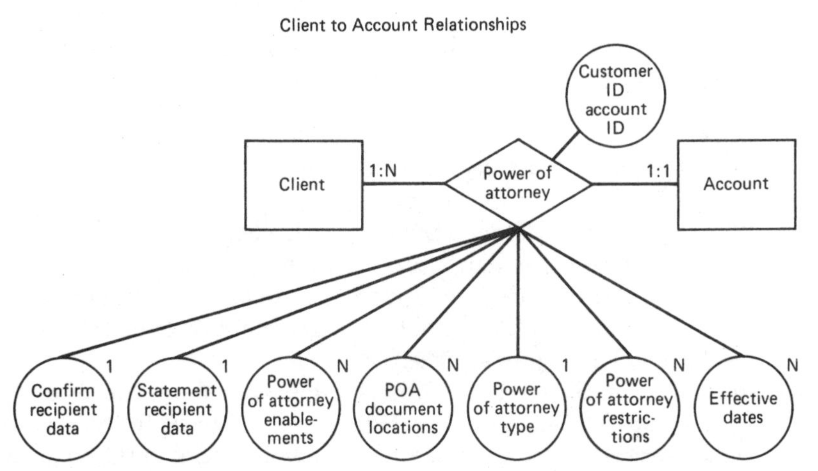

Figure 16.11 Attributes of a power of attorney relationship between a client entity and an account entity.

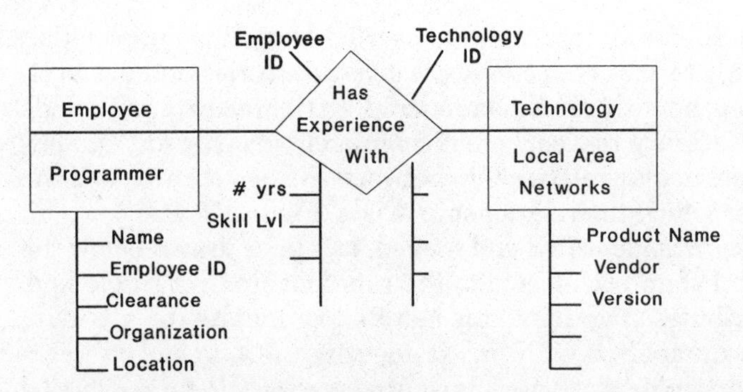

Figure 16.12 Entity-to-entity relationships with specific attributes (alternative form of presentation).

to form more general records, they may be kept separately or in some extreme cases, because of the complexity of the attribute, an attribute may be split into many records. The names of the entities are the names of the logical data aggregates (or structures) of the environment.

A fourth, or data element, level may be added when the models are developed in conjunction with the data processing systems development projects. This is the level which is most familiar to data processing specialists and consists of identifying and defining the specific data elements which are needed to describe each attribute of each entity and each relationship. *Data elements are assigned only to attributes.* In a sense, data elements are the attributes of the attributes.

Additional Rules for ER Model Creation

Regardless of the level being addressed, the following rules apply to the construction of an entity-relationship diagram:

1. Entities:
   a. Each rectangle must represent a single entity, a homogeneous group of entities, or one subset or subtype of the entity.
   b. When developing detailed models, each identified family entity should be decomposed into its component groups.
   c. The mode of decomposition is dependent upon the characteristics of the component entities and the requirements of the firm for information about those entities.
   d. Regardless of the mode of decomposition, care should be taken to ensure that all entity groups can be related back to their base global entity. This may be accomplished by special notation or by including the name of the base entity within the entity group's name.

   e. When the model includes documents, each unique type of document should be included, and the attributes for these documents should include all data field contents which must be validated, processed, and retained by the firm.
   f. When document processing requires that data be validated against preexistent reference files, code lists, spreadsheet or other financial tables, etc., the referenced data items should be treated as if they were entities and included in the model along with their appropriate attributes and relationships.
2. Relationships:
   a. Relationship diamonds are drawn between, and must be connected (by a line from each side of the diamond) to, no less than one and no more than two entity rectangles.
   b. A diamond may be connected back to the same entity, in which case it represents a recursive relationship between unique occurrences of the same entity.
   c. Each diamond must represent a single relationship which is known to exist between the two connected entities *and is of interest to the firm.*
   d. For each line which connects the diamond to a rectangle, at the point where that line joins that rectangle a notation should be made as to whether the two entities being related have a one-to-one, one-to-many, many-to-one, or many-to-many relationship.
   e. This notation should be made in the form *a:b,* where

      a = the entity on the left side of the diamond
      b = the entity on the right side of the diamond

   and *a* and *b* may have any numeric value equal to or greater than 1, or *N* (denoting an indefinite number more than 1)
   f. If the relationship is symmetrical, that is, entity *A* (the left-hand entity) has the same relationship to entity *B* (the right-hand entity), that is, each *A* is connected to many *B*'s and each *B* is connected to one and only one *A*, then the notation closest to each entity should be the same.
   g. If the relationship is asymmetrical, that is, entity *A* does not have the same relationship to entity *B* as entity *B* has to entity *A*, that is, each *A* is connected to one and only one *B*, but each *B* may be connected to many *A*'s, the notation closest to each entity should reflect the view from that entity to the opposite entity.
3. Attributes:
   a. Circles representing attributes are connected to either rectangles or diamonds.
   b. Each circle may be connected to one and only one rectangle or one

and only one diamond and must represent a specific attribute of the entity or relationship to which it is connected.

c. The circles on the diagram contain a name which identifies the specific attribute or set of attributes being depicted.

d. The line connecting the circle to the entity or relationship should be annotated to reflect whether the named attribute may occur only once per entity (or relationship) or many times.

e. Each entity rectangle and relationship diamond must have at least one associated attribute.

f. Attributes which apply to more than one entity, or to more than one relationship, must be diagrammed as if they were unique to each entity or relationship to which they apply. This condition will occur when an entity family has been separated into entity groups, and the members of one or more groups share many of the same attributes. Under these conditions each occurrence of the attribute symbol should have the same name and some notation which indicates that it is identical in format to attributes which appear elsewhere.

If all attributes and all relationships connected to the entity rectangle do not have the potential to apply equally to each and every entity occurrence defined by it, then the definition of the entity being used must be changed and a new entity or entity set, or a new entity subset or subsets, must be created until this condition is satisfied.

Although the above discussion assumed that one and only one model will be created at each level, and for the firm as a whole, most projects are for specific user areas. It may be desirable to create different models for each user area.

Just as an entity can be viewed from many different perspectives, and may seem to be different from each perspective, so too entity-relationship and entity-relationship attribute models can be different from the various perspectives of the firm. Each area of the firm defines the entities of the firm in different ways and relates to them in different ways.

All entity-relationship models need not contain every entity of the firm. The various models need only contain the entities of interest to the particular area being modeled. To illustrate:

1. A model can be built to reflect only the document entities, the entity sources for those documents, and the relationships between both types of entities.
2. A model might contain functional entities and their relationships. Here the functional areas of the firm (managerial concepts) are

treated as entities themselves and the model reflects their relationships to each other.

3. Another variation might contain only the processing entities (groups of people, machines, or work stations) and the document and/or resource entities used by them. This type of model might reflect all the processing stations through which a particular document must travel, or the work stations through which a manufactured part must pass.

   A process model does not reflect what processing is done, or even how that processing is done, but rather a station where processing of a particular type is done. That processing could be complex or simple.

The various entity-relationship approach models are business models, rather than data processing models. That is, they reflect business environments, not methods of processing. The types of entities and relationships selected to be included in each model, the definitions of those entities, and the attributes used to describe those entities and relationships, all combine to describe the environment and the nature of the business itself.

Chapter

17

Data Element Analysis

Element Analysis

Each of the preceding chapters dealt with various aspects of company data model development. The common thread in those chapters was an emphasis on attributes as our lowest-level data aggregate. The final result, however, is a data model as yet devoid of data element detail. It is just that elemental detail that is needed to complete the design.

The chapter on entity-relationship attribute modeling concluded with the statement that data elements are only assigned to attributes. This reinforced the clear distinction which the entity-relationship approach makes between attributes and data elements. The development of an entity-relationship model through the attribution phase is a deductive process, applying rules of analysis and classification to develop the data groupings which must be in place to describe and record data about the members of each entity family.

Because a top-down decomposition approach is used, this process is relatively divorced from considerations of existing systems data file content. Data attribution is developed from analysis of data events, data entity life cycle activities and observation, experience, and empirical knowledge. The data classification techniques develop successively smaller and finer groups of data which are developed using both usage and existence considerations. These attributes are also developed from an analysis of the various characteristics of each distinct kind of member within the family, the family characteristics themselves, and the characteristics of each intermediate grouping between the family and lowest meaningful kind of member group within the family.

On a family-by-family basis, these characteristics and groupings also serve to identify and guide the identification of noncharacteristic physical, logical, and action-based attributes which are common to every member of a family, to each level of grouping within the family, and to each peculiar kind of member group within the family. Since the members of each family can be classified by multiple concurrent means (that is, location, size, and any characteristic which all members share as a family), each classification hierarchy also serves to identify another set of attributes which serve to expand, qualify, and describe the family as classified within that hierarchy.

Because the attributes are developed in a top-down manner, and because each attribute or characteristic data grouping represents a distinct, concise and specific idea or concept, this process can be thought of as a before-the-fact (that is, before elements are added) normalization of data as it is practiced by data base designers. This process however is based upon business usage and business views rather than processing efficiency and data file maintenance considerations.

Attribute Decomposition

Each attribute in its lowest decomposed form is a representation of a group of data which is either completely existence interdependent (that is, all the data comes into being at the same time, gets updated as a whole—and previous sets of values are always archived or discarded) or concept dependent (that is, all the data within the attribute may arise from different sources and may be updated randomly, but all the data elements are interrelated and interdependent because they describe or pertain to a single idea or aspect of the entity).

The system design process is, as previously discussed, in reality always a redesign process, and as such must deal with and account for all current system items (including data elements), all item changes, and must predict to the extent possible the need for new items (including data elements).

The design process may, and usually does, result in these items (especially data) being rearranged, regrouped, relocated, changed or modified in some way (split, combined, recoded, etc.), and supplemented. New groupings of data elements (into attributes, versus old file records and forms) may and probably will result in new grouping identifiers and distinguishing characteristics, and may also result in date and time stamps being added to existence-dependent data groups.

Because entity attributes in a data model represent logical data groupings, each attribute of each entity and each relationship must contain at least one data element otherwise it serves no purpose in the data model. Usually however an attribute represents some group of elements which, when viewed as a whole, describe that aspect, characteristic or action of an entity, or qualifies some relationship between data entities.

Each attribute is complete and self-contained in that all data elements within it relate to the same attribute, aspect, or characteristic. They are complete in that the contents of each attribute should be all that is needed to describe that action, aspect, or characteristic. Since all attributes relate directly to the data entity, they are represented as being directly dependent to, part of, or contained within the entity. Attributes may be repetitive, in that there may be multiple possible occurrences.

Generalized versus Specific Attributes

An attribute may also have variable content, depending upon whether it is generalized to describe all possible members of the entity family, or specialized to describe some specific group of entity family members. They might also be variable in that there might be multiple possible variations of content of a single attribute. For instance, there may be shipping addresses defined for a customer, each of which is complete and each of which is active, depending upon when and what is being shipped to the customer. Again, there might be multiple sets or definitions of customer demographic data, depending upon whether that customer is a doctor, lawyer, teacher, school, or company. Although this representation may be desirable for modeling purposes to show commonality of data, it is usually avoided by giving each specialized combination of elements for a common attribute a different name, in effect making it into a different attribute.

Because the entity is viewed as a family in some cases and as groups of specialized members in others, the names of the data element (each attribute) must be consistent within the entity family, across all common attributes used to describe the various members of the family, and across the attributes which are necessary to describe each specific and specialized grouping of members within the family. Entity families are created based upon the role of their members within the organization or based upon a commonality of characteristics. All members of the entity family share the attributes and relationships common to every entity within the family. Specific family members may have specific attributes or relationships unique to them.

Conditional Attribute Existence

Each data entity and each attribute of each data entity is conditionally existent. These conditions are defined by the entity context, its relationship to its parent, siblings, children and cousins, and to other data entities within other entity families.

Each relationship is constructed such that it defines and supports a specific association or connection between the owner or source (the subject entity) and the target (the object entity). Subject and object are used in the traditional grammatical sense. Each attribute of a relationship contains the data elements necessary to support, qualify, and otherwise define that relationship and the conditions under which that relationship between those two entities is active and valid. The use of each relationship is dependent upon how, when, and under what conditions an association or connection must be established between the two entities. By far the most powerful and complex portion of the data model are the relationships, and thus they are the most difficult to define.

Unlike attributes, it is not enough to determine the name, definition and description, and use of the elements of a particular attribute. The design team must also ascertain the valid format and in the case of representational elements (codes, etc.) the valid and permissible values. These values, while they can be generalized, can be as multitudinous as are the variations in the unique entities which they describe.

The Attribute Equation

A data element is the lowest unit of meaningful information within the data model, however, few elements have meaning or usability by themselves. If an attribute is equated to a grouping of data elements then the data elements relate to that group much as arguments relate to an equation. Thus, the attribute is equal to the sum of its data element components. Each attribute can thus be expressed as an equation in the form:

$$\text{Attribute } A = [\text{data element}(1), \text{data element}(2), \ldots, \text{data element}(n)]$$

Thus the questions to be asked for each element are

Can this element be derived from other data?

Is this data element part of the equation of the attribute within which it resides?

A datum is a fact. Data are multiple facts. The combination of facts yields information, so too the combination of data elements in an attribute yields information about that attribute.

Data Element Aggregation

Data elements are aggregated to groups below the attribute level as well. Thus, month, day of month, and year aggregate into date. Within this context, since month, day and year are all meaningful in their own right, or could be meaningful, we define each separately, and then define the aggregate, with its meaning, and as being composed of three lower-level items. In the same manner phone number is an aggregate consisting of the separate elements area code, exchange, and extension; zip code is an aggregate consisting of sectional center facility (SCF) number, post office number, and zip code extension (plus four).

As a general rule, if an item of data can be broken down into further meaningful parts, each lower-level element should be defined separately and the aggregate element should be defined as well. Thus a data element may be both aggregate data and subelements.

Data in Atomic or Elemental Form

Another general rule states that where possible and feasible, the data model should represent elemental data as opposed to derived data or information. In other words, do specific data elements have to be recorded or can the system "know" that something has occurred simply by the presence, or absence, of some other data element, combination of data elements, or attribute?

As an illustration, if element *A* is defined as the result of element *B* divided by element *C*, only element *B* and element *C* should be defined in the data model, since element *A* can easily be computed.

When in doubt it is generally safer to record the variables or arguments in a computation, rather than only the result of that computation. Sometimes, however, it is more efficient and necessary to record both the arguments and the result, although it is usually done for processing efficiency reasons.

The net amount of an invoice can be recomputed accurately each time by recomputing each line item and adding or subtracting additional charges or discounts, respectively, but only if the item price does not change, or if the item price is recorded by line item. In any other cases the net invoice would change each time any item price changed and orders are usually price-fixed as of the time of taking the order.

Net account balance can easily be recomputed by adding or subtracting all account entries (debit or credit). Point-in-time net account balance can only be consistently computed by time and date stamping each entry.

The composite data attribute model of each entity family within the data model is constructed to contain the complete variety of individual family members. As the model was developed the accompanying narratives described each family member and each family group variation within the family. The data event models described the data that was to be recorded or retrieved from each attribute. The data event model access sequences to each entity and entity attribute described those data elements available in the trigger, or those attributes and those elements which had to be retrieved and which could then be used to access additional entities and their attributes. Each of those expected data elements should have been identified in the accompanying narrative.

Domain versus Context Data Elements

Because data models represent data in the context of their use in describing entities, and because certain kinds of elements are frequently used through the corporate model, most designs distinguish between these two kinds of element usages in the way in which they are documented. This distinction between element types also allows for the creation of a common and modelwide definition which can be used by inclusion wherever the same element is used, but with a different name. These two kinds of elements are called domain elements and context elements.

Definition. A domain element is a data element in its atomic or lowest-level form, which is used to describe the specific type of values to be contained in the element wherever it is used or referenced.

Some examples of a domain element would be

Social security number

Telephone number

Zip code

Definition. A context element is an element that describes a specific named usage of a domain element in a specific context.

The description of a context element must include a "see reference" to the domain element of which it is a specific usage instance.

Some examples of a context element are

Social security number of the spouse of the employee

Social security number of the employee

Social security number of a child of the employee

Naming Data Elements

Each data element, both domain and context, should be assigned a unique name. Name assignment should be in a standard form. One of the most commonly used forms of naming elements employs a format known as the "of-language." Names in this form identify the element, and its next higher-level aggregate plus any identifiers or qualifiers which are needed to make that name unique. A typical name might be

- Date of birth of employee
- Number of line of a purchase order of a customer
- First name of employee

The prime considerations when creating an element name, or element name standard format are that

1. The name should be fully qualified.
2. The name should be fully descriptive.
3. The name should be unique across the universe of names.
4. The name should be meaningful to the user.
5. Where possible, the name should be descriptive of its contents or the values contained within.
6. The name should where possible be indicative of the format, usage, or type of data contained within it (that is, date, name, code, etc.)

Naming Considerations

The above considerations are by no means the only ones, others being

- How much context identification is to be included within the name
- How names are to be grouped when sorted alphabetically within the dictionary (by entity, by type, etc.)
- Whether domain and context elements are to be used
- Dictionary physical limitations on name format and name length
- Dictionary flexibility
- How much meaning the firm wants to incorporate in the name, etc.

Other considerations have to do with programming languages used, data base management systems (DBMS) used, and the personal preference and philosophy of the data administration staff.

Data elements are probably the most frequently used products from the system design, and the most numerous. Many firms attempt to abbreviate them or otherwise shorten the names. While this may be necessary, it is also necessary to ensure that users who need information about data availability can access the dictionary in their context, and find the information they need with a minimum of technical knowledge or dictionary training.

The identification and naming of data elements is almost purely an inductive and enumerative process, since each and every needed data element has to be identified, defined, described, and placed. The omission of one element may in some cases severely impact the design. The misspecification of one element may have an equally severe impact. Although the design team has the inventory of current data elements to work with, the process of renaming each item to the new format, examining and in cases redefining (or defining for the first time) those elements, changing some of the elements, discarding some existing elements (no longer needed or replaced by new ones), and developing the names and definitions of new ones is a time-consuming and tedious task. However it is as critical to the design as the development of user task procedures, and since in many cases those procedures will reference the data elements individually, this task must be completed before procedure development can begin.

Data Element Issues

As elements are assigned to the attributes of each entity, that placement becomes a determinant of all context element names and most of the domain element names. It may in some cases be a determinant of the definition and description of that element as well. The following issues should be examined for each element:

Is it a function of that attribute and of that entity?

Is its value dependent solely on that entity and that attribute?

Were that attribute to represent an equation and would that data element be part of that equation?

Could that attribute be fully described or be meaningful without that data element?

Classification Model Impact

If, for instance, the classification model identified twelve distinct customer types, with twelve distinct demographic constructs, each demographic construct or attribute can occur in the composite entity, although only one will appear on any given unique entity member. Each classification variable form of a common attribute should be identified in some manner by a classification characteristic, attribute, identifier, or code.

All archival data or time-dependent attributes should be dated, indicating both date effective and date of replacement or discontinuance.

Data Element Formats

Data element format or representation consistency should be ensured by type. Format issues include:

Should dates be recorded in Julian format (YYDDD) or in Gregorian (MMDDYY) format, or both?

If recorded in Gregorian format, should that format be standard MMDDYY format? YYMMDD format? YYYMMDD format? MMDDYYY format?

(*Note:* Remember that as we approach the end of the century special consideration must be given to data representation as they span the century mark.)

For numeric data:

- Should the values be recorded to a standard decimal place, that is, .0, .00 or .000, etc., or should it vary?
- Should each distinct type of numeric data have a standard format within that type, that is, all percentages to three decimal places, or four?
- Should all dollars and cents (monetary data) be to dollars and cents or dollars only?

Identifier Attributes

Each entity family must have at least one common attribute whose unique values can serve as the identifier for all members within the family. Many families may have more than one of these common uniquely valued attributes, and groups within the family may also have their own identifier attributes which identify members of the group uniquely. Although identifier attributes are usually more manageable when they consist of a single data element, there is no requirement that they be so. In some cases, it may be necessary and preferable to use multiple data elements as such an identifier.

As an example, each member of the employee family within the firm has a unique identifier called "identifier of the employee." Within the family of employees salespeople are assigned a unique identifier "identifier of salespeople." This identifier is created from a combination of sales region, sales territory, and sales office identifiers plus a sequential number within each office. This combination of data elements is unique across the firm.

Primary Identifiers

The design team must identify at least one primary identifier attribute for each family, and should also identify any potential secondary (which may potentially be nonunique, or not common to all members of the family) identifiers. They must also determine

- Does the proposed identifier attribute always occur, or only occur most of the time?
- Can the potential identifier's values change over time or are they fixed?
- Can the same identifier value be reassigned to other family members or is the identifier a single-use value? For instance, the social security number of an employee is a single-use number, but an internally assigned number may be reused some number of years after the employee leaves the firm or dies.
- Can nonunique identifiers be qualified to entity member uniqueness?

Since each entity in the full data model represents a composite of all members of an entity family, the designers may want to consider extracting certain common data, which are not entity family candidates into a pseudoentity. This pseudoentity is essentially similar to the process control entity we discussed in the chapter on the classification model, but is used to contain the common rates and tables which help to define and control the operations of the business system and its environment.

This "rates and tables" entity family can be used to contain the expanded descriptions or values of common data, such as state code to state name translations, extensive code lists for editing, verification and presentation purposes, etc. This can be used for highly dynamic data which is frequently changed and constantly referenced (such entities as interest rate tables, etc.).

The use of this type of entity family will remove many conversions and tabular searches from the application code and individual processing procedures. These rates and tables become part of the common system data and ease maintenance. Each table entry must however be dated with the dates of effectivity and discontinuance.

The alternative to this type of entity is to include code value and expansion lists with each coded element. This approach is viable when the list of codes is relatively small and static, and is an important part of the system documentation. Entity member attribute values are not ordinarily documented in the system design, since they are not considered part of the design.

Once all data elements within each attribute have been identified, the design team must define each data element. Each element, element aggregate, and attribute should be fully defined and include a narrative or discussion of expected content, expected usage, and potential usage.

Data Element Definition

It is not enough to identify a data element, or to assign it a location or even a name, however meaningful. For all the preceding analysis and work to be meaningful we must define and describe each data element, so that it can be used, processed, and above all be supportive of the business. These definitions support the business requirement for understanding the meaning of data and support the firm's ability to use its data in a consistent and reliable manner.

If data is a corporate asset, that data must have value. The value of data lies in its timeliness, its accuracy, its relationship to other data, and most of all in the ability of the firm's management and operations personnel to understand the meaning, derivation, and source of the data.

From a data processing perspective, which is to a large degree one of data manipulation and data presentation, the primary interest in a data element is its size and format, shape, and value set. From a business perspective, much more is needed. The additional information needed includes

- What it is
- Where it is
- How it is used
- Its format in reports and other presentation methods
- When it is used
- Who uses it
- Where it comes from
- Who can change it, when can it be changed, and under what conditions can it be changed
- Who can see it
- When can it be removed from the files and who can remove it
- Its legal value ranges

Each data element has been assigned a name which represents its location and value type. These names are descriptive in and of themselves. Some data elements named are context specific, while others do not reflect a specific context. These noncontext-specific data elements are more generalized, both in name and content. The definition of a domain element (not context specific) describes its values and derivation, while its specific data model meaning is only available from the context-specific versions. For instance, date represents a specific value range and format. Date of birth of employee represents a particular date, that of a specific employee. Taken as a whole date of birth represents the value range of all dates for all employees. The definition of date is constant, only the meaning of the particular date varies. Date could be any value date in the calendar.

Context Element Definition

The context element definition describes what is unique about this data element occurrence and refers to the domain element for all definitional aspects of date. This approach allows the firm to make one change to the domain element which has the effect of automatically changing the definitions of all context elements. While consistency is desirable it is nevertheless permissible and sometimes desirable to treat each element independently, creating definitions which are appropriate rather than uniform. Thus the full range of data element definitions may become a combination of treatments and the choice is dictated by the elements rather than adherence to rules.

Each data element is described at its lowest level of occurrence as a self-contained unit. In addition, any grouping of elements which has meaning below the level of attribute should be defined as well and related upward and downward to its superior or subordinate parts. To illustrate: The data element "date of birth of employee" is composed of three subelements, "month of birth of employee," "day of birth of employee," and "year of birth of employee." All four elements have meaning and all four should be defined.

What then are the components of an element definition? Another way to phrase the question and perhaps a more meaningful question is what do the managers and operational personnel of the firm need to know about an individual data element, and moreover, what should they know about that element.

Definition Components

This phase of data element analysis is the one which ties together all of the documentation narratives from all other design products. The definition of each data element consists of the following parts:

1. Physical and logical format definition
2. Narrative definition
3. Cross reference information
4. Value ranges and code lists
5. Source and use information
6. Context-specific meaning
7. Derivation or calculation
8. Time reference or time frame information
9. Individual element editing, verification and validation information
10. Multidata element or context editing, verification and validation
11. User alias and context alias names
12. Attribute, entity group, and entity family context
13. Default values
14. Data content, usage, source, or other critical design assumptions with respect to this element

Each data element must be examined both from an overall design perspective and from a context-specific perspective. Data elements must be examined for consistency of form and and definition. Derived elements must be consistent with the elements from which they were derived or which were used to derive them.

Code structures must be examined to determine if all possible values have been accounted for (both current and projected).

Each data element should have a narrative description that is as complete as possible. That description (or definition) should indicate exactly what the contents of the element represent. The description should reflect a single occurrence of the element if it is a repeating element. These narratives should reflect all the assumptions, comments, and specifications from all the narratives generated in all previous design products.

Derived Element Definition

For each calculated or derived data element the formula for calculation or derivation should be included in the data element documentation description. Each element that participates in the calculation and that are functions of the calculation should be listed. The definition of each of those data elements should in turn indicate the name of each calculated data element that references them.

Once the data element definitions and descriptions are complete, they must be examined within the context of each place this element is used, if it appears more than once. The design team must ensure that the definition, exactly as written, is applicable where this element is used.

Any inconsistencies in definition or usage should be resolved. If necessary, new elements should be created to ensure complete consistency of meaning and use.

Format definition describes the length, number of characters or digits, number of decimal digits, precision, and format editing criteria (planation, dollar sign usage, use of commas and periods, use of spaces, justification, etc.) of the data element from the user's perspective.

The length of each element and its precision, if applicable, should reflect its current and anticipated value ranges. The design team must determine

The largest value the element can assume

The largest number of characters in the longest name

The largest amount that can be anticipated

The most number of characters necessary

For identifiers:

What is the largest projected number of entity occurrences?

For attribute identifiers:

What is the largest number of occurrences of this subset we can have?

For coded elements:

What is the maximum anticipated range of each code?

Element Sizing

As a general rule, if more than 75 percent of the capacity of an element with known data values has been used, it should be expanded, unless by its nature it can be determined that the current capacity is sufficient.

For each element:

Determine whether or not it must be present and if it is present what are its editing criteria?

What are the maximum and minimum values permissible?

What is the default value if no user-supplied value is given?

What actions are to be taken if the element does not pass the editing tests?

If this element value is dependent upon or derived from the value of some other element, how are those dependencies found? What are those derivations?

If this element is conditionally present, based either on the presence or absence of some other element or elements, what are those conditions and data elements? Conditional presence and conditional contents should be noted both in this element and in the definition of the other conditional elements.

Where an element is coded, all possible values or functions of that code should be listed in tabular form with the code value as the argument and the description or definition or meaning of that code as the function.

All the data element definition and description documentation should be reviewed by all user areas of the organization. This will ensure that all users agree that the definitions supplied are correct, accurate, and complete. All code value lists and all derivation calculations or rules must be verified with the users. All documented assumptions should be reviewed and approved by the user community.

Any discrepancies, misrepresentations, or incorrect definitions should be revised, corrected, and submitted for reapproval. Each user area should "sign-off" on the documentation. Any later amendments should be reviewed by any users who have previously "signed-off."

Chapter

18

Entity Families, Attributes, and Normalization

Regardless of how well the definitions are written or the entity groups and entity families constructed, not all members of a group will be exactly alike. A model where all group members are exactly alike would be excessively cumbersome and would in all probability result in an overly large number of very small groups. Thus the data model seeks composite descriptions—descriptions which cover all possible member attribute configurations.

However, each entity occurrence is also unique in that it has its own distinct set of physical attributes (descriptors), operational attributes, and relationships. Thus the assumption cannot be made that all data elements within the composite model of the entity family will, or even should, be present or active for any given entity group or entity occurrence of the entity family. On a composite basis, however, all the attributes and data elements are needed to describe the entities in the family.

Just as there are various groups of entities within a family, there are also various groups of attributes within the data model which correspond to those groups. For instance, all customers have demographic attributes, however the demographic data for a doctor and a teacher are different and these in turn are different from the demographics of a school which in turn is different from those of a hospital. If doctors, teachers, schools, and hospitals are all customers then the demographic attributes for each kind of customer are determined by a characteristic of that customer—*type of customer* (doctor, teacher, school, hospital).

The attributes of entity occurrences, entity groups, and entity families are determined partly by the characteristics of each, and partly by the data indicated by the business rules of the firm states. Different types of attribute data are dependent upon the characteristic value. In the same manner that characteristics are cumulative (they chain together in increasingly longer chains), attributes also chain together in increasingly longer chains.

Attributes, Characteristics, and Data Elements

For purposes of explanation and further discussion we will repeat our earlier definitions of attribute and characteristic and add a definition for data element.

Definition. An *attribute* is some aspect or descriptor of an entity. The entity is described in terms of its attributes. An attribute may contain one or more highly interrelated data elements. Attributes have no meaning, existence, or interest to the firm except in terms of the entity they describe.

Definition. A *characteristic* is a special multipurpose, single data element attribute whose *discrete values* serve to identify, describe, or otherwise distinguish or set apart one thing or group of things from another.

Definition. A *data element* is the smallest, meaningful unit of data within the data model.

A *data group* is a collection of data elements which have been given a group name for purposes of documentation, reference, or processing convenience. A data group may be as small as two data elements or it may be a reference to a very large (defined or undefined) group of data elements. Some examples of a data groups are *date* (month, day, year), *address* (first address line, second address line, city, state, zip code), *company financial data* (undefined).

An attribute is a data group containing very specific, interrelated data, and is treated in much the same manner as we treat entity groups. Figure 18.1 illustrates the relationship between attributes, data groups, and data elements. We break down or decompose attributes in the same manner as we break down the entity family. In fact since the entity family is a data model construct we can say that the entity family represents the label of all data needed about the entities in that family. The entity group represents only the data which is specific to that entity group. Thus, as we group entities within the family we are also grouping data at the same time, since each entity group also iden-

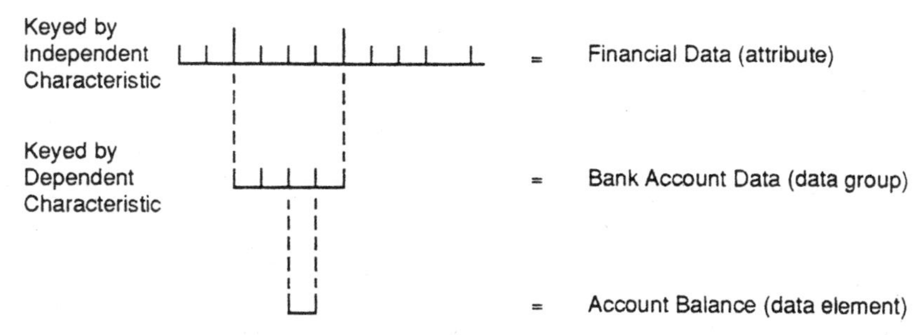

Figure 18.1 Attributes, data groups, and data elements.

tifies some specific type of data which makes it different from other entity groups. The minimum data difference between entity groups is the characteristic value which determined the group membership.

An attribute may be a very abstract or general category of information (at the entity family level), a specific element of data (at the entity occurrence level), or a level of aggregation between these two extremes (at the entity group level). Most attributes appear as clusters of highly interrelated elements of data which in combination describe the specific aspect of the entity as represented and identified by its characteristics. Each characteristic identifies a different group of data elements. Even attributes or data groups which appear not to be characteristic-based are (for the most part they are based upon the entity occurrence identifier characteristic). The data values of attribute data elements are not critical to the development of the data model and in most cases they are unique to an entity occurrence. Only characteristic values are critical. The data model must however document the valid ranges of the data element content, their format, editing rules, etc.

The following will illustrate the relationship between attributes, characteristics, and data elements.

In a previous illustration (Figure 18.2) we had two named groups—exempt employees and nonexempt employees—classified by *pay status* (nonexempt, exempt).

Nonexempt employees are entitled to overtime pay, which is calculated through a series of formulas established by the business rules of the firm. One attribute of nonexempt employees could be called *nonexempt pay factors* which is identified by the *pay status* characteristic value *nonexempt*. This attribute includes all data elements used to determine how the employee is to be compensated (agreed-upon work week, agreed-upon work hours per day, agreed-upon work start time, agreed-upon end time, base hourly rate, rate per overtime hour, rates/shift, etc.) all of which are needed to determine what the base pay is, when overtime is to be paid, and how much is to be paid for overtime.

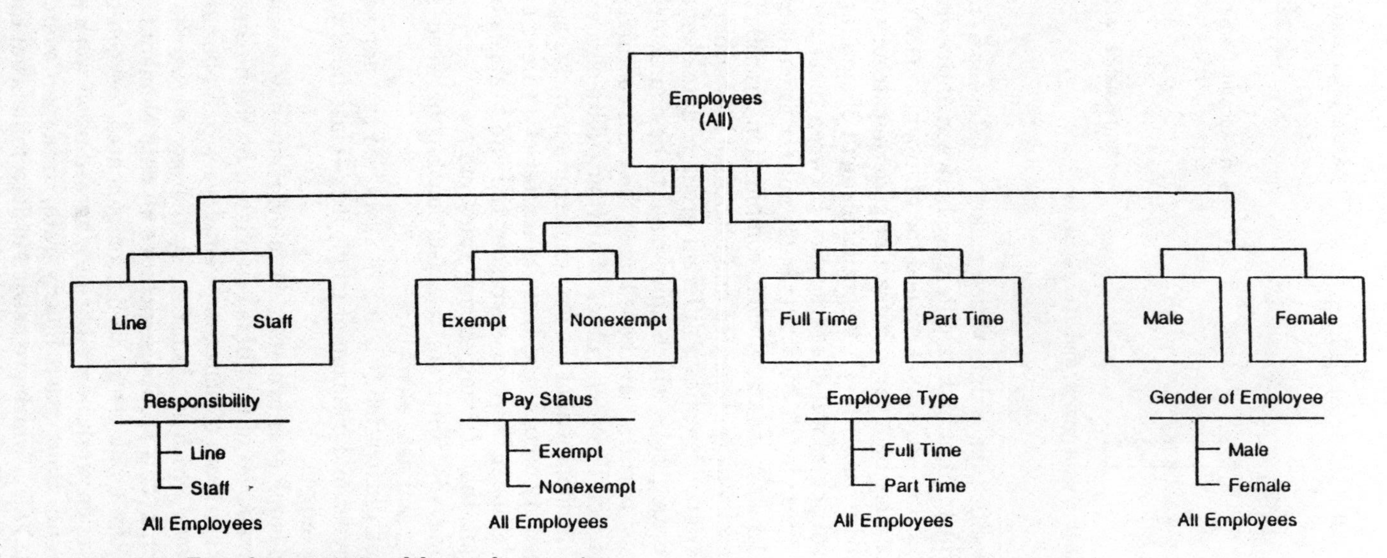

Figure 18.2 Four characteristics of the employee entity.

This characteristic-dependent group of data (attribute) could be expressed as a formula (with illustrative values) as follows:

Attribute name – nonexempt pay factors
= [pay status = nonexempt, agreed-upon work week = 5 days, agreed-upon work hours per day = 8, agreed-upon work start time = 8:00 A.M., agreed-upon work end times = 16:00 P.M., base hourly rate = $12.50, rate per overtime hour = $18.75]

If the business rules determined that overtime was based upon the shift worked instead of a rate for each hour over the agreed-upon hours, then an additional characteristic would be needed—*shift worked* (first shift, second shift, third shift, fourth shift) and there would be one attribute for nonexempt (data common to all nonexempt employees), and one attribute for each shift.

These characteristic-dependent groups of data (attributes) could be expressed as a series of formulas (with illustrative values) as follows:

Attribute name – nonexempt
= [pay status = nonexempt, shift worked = shift number, agreed-upon work week = 5 days, agreed-upon work hours per day = 8]

Attribute name – nonexempt first shift pay factors
= [pay status = nonexempt, shift worked = first shift, agreed-upon work start time = 8:00 A.M., agreed-upon work end times = 16:00 P.M., base hourly rate = $12.00, rate per overtime hour = $18.00]

Attribute name – nonexempt second shift pay factors
= [pay status = nonexempt, shift worked = second shift, agreed-upon work start time = 16:00 P.M., agreed-upon work end times = 24:00 P.M., base hourly rate = $18.00, rate per overtime hour = $24.00]

There would also be attributes for third and fourth shift pay factors. Each attribute illustrated above is identified by a specific set of values of a specific set of characteristics. The combination of independent and dependent characteristic values (pay status and shift worked, respectively) is the chain which identifies that attribute. All the elements in each attribute work as a group, and each attribute is relevant to a specific fact of the employee. It should be obvious that (repeating) characteristic-dependent data groups in reality could, and do, represent smaller groups of employees (a further qualification of pay status by the characteristic shift worked).

Classification and Normalization

Normalization is an after-the-fact process for correcting the grouping of data when a design is developed inductively. Classification is a before-the-fact process for grouping data when a design is developed deductively. Put another way normalization is classification performed in bottom-up design, classification is normalization performed in top-down design.

Both processes attempt to determine the proper groupings of data for maximum data integrity. The term *data integrity* is used to describe that property of data which refers to its resilience to inadvertent and unintentional change. Inadvertent change may occur when a change is made to one type of data and that change also changes the meaning, but not necessarily the values, of other data associated with it. For instance, assume that an address is associated with a customer record. If we also assume that the customer's telephone number is stored in another part of the file, it is possible to change either the address or the phone number, which are dependent upon each other, without changing both. This causes a data inconsistency. If each address has a city name, state, and zip code associated with it, it is possible for the zip code in one record to reflect a different city and/or state than in another, when in fact a zip code uniquely identifies both city and state. Again there is a data inconsistency within the file.

Another kind of data integrity problem manifests itself when one part of related data is removed from the file while another remains. For instance, if we assume that vendor invoices are stored in one part of the file and vendor information is stored in another, then it is possible for the vendor information to be removed while the vendor invoice still remains.

Another more subtle form of data integrity problem may arise when seemingly independent data is stored independently and is subsequently found to be dependent. For instance, assume an order is written for a particular part, and the customer is quoted a price from the part description file. If that is the only place the price is stored, then if that price subsequently changes, it may retroactively change all orders which use that file for reference. In this case the quoted price for the part should have been stored with the invoice line item since it is dependent on the order and date, or the prior prices for the part should have been saved with their effective dates (from and to) so that the original quoted price for the invoice could be retained.

The topic of normalization was first proposed in 1970 in the *Communications of the ACM* by E. F. Codd within the context of his description of the relational data base form. Normalization has been expanded upon and commented upon by both C. J. Date and William Kent. Today, there are many variations of the normal forms, but the most popular is known as the Codd-Date-Kent normal forms. These normal forms are expressed as a set of rules, which if followed will arrange data for storage in a manner such that its integrity is virtually assured. There are three basic rules, corresponding to the three basic normal forms, as well as more advance rules which if followed place data in what is known as fourth, fifth, and higher normal forms. The effect of normalization is to organize data around identifiers and characteristics, in successively finer and more restrictive groupings. If followed to its ultimate end normalization could result in data groupings of one or two data elements each. Data processing systems and data modelers should use these rules judiciously and should strive to achieve a balance between data models which ensure a high degree of integrity and data models which are practical from an implementation sense.

There are several other factors which should influence the grouping of data within a file. These include user access, data ownership, data maintenance requirements, data acquisition constraints, and the performance requirements and constraints of the DBMS under which the data file is implemented.

In a 1986 article in the *Auerbach Systems Development Management Series,* Kent discusses normalization within the framework of normal forms, that is, levels of grouping. He states that "the aim of normal forms is to ensure that if a record represents more than one fact, they are all single-valued facts about the same subject, and nothing else."

A single-valued fact is, as its name implies, a data element that has one and only one value. For instance, an employee's records may provide for educational courses taken. Since the employee may take several courses, the course-taken element can have multiple values. This may be represented by a repeating field (course-1, course-2, etc.) or it may be represented by multiple records each of which indicates the employee identifier and the course name. Since multivalued facts are common in the real world, and since most DBMS products allow for multivalued facts this is not normally a problem. However, the need to identify these elements and to store them properly is necessary, and since each DBMS treats these multivalued facts differently, and since some place severe restrictions on their use, the model must allow for all treatments.

Many of these constraints on data, such as when a data element may or may not have multiple values, may be designed into the DBMS or they may be handled procedurally.

The end result of the normalization process, as with the classification process, is to ensure that each data element is uniquely identifiable, that all data elements used to describe a given entity are grouped together, and that data about multiple entities are not intermixed within the same records.

The first normal form consists of grouping atomic form data around a single key with all repeating groups eliminated. The first normal form also specifies that all records of a given type must have the same number of data elements. This condition is usually interpreted to mean that repeating groups with variable numbers of repetitions are eliminated. Since these variable repeating groups or multivalued facts are both common and necessary, the first normal form restructures the data to break repeating groups into multiple single element records which can themselves repeat multiple times. The classification step which most closely corresponds to this is the development of the entity families and the grouping of entities and data by characteristic value.

Second normal form ensures that no single-valued facts are dependent on only part of a key (identifier). Many designers develop records with composite keys, that is, keys which combine the identifiers of two separate entities. These records are then used to store mixed data, data about each entity independently and data about the composite keyed entity. For instance, a record may be constructed with the composite key of vehicle identifier and garage identifier. The data elements in that record may describe the garage name, the vehicle name, and the date and cost of storing that vehicle in that garage. This poses a maintenance problem since the garage name may change and thus all records containing that name will also have to change.

The modeling techniques described in this book remove that problem since only records that represent relationships are allowed to have composite keys. All other records have as their key the entity identifier and one or more characteristics.

Using classification, data groups are determined by explicit or implicit characteristics. Repeating data groups are sets of data which occur in identical form more than once. Since each data group contains an identical set of data elements, and each occurrence means something, there must be an implicit or explicit characteristic associated with each occurrence to distinguish one from another. Each occurrence is distinguished by a unique value which determines data group element contents and usage. A complete data model should show these as separate groups of data each keyed by the characteristic. Characteristic analysis and identification and characteristic value-based data grouping eliminate the need for this step. Since data is grouped about a characteristic chain and grouped at each level about the characteristic values at that level, second normal form is always ensured.

Third normal form removes data dependent upon the other data within the data group. The use of both independent and dependent characteristics to identify the key structures for every data group, and the use of attribute and data group logic, ensures that every data grouping is accurately identified, and that subsequent data element assignment of all data in a data group is fully key dependent. Although these are usually referred to as functional dependency data groups in the normalization process, they are in fact characteristic-dependent data groups, a condition much more clearly represented and understood from the classification viewpoint.

The ER model development segregates data about each entity into sets of records which describe only that entity. When data is necessary about two entities as a pair, a relationship is established. Thus in the example above the composite key of vehicle and garage would be replaced by a relationship "vehicle is stored in garage" and any data pertaining to the storage of that car in that garage is maintained in the relationship record which by definition must have multiple keys. Fourth normal form removes multiple multivalued dependent data from a given record. Most multivalued data elements are also characteristics.

Classification is completely value dependent, and each classification data group is dependent not only on a chain of characteristics (data elements) but on a chain of characteristic values.

A data model developed using classification techniques will not require a subsequent normalization step since all data is completely and logically classified and organized. This complete and logical classification and organization of data is the goal of both normalization and classification.

ER Models, Classification, and Normalization

Many of the problems of data grouping which normalization attempts to rectify are eliminated by data models which are based upon the ER model and on classification analysis. The data models described above use classification of data within the entity and intensional characteristics.

Many of the same techniques and much of the same logic are used to analyze the relationships between entity families (and entity groups within a family). The relationships of interest to the firm and the expression of those relationships are dependent upon the business rules of the firm and the entity family characteristics.

Although classification removes much of the need for normalization, a normalization pass should be made on the final design to detect and correct any errors within the characteristic value-dependent data groups. Any errors detected should only be violations of fourth and fifth normal form, although some third normal form violations may slip through undetected by the classification analysis.

Chapter

19

Translating the Data Model for Implementation

Each of the data structural models has different operational and implementation characteristics, and these differences influence the capabilities and restrictions of the data structures themselves. The natural structure of the data is one of the major factors in the determination of which DBMS is most appropriate; thus, it is important to understand how each structure looks at data and which kinds of data are most suited for each structure.

Each DBMS allows data to be fragmented, according to the same or very similar sets of rules, and in roughly the same manner. They differ in the manner each employs for connecting those fragments into larger logical data structures. Each DBMS uses a different type of data structure diagram that depicts

1. The mode of connection of the data segments within the larger data aggregates
2. The dependencies of the data segments within the larger data aggregates
3. The allowable or supported data access paths between each of the segments
4. The structure model of the logical data record (or entity) for that DBMS
5. How these data aggregates are defined to the DBMS itself

The Data Model View of the Hierarchic Model

The hierarchic diagram (Figure 19.1) presents the data fragments in a an inverted tree structure. This inverted tree represents the data segmentation, the segment connections, and the inherent dependencies of those segments. Each tree structure represents the collection of data about one type of entity and is also called a logical data record. There can only be one hierarchic structure per data base. A special implementation of the tree structure allows multiple tree structures to be combined into a larger tree, which is also called a logical data record; however each component tree is still defined as a separate data base.

All access to the logical data record is through the base (Figure 19.2) or root segment. It is this segment that contains the unique identifier(s), or keys, for the entity occurrence being described. A data base contains multiple tree occurrences, each of which pertains to a specific entity occurrence. Each unique entity within a given data base may have its own configuration of occurrences or nonoccurrences of each segment type defined for the general entity hierarchy.

The tree structure diagram depicts each segment type only once. However, aside from the root segment of each structure, there can be multiple occurrences of any given dependent segment type within the structure. Each data segment beneath the root segment describes some aspect of the base entity. These dependent segments may be keyed, or unkeyed, depending on their contents, usage, and number of occurrences. Dependent segment keys may be unique, or duplicated, both within and across occurrences.

Within the hierarchy, root level segments relate only to segments directly dependent to them. The access path to any segment beneath the root segment must include all of its immediate hierarchic predecessors,

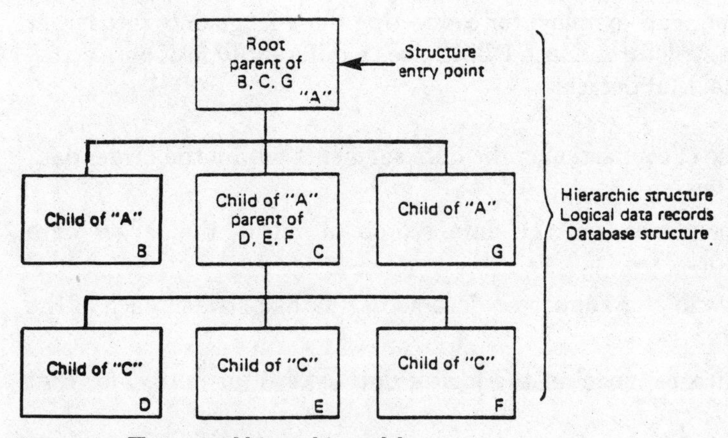

Figure 19.1 The general hierarchic model.

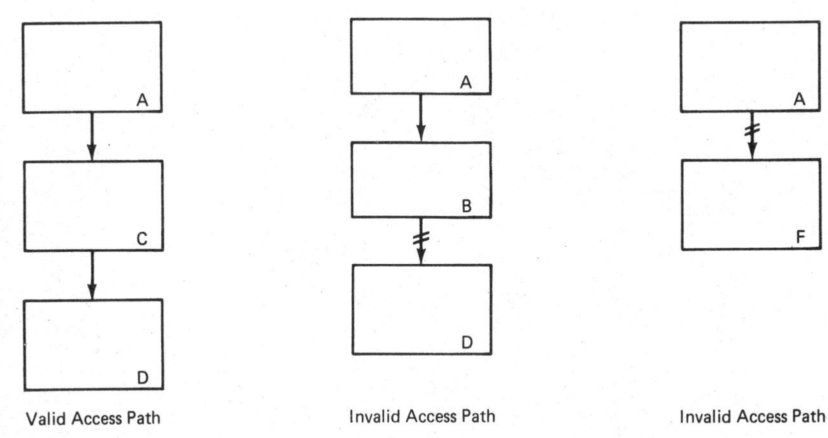

Figure 19.2 Access paths for the hierarchic model.

or parents, on a direct path from the root, as defined in the hierarchic structure.

Segments at the same level below the root (1) cannot relate to each other, (2) must relate as children to only one parent segment at the next higher level within the hierarchy, or to the root itself, and (3) may relate as a parent to any number of child segments, each of which must be one level lower in the hierarchy. These level-to-level, or parent-to-child, dependencies, imply that the lower-level segments (children) have no meaning and, indeed, cannot exist without the higher (in terms of position within the hierarchy) level segments (parents). The hierarchic model is most effective when

1. Each hierarchic structure contains data about a single entity and each entity is relatively homogeneous, having few distinct subtypes.
2. The primary access to each hierarchy is via the identifier of the entity.
3. The entity being described is rich in descriptive attributes, and these attributes occur in multiples, or not at all.
4. Entity occurrences are processed one at a time.

The Data Model View of the Network Model

The network diagram (Figure 19.3) has no implicit hierarchic relationship between the segment types and in many cases, no implicit structure at all, with the record types seemingly placed at random. Record types are grouped in sets of two, one or both of which can, in turn, be part of another two-record type set. Within each set, one record type is

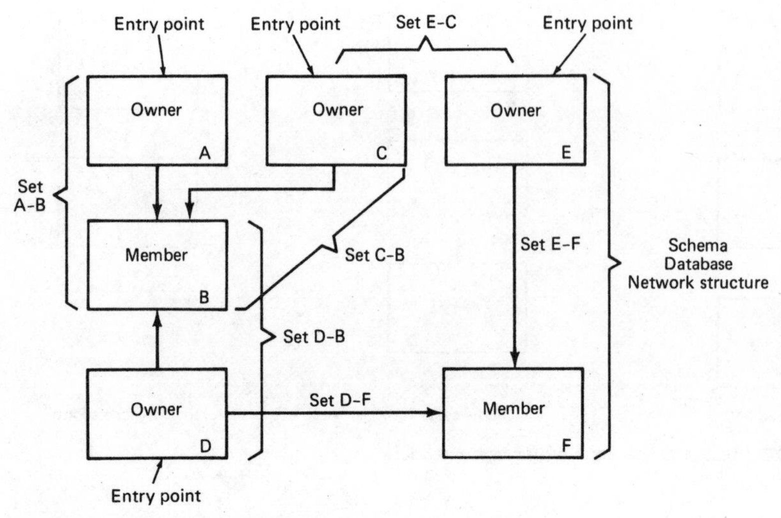

Figure 19.3 The general network model.

the owner of this set (or parent) and the other is the member (or child). Each record type of these parent-child (or owner-member) sets may, in turn, relate to other records as a parent or a child. Each set represents data about a specific entity, and thus each owner is keyed uniquely.

Each record within the overall diagrammatic structure must be either an owner or a member of a set within the structure. Normally, each set is accessed through the owner record type, each of which contains the identifier, or key, of a specific occurrence of the set type. Each record type may be keyed or unkeyed, and key fields may contain unique or duplicated values. Because each record type in each set can be joined to any other record type in any other set, this structure allows highly flexible access paths through the various record types for processing purposes.

Because each record can be related to one or more other records, a network diagram depicts a web of data records with their various interconnections. This composite of all records and all relationships is said to be a schema, and the entire schema is considered to be the data base. Firms using network-based DBMSs usually have all data defined under one master schema. A schema may have multiple entry points, one at each owner of each set.

Unlike the hierarchic model, where each tree structure is a logical data record, there are no discernible logical data records within a network diagram. Instead each application can create its own logical data records from any combination of sets. These logical data records can then be segregated from the master schema by means of a subschema definition.

There are no levels within the network model and thus no level-to-level or parent-to-child dependencies beyond those of owner to member. Access to any segment may be direct or through its owner. Any given segment may own or be owned by (be related to) any number of other segments, with the restriction that (1) any pair of segments thus connected must be related through a uniquely named set and (2) any given segment occurrence within a set may have only one owner.

Within the network model, hierarchic relationships (Figure 19.4) may be depicted by having one segment own (through multiple sets) many other segments; each of these owned segments (members) may, in turn, own multiple other segments, again through named sets.

Within this hierarchy, however, and subject to set construction restrictions, segment types at the same level may relate to each other as either owners or members of sets, and segments at any level may relate directly to segments at any other level. Segment types may be directly related to segments at multiple other levels, either above or below the immediate level of the segments, may be related to segments outside the hierarchy through named sets, and may have multiple hierarchic parents and multiple hierarchic dependents or children.

The network model is most effective when

1. Used to contain data about multiple entities that are connected in complex relationships.
2. The multiple primary accesses to the data structure may be through the identifiers of the entities themselves or through their relationships with other entities.
3. There are multiple entity groups, each with different attribute descriptors and the dependent attributes of these entity groups occur in multiples, or not at all.

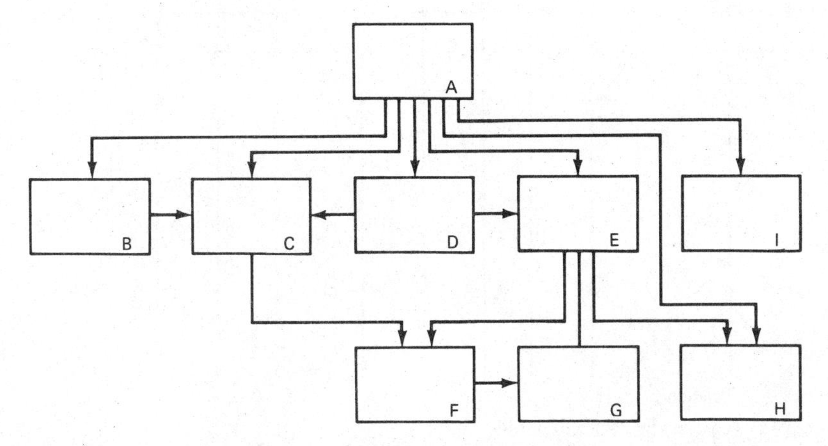

Figure 19.4 A hierarchy within a network model.

4. There are few, if any, hierarchic relationships between the entity attributes.
5. The applications need to see the universe of data entities and their relationships and process transactions that are aimed at many interrelated entities.

The Data Model View of the Relational Model

The relational diagram (Figure 19.5) represents each record type in tabular form, and all records of the same type are contained in a single table. Thus the relational model is organized around record types and not around entities.

The relational model has no implicit structure aside from the table. There are no fixed parent-child or any other relationships within a relational environment. Instead, each table may be related to any or all of the other tables in any number of ways. Any single table, or any combination of two or more tables, may be accessed by any application. Unlike the network and hierarchic models the relational model does not support any physical record-to-record connections. Each freestanding table is known as a relation, and each entry within each table is known as a tuple, or more commonly, a row. Whereas all data manipulation op-

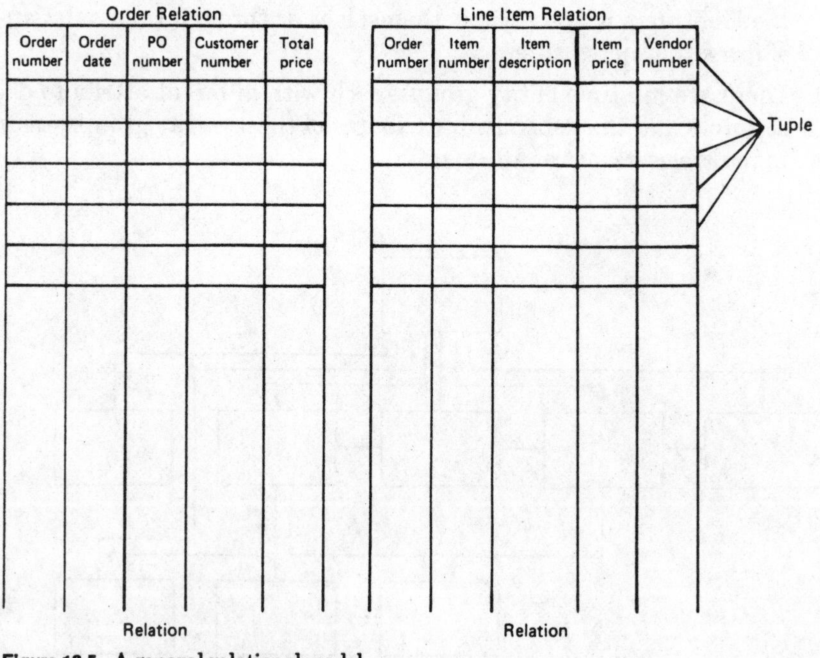

Order Relation

Order number	Order date	PO number	Customer number	Total price

Relation

Line Item Relation

Order number	Item number	Item description	Item price	Vendor number

Tuple

Relation

Figure 19.5 A general relational model.

erations are "record at a time" (where each record must be accessed through its key or through its relationship with, or proximity to, another record) within the network and hierarchic models, data manipulation within the relational model is "set (or table) at a time," where the set of rows accessed may be as few as one or as many as exist in the table.

Each application can create its own logical data records (Figure 19.6) from any combinations, or portions, of tables as needed. These logical data records can then be accessed and manipulated by means of user views or "projections." Although each data table contains data assigned according to a primary key for the entries of the table, there is no ex-

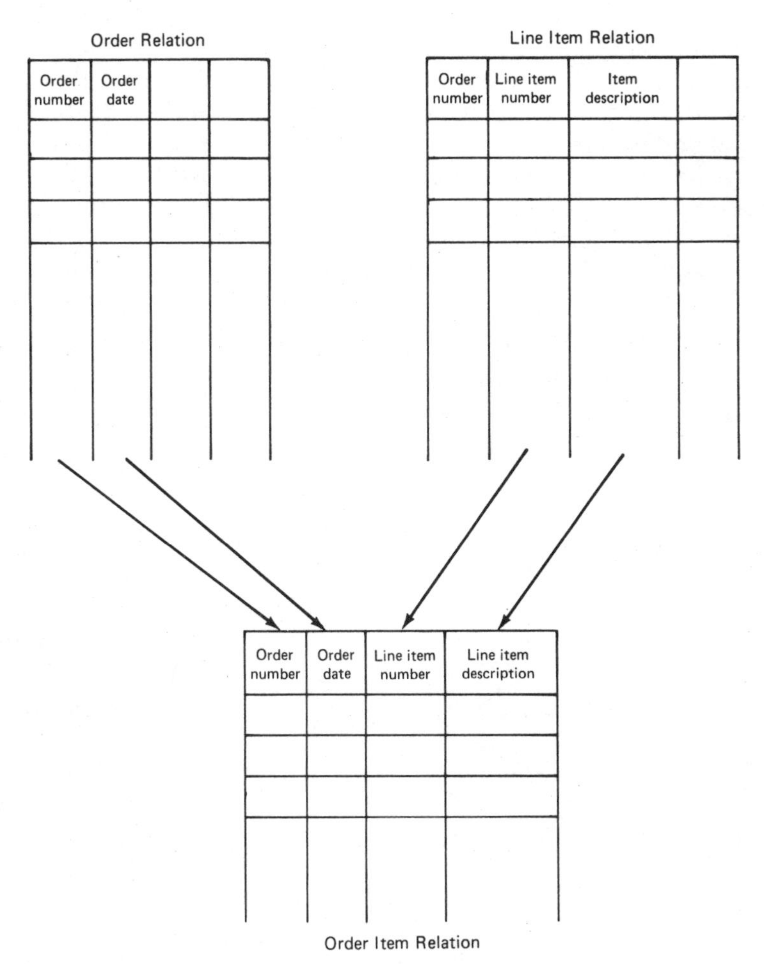

Figure 19.6 New tables created from portions of others.

plicit sequence to the entries of a table, and the table may be accessed via the contents of any field (or column) of data within it.

A table may contain any number of rows, and a row within a table may contain any number of data elements, with the restriction that all data elements must be atomic, that is, they must be defined at their lowest possible level of decomposition, they must be nonrepeating, and they must be uniquely named within a table. Each table must have a data element column(s) defined as a primary key, to permit each row to be uniquely identified, and the primary key field of each row must contain a unique value. All occurrences of a data element within a given column of a table must be identically defined and must contain a data value or a null entry. Each row of a given table must have an identical set of data elements.

Tables may be related, or joined, in any sequence, any table may start the sequence of joins, and a table may be joined to itself. Any number of tables (Figure 19.7) may be related together, provided that each table, or each pair of tables, to be joined has a column of data that is identical in definition and is populated from an identical range of values (or domain). Any given table can be directly joined with only two other tables at any one time and the tables must be connected in sequence, although the sequence of table joins is immaterial.

The relational model is most effective when

1. Each table contains data about a single entity group.
2. Each entity family is homogeneous with little, if any, difference between entity groups.

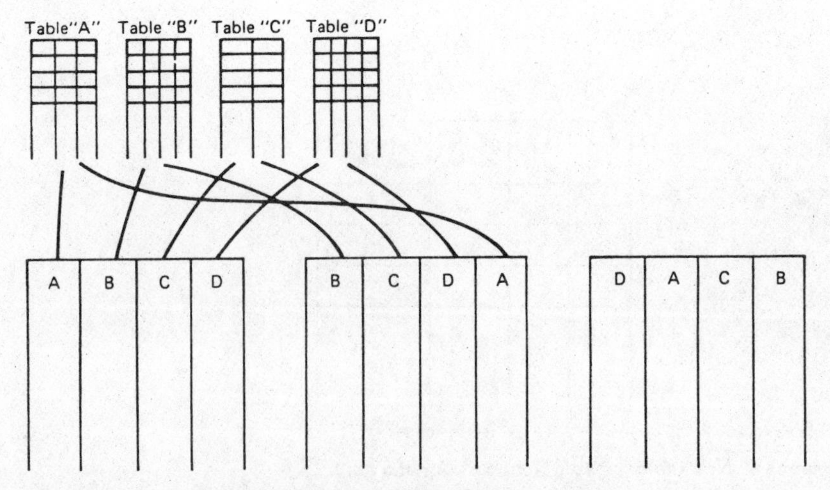

Figure 19.7 Any number of tables may be joined in any sequence.

3. All data elements within a given table relate only to the primary key of the table.
4. The table data must be accessed in multiple sequence or via the contents of any data element within the table.
5. There are multiple entities or entity groups, each with different attribute descriptors and all of which are related to each other in some way.
6. The dependent attributes of each entity occur singularly or not at all.
7. There are no intervening or hierarchic relationships between the entity and its attributes.
8. The applications must see the universe of data entities related in complex ways for retrieval purposes.
9. The applications process update transactions that can be applied to one entity table at a time and not to more than one table.

Translating Attributes into Records

The entity-based data model calls for the representation of each distinct attribute for each entity (Figure 19.8) and each relationship. An attribute may be a descriptor or an identifier or it may be some physical characteristic—a record of some action taken or a status descriptor. Generally, an attribute refers to a distinct category of data or information of interest about the entity, or some category of data that describes or qualifies a relationship. An attribute should not be equated to a data element, although in some cases a single data element may suffice to describe the attribute. Generally, an attribute will require more than one data element for full definition.

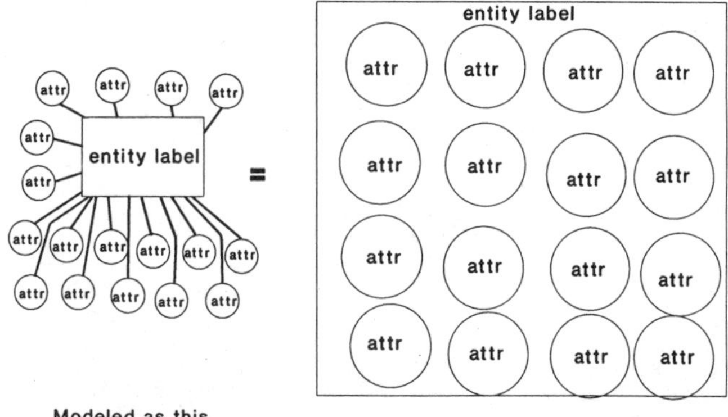

Figure 19.8 Entity attributes.

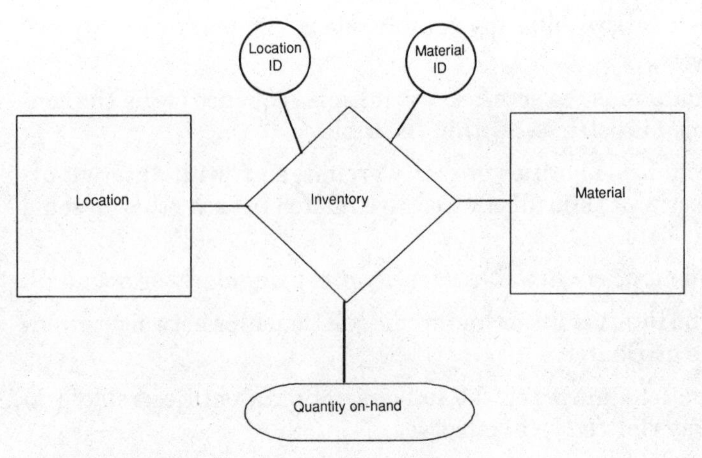

Figure 19.9 Simple relationship—three attributes.

Relationships usually have very few (Figure 19.9) attributes, although a complex relationship may have as many as a dozen or more. Entities, on the other hand, may have several dozen (Figure 19.10) attributes. The number of attributes depends on the level of interest that the firm has in the entity, the number of things the firm must know about the entity, and, more importantly, how the attributes were named and defined [the number of data elements needed to store the desired information (Figure 19.11) about the attribute].

For instance, an employee entity may have a single attribute called education, it may have two different education attributes—one internal and one external—or it may have a complex set of education attributes such as high school, college, graduate school, vendor courses, and com-

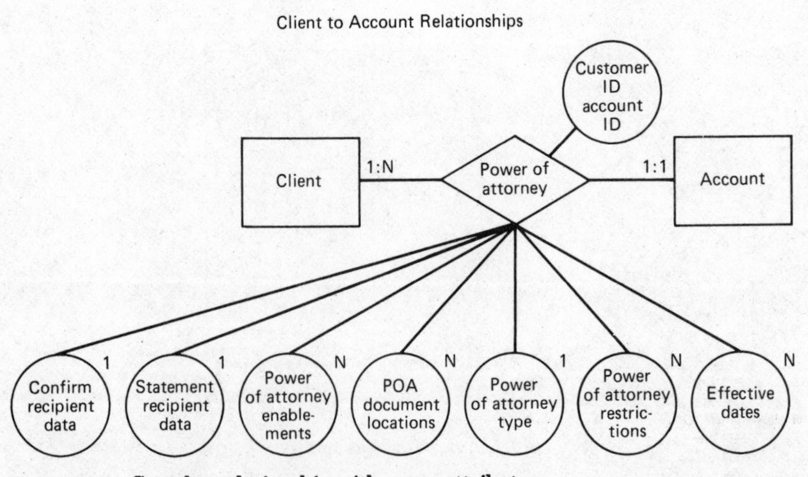

Figure 19.10 Complex relationship with many attributes.

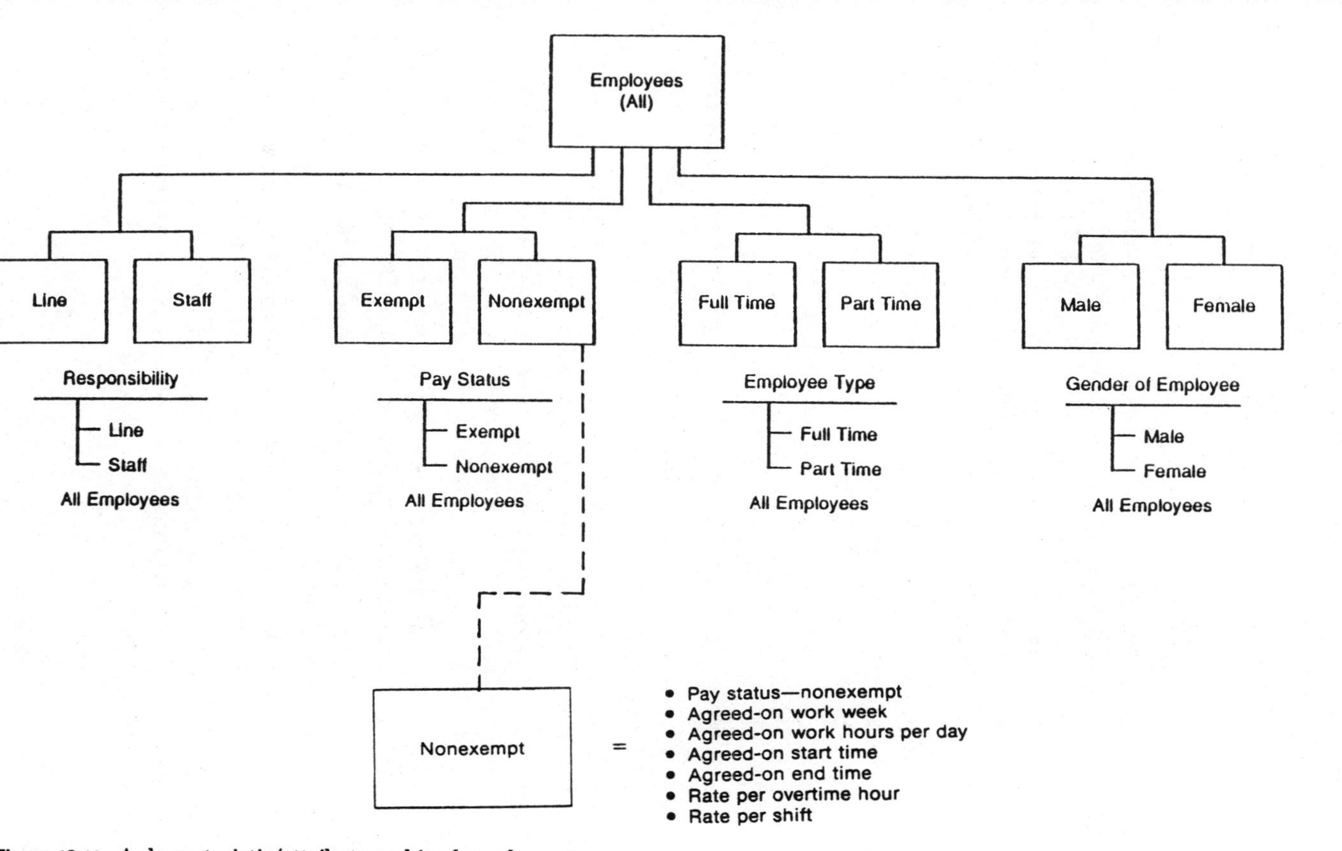

Figure 19.11 A characteristic/attribute and its data elements.

pany courses. Each of these three variations may contain the same information or may be represented differently, but they all describe the employee's education.

Because each attribute describes a different aspect or quality of the entity or relationship, conceptually each attribute is different. From an implementation perspective, however, it may be more practical to combine attribute types into more general record types. Combining attributes only serves to reduce the number of dependent segments in the hierarchic implementation, or the number of sets owned by the entity in a network implementation. Combining attributes into more generalized record types does not and should not reduce the number of data elements needed for each type of attribute. In fact, combining attributes may create the need for additional code or identifier data elements to distinguish between different attribute groupings.

There are no hard and fast rules for consolidating attributes; however the following guidelines may assist:

1. All attributes that always occur and occur only once can be combined.
2. All attributes that may occur, and if they occur, will occur only once, may be combined.
3. Attributes that originate on the same form, or are updated by data from the same form or source, may usually be combined.
4. Attributes that look the same but represent different categories of information, such as various customer address (legal, primary residence, mailing addressees, etc.), may be coded and combined.
5. Attributes that are always accessed together and change or vary according to the same set of business rules may be combined.
6. Attributes that have the same access or update restrictions (security) may be combined.
7. Attributes that have the same identifier or sequence characteristics, such as attributes that record actions by date, may be combined.
8. Attributes that contain textual data, such as special handling instructions, special shipping instructions, customer service notes or special billing instructions, may be combined.

Translating the Data Model into Hierarchic Data Structures

Within the hierarchic model, the name of the entity family or group becomes the name of the hierarchic structure. All name or identifier attributes for the entity family or group should be collected and aggregated into the root segment of the hierarchic structure. Any uniquely occurring identifier attribute can be chosen as the structure access key (root key). All other attributes of the entity become, either individually or in combination, the dependent segments of the root. Because of their direct relationship to the entity, entity hierarchies normally contain two levels, the root and the dependent. If any of the dependent segments represent data about characteristics which are further qualified by dependent characteristics then a third or even a fourth level of segment may be used. Third- and fourth-level segments may also be used for history segments.

Relationships within the hierarchic model can be implemented in a number of ways. They can be either DBMS, or programmatically maintained, and can reside within the hierarchic structure of each entity of the pair or independently of either entity. The relationships between each related pair of entities (Figures 19.12 and 19.13) must be examined one at a time.

If the relationship being examined is simple, that is, if it has few attributes, all of which are nonrepeating, a segment type should be created for it to contain the nonkey data elements that describe and qualify the relationship. That segment is then treated as if it were an attribute of each of the entities of the pair. As such, it must also contain the key or identifier of the target entity. The target entity is the opposing entity of the related pair.

If the relationship is complex, containing multiple or multioccurring attributes, it should be maintained independently of each entity. In this case, a hierarchy is set up for the relationship as if it were an entity itself, the attributes of the relationship become dependents of the relationship, and the paired keys of each entity involved are used as the combined identifier of each occurrence of the relationship. Selection of an entity for hierarchic implementation is appropriate if

1. The entity has attributes that occur multiple times.
2. Access to the entity is primarily through its primary key.

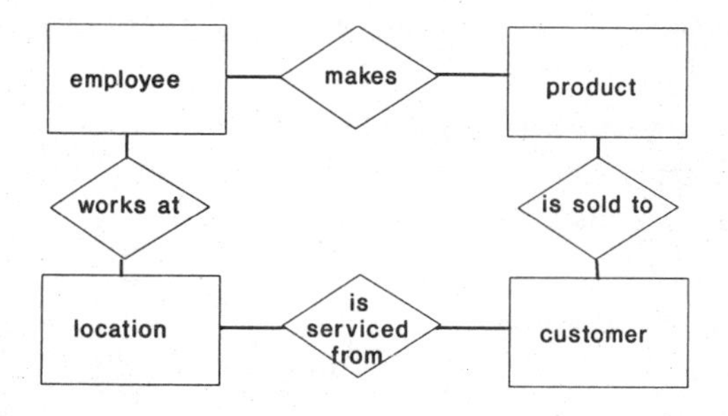

Figure 19.12 ER models—classic Chen notation.

But... what happens when

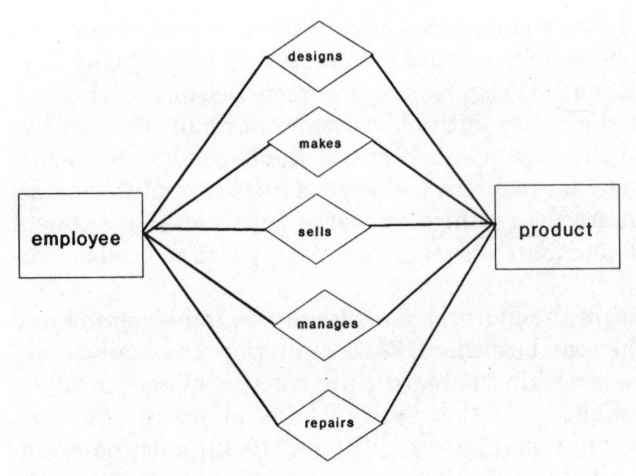

How does this affect the complexity of the model ?

Figure 19.13 ER models—classic Chen notation.

3. There are few relationships between the entities, and the relationships are well defined and relatively simple in that they require few attributes for description and qualification.
4. The relationships between the entity and any other entities are symmetrical, in that the same data can be used to support and qualify the relationship from either side of any given related pair.
5. Processing occurs against a single entity type or small group of entity types, that is, only a small number of entities (not entity occurrences) are needed by an application for reference or processing purposes at any one time.
6. Processing of the entity is either random, sequential, or both, entity at a time, and requires that all or most attributes of the entity be available at the same time.
7. The data about the entity are volatile and are changed frequently within the processing streams.
8. There are numerous entity groups within each family, each with differing attribute characteristics, and the application processing dictates that the entity family members be processed as a set.

Translating the Data Model into a Network Data Structure

Within the network model, each entity is set up as the owner of multiple sets, and that owner record contains any names or identifiers for the entity occurrence. Each attribute or combination of attributes becomes a member record of a set with the entity record as its owner.

Relationships within the network model can be implemented in a number of ways. They can be either DBMS or programmatically maintained and can reside as a set within the structure of each entity of the pair or independently of either entity. As with the hierarchic translation, the relationships between each related pair of entities must be examined one at a time.

If the relationship is simple, that is, if it has few attributes, all of which are nonrepeating, a record type should be created for it to contain the nonkey attributes that describe and qualify the relationship. These records become intersection records, which are owned by each of the related entity occurrences.

If the relationship is complex and contains multiple or multioccurring attributes, it should be maintained independently of each entity. In this case, a hierarchy or cluster is set up for the relationship as if it were an entity itself, the attributes of the relationship become members of sets of the relationship entity, and the paired keys of each entity involved are used as the combined identifier of each occurrence of the relationship entity owner. That owner record is then treated as if it were an intersection record between each of the entities of the pair.

Selection of a network implementation is appropriate if

1. Some or all of the defined entities have attributes that occur multiple times.
2. Access to each of the entities is primarily through the primary key of the entity.
3. There are many relationships between the entity families and entity groups, and the relationships are well defined and complex, requiring multiple attributes for complete description and qualification.
4. Processing of the entities usually requires that most, if not all, entity types (not entity occurrences) are needed by an application for reference or processing purposes at the same time.
5. Entity processing is either random, or sequential, or both, entity at a time, and requires that all attributes of the entity be available at the same time.
6. The entity families have been split into multiple groups, which share common attributes.
7. Entities are processed in terms of their relationships with some other entity or category.

8. The data about the entity are volatile and changed frequently within the processing streams.
9. There are numerous entity groups, each with differing attribute characteristics, and the application processing dictates that the entity be processed both as a family and by group.
10. Processing requires multiple paths through the entity structures where paths are guided by entity attribute data element values.

Translating the Data Model into Relational Data Structures

Within the relational model, only entities with certain characteristics, and without others, can translate into relational tables. The attributes of the entity, the number of occurrences of each attribute, the complexity of the relationships between those entities, and the number of groups into which each entity family has been decomposed all become determining factors.

Each distinct entity family or group becomes a relational table. The columns of the table include the identifiers of the entity and the data elements of its nonrepeating attributes. In cases where some of the entity attributes occur multiple times, each distinct attribute type that does so must be established as a separate table and keyed with the identifiers of the entity family in addition to any other characteristics or data elements required to distinguish between repetition occurrences

As with the network and hierarchic models, simple and complex relationships must be handled differently. If the relationship is simple, that is, if it has few attributes, all of which are nonrepeating, a single table can be created for it. Each row of that table implements a specific relationship occurrence between the two entities. The table should contain a pair of columns, where each column contains one of the paired keys of the related entities. These paired keys act as the identifier of each relationship occurrence. The remainder of the columns in the table contain the data elements of the attributes that describe and qualify the relationship. Each separate relationship type between each entity pair should be converted to a separate table.

Complex relationships, or those containing multiple or multioccurring attributes, should be treated as if they were entities with repeating attributes. The base table of this relationship entity should contain the data elements of all nonrepeating attributes, and a separate table must be set up for each repeating attribute type of the relationship. Each table of the relationship set must contain a set of columns, each of which contains one of the paired keys of the related entities.

Selection of an entity for relational implementation is appropriate if

1. The entity has few, if any, attributes that occur multiple times.
2. Access to the entity may be through the primary key of the entity or through any data element defined within the table constructed from the entity's attributes.
3. There are many relationships between the entities, and the relationships are well defined or poorly defined and simple, requiring few attributes to define and qualify them.
4. The relationships between the entities may be maintained by data elements that reside wholly within each entity.
5. Processing of the entity usually occurs singly or in combination with small groups of other entity types, that is, only a small number of entities (not occurrences) are needed by an application for reference or processing purposes at any one time.
6. Entity occurrence sequence is unimportant to processing.
7. Entity processing is set at a time.
8. Entity processing does not require that all attributes of the entity be available at the same time.
9. The data about the entities are stable and do not change as a result of processing.
10. The entities have been split into multiple groups, which do not share many common attributes.
11. There are numerous entity groups, each with differing attribute characteristics, and the application processing does not dictate that the entity set be processed as a whole.
12. Processing does not require multiple entity types to be related to any one given entity at the same time.
13. The data about an entity are contained within one or two tables, and updating the entity data attributes of any given entity is not dependent on the data within any other entity table.
14. Updating the data within one table does not affect its relationships with any other table.

Epilogue

The techniques of data analysis and data modeling continue to evolve. Unlike some of the more popular techniques which are applied to the processes and functions of the business these data oriented techniques have relatively few standards, and few accepted ways of doing things. Work is being done to develop new and more effective techniques as the existing techniques continue to evolve.

Until there are standards and accepted ways of doing things, each practitioner is of necessity more or less free to produce work products according to his or her own understanding. The practitioner should remember however that these work products, the models and narratives, are designed to communicate information. The information to be communicated is the understanding that the analyst has developed and the design that the designer has produced.

Many model developers give in to the tendency to develop complex models by incorporating many ideas in a single model. The same holds true for for the tendency to use many different symbols in the same model. These tendencies should be resisted at all costs. Models are most effective when they are simple. A model which must be explained by the modeler is not an effective model. For the same reason a narrative which must be explained is not any effective narrative. How many times have you heard someone say "what I was trying to say is . . ." or "what this model means is . . ."? Thus my final advice to the model developer is follow the KISS principle—keep it simple stupid. Make sure that your models are self-explanatory and that your narratives are clear, complete, and unambiguous.

Index